THE GURKHAS
THEIR
MANNERS, CUSTOMS AND COUNTRY

THE GURKHAS
THEIR
MANNERS, CUSTOMS AND COUNTRY

W. BROOK NORTHEY
C. J. MORRIS

WITH A FOREWORD BY
C. G. BRUCE

GYAN

Published by

Gyan Publishing House
5, Ansari Road
Daryaganj, New Delhi-110002
Phone: 011-47034999, 9811692060
E-mail: books@gyanbooks.com

Distribution Network
gyanbooks.com
India, USA, Canada, UK, Australia, France

ISBN : 978-81-212-3453-5 (PB)

2nd Impression 2020

Printed at: Gyan Press, Delhi.

The Gurkhas their Manners, Customs and Country
Authors: W. Brook Northey; C. J. Morris

THE GURKHAS

THEIR MANNERS, CUSTOMS AND COUNTRY

BY MAJOR W. BROOK NORTHEY, M.C.
Late 1st K.G.O. Gurkha Rifles

AND CAPTAIN C. J. MORRIS
3rd Q.A.O. Gurkha Rifles

with a foreword by

BRIGADIER-GENERAL THE HON. C. G. BRUCE
C.B., M.V.O., late 5th Royal Gurkha Rifles and 6th Gurkha Rifles

With Illustrations from Photographs by
the Authors and others, and a Map

LONDON
JOHN LANE THE BODLEY HEAD LTD.

KINCHINJUNGA FROM EASTERN NEPAL

THIS BOOK IS DEDICATED, BY SPECIAL PERMISSION,

TO

HIS HIGHNESS MAHARAJA SIR CHANDRA SHAMSHER JANG BAHADUR RANA

G.C.B., G.C.S.I., G.C.M.G., G.C V.O., D.C.L.

Honorary General, British Army; Honorary Colonel, 4th P.W.O. Gurkha Rifles; Thong-Lin-Pimma-Kokang-Wang-Syan; Grand Officier de la Légion d'Honneur; Prime Minister and Marshal and Supreme Commander-in-Chief of Nepal,

WITHOUT WHOSE HELP AND PERSONAL ASSISTANCE IT COULD NOT HAVE BEEN COMPLETED

PREFACE

THIS book, except for the two chapters under our respective initials, is a word-for-word collaboration. The bulk of the material was collected during service on recruiting duty, and has been carefully checked by reference to all possible authorities.

Except in Chapter IV, diacritical marks have not been employed in the text, but for the benefit of students they have been added to the Nepali words in the Index. The system adopted is that advocated by the Royal Asiatic Society, and place-names have been spelt in accordance with the rules laid down by the Royal Geographical Society for the transliteration of foreign alphabets.

The illustrations, with the exception of one or two of the interior of Nepal, which were kindly supplied by the Darbar, are all from photographs taken by us, and we have to thank the council of the Royal Geographical Society and the Mount Everest Committee for permission to use a few copyright pictures, which were, however, also taken by us.

To Captain C. G. Borrowman, 4th P.W.O. Gurkha Rifles, we are indebted for the most attractive picture of a Gurkha which adorns the wrapper of this book.

In writing the history chapter we have borrowed heavily from all the published works on the subject, and particularly from Professor Sylvain Levi's monumental treatise.

We have to thank our friend, Captain R. L. Turner, M.C. (Professor of Sanskrit in the University of London), not only for the chapter dealing with the languages of Nepal, but also for much kind help and suggestion throughout.

The map has been drawn from the recent survey of Nepal, and we are indebted to His Highness the Maharaja and to the Surveyor-General in India for permission to reproduce it. The districts in the map have been shaded in to show the habitations of the various tribes.

Owing to the fact that Nepal is closed to European travellers, it has not been possible for us to give a detailed description of the interior of the country. His Highness did, however, as a special favour, very kindly permit us to visit certain portions of the country on the eastern and western borders, and from these journeys we were enabled to gain a good general idea of what the rest of the country is like.

As will be seen, we know practically nothing about the origin of the inhabitants. Although, as Professor Turner points out, language is not an infallible guide in this respect, it does help to trace the growth of a people. There are a number of languages spoken in Nepal to-day about which we know nothing beyond their names, and if we can stimulate interest in this very important subject, and can also bring to notice the magnificent work done by the Gurkha nation during the Great War, we shall feel that our labours will not have been in vain.

W. B. N.
C. J. M.

CANNES,
December 1927.

FOREWORD

BY BRIGADIER-GENERAL THE HON. C. G. BRUCE, C.B.

I DO not think that, up to the present time, any work has been issued to the public which gives a view, as a whole, of the kingdom of Nepal. By far the greatest writer on Nepal and its inhabitants, and by far the greatest scholar, who gave nearly his whole life to its problems, was Brian Hodgson ; but his work is not now available for, nor would it interest, the general reader. He touches so many sides of research, and writes so much as a scientist, that it would be impossible to collate or to reconstruct his labours in any concise form ; nor would they represent the problems of Nepal as they are to-day.

In the present work the authors have attempted to give a picture of the country as a whole, and a description of the manners and customs of the various races inhabiting Nepal at the present time, a country very different to that of Brian Hodgson's time, for the advances made even in the last thirty years are greater than during its whole history.

Considering that the Indian Government has had intimate relations with Nepal for more than a century and a quarter, it is astonishing how little that country is known, even in India. I have met civilians and soldiers in different parts of India who have no conception of its conditions, and who knew, in fact, very little more than that the kingdom of Nepal, as it now is, occupies a stretch of the Himalayas ; and that in the Nepal Terai, the belt of forest at the foot of the hills, great shooting parties were sometimes given to Royalty, or other distinguished visitors. Indeed, although it was vaguely known that Gurkhas come from Nepal, I have actually heard wonder expressed by servants of the Indian Government that Nepal was an absolutely independent kingdom, and that Gurkhas were not born subjects of the British Empire.

Besides giving a full account of what this intensely interesting country is like, the authors have provided full details of its government and of the life of its people. There is, of course, for official use, the handbook for the recruitment of Gurkhas, which was originally written by Major Vansittart ; but that is a work which, naturally, does not appeal to popular taste, and is essentially technical, full of information though it is.

To turn to the geographical aspect of Nepal. It is a very remarkable thing that there should still be in the world a kingdom which has somewhere in the neighbourhood of six million inhabitants and yet is cut off from contact with the outer world. This condition of isolation would have been entirely impossible if its geographical situation was other than it is. To give a rough outline, Nepal occupies a stretch of the Himalayas, bounded on the east by the long Singalela ridge, which descends due south from the Kinchinjunga group, which again divides the British territory of Sikkim from Nepal ; and bounded on the west by the Maha Kali river, which forms the boundary between Nepalese territory and the British district of Kumaon. A great tropical belt of jungle runs the whole length of its southern border, and effectively cuts off the lower hill tracts from contact with the plains ; for not only is this jungle of the greatest tropical density, but for six months of the year it is intensely unhealthy.

Then, again, the long ridge of the Mahabharat range forms a barrier beyond the Terai jungle itself. The present dominions which form the Nepal kingdom have now certainly been given the name of the Kingdom of Nepal, but that name is of very recent date. For innumerable centuries, the only part of this long stretch of country to which the name of Nepal can be truly applied is that of the valley situated, roughly speaking, in the centre of the kingdom, which is the seat of the present Government. This valley is known as the Valley of Nepal, and, except in our own geographies, and for the sake of convenience, it is the only part of the kingdom to this day which would be referred to, under any condition, by its inhabitants, as Nepal. This valley, though shut off from India by the afore-mentioned dense jungles and mountain ranges, has been from time immemorial a place of religious pilgrimage and veneration.

It has a very ancient history and a very ancient civilization. For centuries and centuries, before the present rulers of the country emerged from a condition of barbarism, Nepal had a highly developed civilization of its own. Probably the climate may have had something to do with this, for the average height above sea-level of the whole of the valley is roughly 4,500 feet. It was therefore likely, with its mild and not rigorous climate, that it should form an attraction in early days. Further, from the earliest traditions, the home of the gods has always been located in the Himalayas.

Again, long after the establishment of Hinduism in the valley, when the religion of Buddhism came into being, it is there that Sakyamuni, *i.e.* Gautama, a scion of a Rajput clan, and the son of a king, was born, on the confines of the country. Therefore, what was more natural than an influx of Buddhism, when his great apostle, the King Asoka, marched to the foot of the Nepal hills about 250 B.C.?

After the establishment of Buddhism in India, and after the journeys of King Asoka, Hinduism and Buddhism flourished side by side in the Nepal valley, and that place has been a centre of orthodoxy for both religions.

Up to the present day, and as far back as authentic history goes, the valley has been occupied by a Mongoloid clan known as the Newars. This race, owing no doubt to a desire to justify itself in the presence of orthodox Hinduism, claims that it is of Aryan descent, and connected with the Nairs of Southern India, a claim, however, which has never been fully substantiated.

For many centuries the Newars formed the sole cultivated race, with a civilization of their own, of this part of the Himalayas, and, to this day, all arts and crafts and trade have been in their hands. During the whole of this period, this tract of the Himalayas has been occupied by different tribes of more or less barbaric hillmen, and it was not until many centuries after Newar civilization had been established that these hillmen showed any signs of corporate government.

There are few Englishmen who, spending their service in India, have any conception of what a visit to Nepal is like. When once the Terai has been crossed, when once the lower foothills are entered on, one is in an entirely new world. The note that is touched is almost Chinese. The type of house; the agriculture; the features of the people; their habits, their bazaars, their trading, are all quite different. Women preside at the shops, living a perfectly free and open life. One sees strange mixtures of types, non-Indian, and, above all, a different architecture. In fact, in just a few hours of travel one is ushered into quite a new world.

Although Nepal is but a small kingdom, long and very narrow, it contains a wonderful mixture of races and clans. It seems to have been in the past ages a kind of refuge or dumping ground for numerous emigrants, both from the south and north. That strange race one hears of in the dim past, known as the great Khassia race, mentioned often by scientists who deal with these problems, has especially left its mark on this part of the world.

The descendants of the section of this great Khassia mixed race which occupies the kingdom of Nepal now form the Rajput or Kshettriya clans which are the governing class of the country, and from which all their aristocracy, even the King himself, the Prime Minister, and the other noble families of Nepal are drawn. They now claim for themselves rights in the second rank in the Hindu hierachy, that of true Kshettriyas, and wear also the sacred thread. This, of course, is but one example of the extraordinary elasticity of the Hindu religion under certain conditions, for a glance at their features will show their Mongolian descent. For all that, they bear other distinguishing marks—a quicker, although probably not a greater, intelligence than other clans, and many have, as might be expected, a finer type of feature also.

In their hands, too, for some generations, has been vested the powers of government; in fact, they have succeeded to the old traditions of governing, which count for so much.

Until the middle of the eighteenth century, the Gurkhas had hardly been heard of. The only civilization of the country was still centred in Nepal and its valley, although the Newars had pushed communications east and west, as may be seen from some of the older buildings as far east as Dhankuta. But the true civilization of the country was, as I have already said, in the valley of Nepal, and the hill country to the north, west and east of the valley was then occupied, from one end to the other, by different tribes of hillmen.

In order to show the reason why these different hill tribes were kept so long isolated—for, in fact, they never made themselves felt until about the middle of the eighteenth century—it will be necessary first to explain what the geography of the country is like.

As I have already said, the main backbone of the country is the 500 miles of the Central Himalayas. This forms the northern boundary of the kingdom for its eastern half. Thence it dips down in a curve south, and finally rises again to form its northern boundary. Innumerable rivers either cut through it or rise on its southern slopes, and the valleys and countries drained by them are most precipitous and broken. In consequence, the valleys in the old days must have been very much isolated one from the other.

Nepalese geographers divide their country as follows: The eastern part—known as the Seven Kosis—that is, the country drained by the Kosi river and its seven great tributaries; and then Nepal and its surroundings, locally described as everything between the four passes, that is, the four passes that lead from the valley, north, south, east and west, namely, to the north, the Pati Pass; to the south, the Pharping or Khăsi Pass; to the east, the Sāgā Pass; to the west, the Pānch Mārsi or Bédunga Pass. Then we have a great tract of country drained by the Gandak, known as the seven Gandakis. And finally, on the west, the basin of the Karnali. The whole of this country is extremely mountainous, and communications all through it, even to this day, are very primitive indeed.

Now we come to another feature which forms a most important tradition in the family history of the reigning line of Nepal. When the Emperor Allah-u-din, leading his Mohammedan army, sacked the fortress of Chittore, many of the family of the Rajput King, after the sack of the city, fled north to the hills. Tradition says that these, true Rajputs of the purest blood, took refuge amongst the hillmen, and that from their progeny descends the family of Gurkha, the present reigning family of Nepal. Of course, such a tradition as this, without written proof, is difficult to accept altogether, but there is no doubt that there was an infusion about this time of good Rajput blood into the hill tribes. It must not, however, be imagined that the Kshettriya clans of Nepal took their rise entirely from these refugees. The main body of that race had already been in existence for a very long time, but that does not preclude the fact of a further modification caused not only at that time, but also at later periods, under the stress of the various Mohammedan invasions of India.

We now come to the period from which the modern development of Nepal may be traced. This prolonged development is due to the gradual rise to power of the reigning family of Gurkha. Over that small state, about the middle of the eighteenth century, was a remarkable ruler whose name was Prithwi Narayan Sah. He was, no doubt, a remarkable man, and organized his country so well, from both civil and military points of view, that he was able, having also obtained power over some of the other small neighbouring states, to invade the Nepal valley.

For nearly twenty years the war between the followers of the King of Gurkha and the different kings of Nepal was carried on with varying successes, but after many setbacks, and a great deal of hand-to-hand fighting, and dramatic, but rather horrible, incidents, Prithwi Narayan brought the whole of the valley of Nepal completely under his sway, and established himself there as the sole ruler of the surrounding country.

Prithwi Narayan's little hill state of Gurkha gave its name to all the followers of the King in his adventure, who were known as Gurkhalis, or followers of the King of Gurkha—the town Gurkha taking its name from its patron saint, Gorakh Nath—and these were all the races that inhabited that state—Brahmans, Rajputs, the Mongolian hill tribes, the menial clans, and even some of the Newar merchants, whose property happened to lie in the state of Gurkha.

Shri Gorakh Nath is the patron saint of all Gurkhas, and the saint they invoke and praise in all times of stress and exaltation. He is to the Gurkha nation far more present and infinitely more of a living force than ever St. George was to " Merrie England." He is also supposed to preside in person when the Gurkha army takes the field, or when Gurkha regiments go to war. So much so is this a living belief that there are persons still living who profess to know that in the small war with Tibet, which took place just before the Indian Mutiny, the Tibetans were astonished to see him marching at the head of the Gurkha troops, and the Gurkha victory over the Tibetans is largely put down to this conviction.

The small neighbouring kingdoms which had not come under Prithwi Narayan's rule so far, but whose subjects were precisely the same as those of that ruler, were not as yet allowed to call themselves Gurkhalis. But when, during the period of conquest and annexation, nearly the whole of the Chaubisia Raj, *i.e.* the twenty-four kingdoms (small hill states), joined its fortunes to those of Gurkha, the great fight in the Nepal valley between the wild and uncultivated hill tribes and the much more highly educated and cultivated Newars was pursued with great ferocity.

Such was the resistance of the Newars, in some sort despised by their Gurkha conquerors, in the same way that all wild people have always despised the, to them, softer and less manly town dwellers, that they were never forgiven by the Gurkha king for the stubbornness of their resistance.

Prithwi Narayan, having established himself firmly in the Nepal valley, and having thereby enormously increased his resources, proceeded to spread his conquests east and west, and after his death his successors carried on the same policy.

Finally he annexed the whole of the hill country so far afield as the present border of, and even beyond, Sikkim, and also by degrees swallowed up and assimilated those of the little kingdoms lying far to the west of the Nepal valley.. Wild, uncultivated men as they were, and inflated with the successes which had crowned their ambitions, the successors of Prithwi Narayan suffered terribly from over confidence in themselves and their power. Their lust for conquest was far beyond their real power, and they were undoubtedly rapidly riding for a fall.

They first pushed up into Sikkim in 1792, and followed that up with an invasion of Tibet, where they came into contact with the Chinese. The Tibetans, in fact, called the Chinese to their assistance, and a great army of Tibetans and Chinese drove the Gurkhas out of Tibet back over the open passes of Kuti and Kerong, and followed them right into the heart of Nepal, where a treaty was concluded within a single day's march of Kathmandu.

By 1803 practically the whole of the district now included in the kingdom of Nepal had been taken over, but even this great extension of their government did not satisfy the Nepalese. Quite naturally, for a people so shut in, owing to their great successes, they considered themselves unconquerable. Their arrogance was prodigious, and an account of their

Court, left by Kirkpatrick and others, shows them to have been almost impossible to deal with. Their lust for conquest was unquenchable. They pushed their troops west, their outposts reaching almost as far as the Kashmir border. They completely occupied the district of Kumaon, and also Garhwal ; and passing through what are now the Simla Hill States, they dominated, for a short period, the Kangra valley. There are the remains of a Gurkha fort of the period to this day at our military station of Bakloh, itself now the headquarters of a Gurkha regiment.

But pride comes before a fall. They quarrelled with all their neighbours, both the Sikhs and the British, and losing to the Sikhs in the Kangra valley, they had to draw in their horns very considerably. Their arrogance, however, did not abate, and it was due to the continual differences that arose with the British Government that war was finally declared in 1814.

Out of evil sometimes comes good, and from the defeat of the Gurkhas and the consequent Treaty of Segowli dates the continuous good terms and the present excellent relationship which have existed between the British Empire and the kingdom of Nepal ever since.

The details of that war make good reading to the present day. The most conspicuous feature of the war was the bravery of the Gurkha troops themselves. It was, in fact, an eye-opener to our army in India to find another race which, given certain conditions, could meet them and beat them on equal terms. It is strange to think that many of the Gurkha troops of those days, though their army had been, in a manner, copied from our own, were still armed with bows and arrows, and employed some flint-locks.

Many engagements were fought in the war which

reflected the greatest credit on both sides, but I doubt whether up to that date such a fight against purely indigenous troops had been contemplated as the resistance made at the fort near Dehra Dun, which resulted in the death of General Gillespie, and the repulse of the many attacks of the force of all arms under his command. The Gurkha survivors who were left in the fort—some seventy or so, including some women—escaped and made good their retreat before the fort was finally taken.

The war was brought to an end at last under the most competent leadership of General Ochterlony, who out-manœuvred and defeated the Gurkhas on what is now the main road to Kathmandu, at the defile of Bichia Koh.

With the Treaty of Segowli, the Indian Government established permanent relations with Nepal, a representative of the British Government was to remain at their capital, and over and above, and of still greater importance, the Gurkha Government allowed three regiments of Gurkhas to be raised and incorporated in the Indian Army, a proviso of the treaty specially stating that they were to be officered entirely by British officers.

After the death of Prithwi Narayan, his heirs and successors appeared on the whole to have become degenerate, and in a very curious way history repeats itself, for by degrees all the executive power of the Government became vested in the Prime Minister and his immediate supporters, usually men of his own clan. From that day to this that particular arrangement has gone through a clear course of evolution. Since the first Prime Minister of any great importance, Bhim Sen Thapa, the history of Nepal has been mainly the history of the struggles for power of the various Prime Ministers. To this present day we have a condition in a way resembling that of old Japan, and still more resembling the old

French Court under the Carlovingians, when Pepin was *Maire du Palais*.

Until the great Maharaja Jang Bahadur firmly established himself as Prime Minister, the history of Nepal was made up of continual factional fights for power, and for the permanent position of Prime Minister, and all that it carried with it.

The greatest character in Nepalese history was this same Jang Bahadur, himself the son of a Nepalese general chiefly noted for his piety. He came on the scene about 1845, and he was so placed as to be brought into opposition with the followers and clan of the then reigning Prime Minister, and as an adherent of the reigning Queen, a very able lady, but a tigress. His own party, headed by himself, made a clean sweep of the opposition in a free fight, followed by a massacre in the palace precincts. There were other rather horrible incidents in the rise to power of this exceptional character, but they must not be taken too seriously in judging him. He was essentially, both in his ideas and in his capacity, far superior to his time and surroundings, and the many terrible incidents of his early career were forced upon him.

It must be remembered that it was but a short period from the time when his forebears had emerged from an almost barbaric condition, that they had been completely and entirely isolated from the world, that the state of the country was always at that period turbulent, and that the only way to preserve one's own life was to remove those who threatened it.

Jang Bahadur, as soon as he was firmly settled, rose rapidly above his surroundings. In addition to being Prime Minister he was a noted hunter, quite fearless in facing big game of all kinds; an athlete, so far as such exercises were indulged in in that country; and a regular dare devil when he was a young man, as many of the traditions and stories told about him bear out.

When once in power he showed his capacity in many ways, and he also showed that he was by no means the savage that many people were inclined to consider him.

In 1850 he was strong enough to overrule all the prejudices of the country, and undertake a journey to England, and it was due to the enormously educative results of that journey, probably, that Jang Bahadur was able to induce the Nepalese to throw in their part with us at the time of the Mutiny. For until that time, the Nepalese had not the faintest idea of what lay in the world outside. Really, their only experience beyond their own land consisted of those few members of the Nepal Government who were sent once every five years travelling to Pekin overland to offer a tribute to the Chinese Government, in accordance with the terms of the treaty completed with China in the year 1793. Probably, the farthest point in other directions reached by Gurkhas of any standing was Benares, for this was a place of pilgrimage for Hindus all over the country, in addition to being a place often selected as the residence of various Nepalese who were, from time to time, exiled from their own country.

Jang Bahadur died, it is believed, while actually hunting in the Terai, in the year 1877, leaving behind him a very different government, a very different army, and a very different organization to the one that he took over when he became Prime Minister in 1845. In all ways his career shows him to have been a very remarkable man.

Since his time, members of Jang Bahadur's family have continuously been Prime Ministers of Nepal, and nearly the whole of the ruling power has been in their hands ; the Maharaj Adhiraj, to give the King his full title, taking but a small part in the affairs of the State. By a curious arrangement, Jang Bahadur decreed that on the death of a Prime Minister he should be succeeded by one of his brothers. Since his death there have been four ministers, three of whom have been brothers and nephews of Jang Bahadur, of whom by far the most enlightened is the present Maharaja and Prime Minister, Sir Chandra Shamsher Jang Bahadur Rana, under whose rule Nepal has made advances far beyond the conception of any of his predecessors.

His Highness has been throughout his career a firm friend of the British Government, and although he holds in his hands almost complete power, he is not an autocrat. Behind the priestly and noble classes of Nepal lies an intensely strong and conservative feeling, no less strong for being in small numbers. For Nepal is now the headquarters, one might almost say, of orthodox Hinduism, and yet His Highness, through sheer force of character, has brought about reforms and encouraged a liberal outlook in the country such as could not have even been dreamed of by his uncle, Jang Bahadur.

Sir Chandra himself has visited England, and although he took this very daring step, it was not in his time such a shock to his people as the journey taken by his uncle before him, and, indeed, nowadays Nepal is in a very different state to what it was even thirty years ago.

When he first succeeded to the premiership travel in Nepal to the outside world was forbidden. Communications with it were therefore kept in the most primitive state. When once the hill barrier was reached only a mule track led into the country, and yet we now find excellent roads, electric light installations, a water supply, and motor-cars, where in the old days the only method of travel was on foot, or on the backs of hill ponies, or carriage by the very excellent local method of hammocks slung on a pole. It is strange to think that all the heavy and delicate machinery required for these improvements has been brought either on elephants or man-handled through the hills, the whole way from the plains of India to Nepal.

Until quite lately there was a great prejudice against the introduction of railways, even into the Terai jungle at the foot of the hills, but now the Terai belt is crossed by a short railway owned by the State, which connects the frontier posts of Raxaul with the motor road on the far side of the forest. This obviates many of the dangers and difficulties in passing through this Terai belt during the unfavourable parts of the year. It must be remembered that this policy of isolation was the deliberate policy of the Nepal Government, and is so still, and that the improvements which they have made are not for the benefit of the foreigner, but purely and simply for their own benefit. Meanwhile, even entry by the main route to the capital is confined strictly to the very, very few officials who are occasionally permitted to visit the country, or to specially invited guests of the Maharaja himself.

The Government of Nepal is run on purely militarist lines. Its laws and its religion are entirely and absolutely interwoven. The religious law is the base of the civil law, and the civil law is based on the ancient Hindu Laws of Manu, which has a truly orthodox Hindu outlook. But the Gurkha Government itself is the purely militarist government of a purely military people, and therefore, although closely adhering to those same laws, the whole attitude to life is a militarist one. All officials, or very nearly all of them, bear military titles.

By far the greatest expense of the State is that of keeping up the army. In comparison to the size of the country and its income, it consumes, what we should consider, far too great a proportion of the available funds, but this does not seem to be resented by any part of the population, and the soldier, no matter on what business he may happen to be, if bearing the badge of his rank, expects and receives consideration everywhere. The people seem intensely interested in everything to do with military matters, although among the peasants there are very few signs of a naturally pugnacious tendency. Military tradition and military reputation is the one thing which interests all classes.

I have already said that the State is the headquarters of a certain Hindu orthodoxy; that being the case, it is natural, when the Government is so extremely concerned with these matters, that caste, as known amongst the Hindus of India, should be regarded by them with the utmost concern.

Dividing the population of the country into the priestly classes: the Kshettriyas, or warriors, the second great class in the Hindu hierarchy, come first; then the Mongolian clans (also classed as military clans); and finally, the inferior Mongolian, or non-fighting hill tribes and menial classes; so it will be seen that it is a fact that the Kshettriya clans keep in their hands the whole power of the administration. When it is stated that the Gurkhas do this, or the Gurkhas do that, it refers entirely to the habits, customs, prejudices, or orders of this Kshettriya race. Beyond them are the Mongolian military clans who form by far the greater bulk of the soldiery of the Gurkha regiments in the Indian Army.

Several of these clans are also enlisted freely in the Nepal Army, with the exception of those living to the east, from whom we draw many of our best soldiers. Socially these men have little consideration in the country. In appearance they are generally Mongolian in type, more markedly so than the races socially superior to them.

All these different clans, at different times, have been induced to submit themselves to the Hindu ceremonial laws, but there is no doubt whatever that in their observances of these ceremonies they are infinitely more lax than the clans superior to them in the Hindu hierarchy.

The whole population of Nepal is, in fact, extremely mixed, the belt of Terai and its neighbourhood, especially the large tract of country ceded to Nepal as a reward for its services during the Indian Mutiny, contain exactly the same class of people as we have in our United Provinces and in Bengal. But the mountainous tracts have a still more mixed population. For, besides the ruling classes, there are the different Mongolian military clans, who have entered Nepal at different periods in its far past, speaking each their own language and differing greatly in all their customs, and other like Mongolian clans, who, for some reason, are considered militarily inferior, but who have arrived in the country probably much under the same conditions. There are also a host of menial clans ; and, to the west, other tribes of a rather interior type of hillmen not suitable to be classed with the military tribes. Beyond that again, there are certain relics of a bygone forgotten age, whose habitat is in the great forests.

The languages spoken amongst all these tribes are almost innumerable, but are, generally speaking, Mongolian in origin. The cultivated classes speak the Hindi dialect, generally known as Nepali, which has now become the official language of the whole country.

Besides the above-mentioned races there are also living in Nepal a very considerable number of pure Tibetans, who follow the Lamaistic religion. These are settled for the greater part close to the Tibetan border, but are often to be met with, as well as many other pilgrims from far Tibet, in Kathmandu itself, for in that place, so long a great centre of orthodox Buddhism, are still some of the most sacred shrines and places of pilgrimage.

Although the policy of reform adopted by the Prime Minister is bearing great results, there are certain defaults which will some day have to be faced seriously. Such is the expenditure on the army that little can be left for other and more essential services of the State. Communications are still very primitive, especially from east to west, where there is only one great roadway, and that roadway, from our point of view, is not a high-road at all, but a rather indifferent mule track ; the only made roads in the whole country are those leading to the valley from the plains of India and in the valley itself.

Perhaps nothing brings home to us more the attitude of the Nepal Government to the Indian Government, and to the British Empire, than the efforts made to help us during the Great War. We had, at the commencement of that war, no less than twenty battalions of regular Gurkha regiments serving in the Indian Army, as well as numerous military and civil police, employed, not only in India, but in Burma as well. We were enabled to keep all these up to full strength during the whole of the war, and the number of the regular battalions was also increased to thirty-three, and notwithstanding terrible losses from death, wounds and sickness, never did the supply of men fail, and when we were in urgent need of more men in India, a Nepalese contingent of 12,000 of their best troops was sent down in order to help in the internal defence of the Indian Empire.

It is strange to think that in the war of 1814, the entire Gurkha army consisted of but 12,000 men, and it was practically this number of men who formed the Nepalese contingent a hundred years later, and which was commanded by General Sir Baber Sham Sher Jang, a son of His Highness the Maharaja, the Prime Minister.

The war, as everywhere else, has brought difficulties to Nepal. It owes its prosperity, naturally, other than trade with India, to its peasantry, and the greater number of its peasantry belong to the military clans. They suffered terribly. Revenue, of course, diminished, and according to what happened in every country throughout the world, engaged in the war, pressure had to be brought to increase this loss of revenue. Further, immense numbers of Gurkhas had been across the sea, had had hard work, but had also received good pay, and when the war ended, a very serious problem arose. The standard of living in Nepal is, naturally, low, for wages are low, but, generally speaking, food is cheap ; but still, work is very hard. In consequence, ever since the war there has been a greater difficulty than ever before in getting discharged soldiers to return to their homes. Looked at in a broad way, this is, no doubt, due very much to the isolation of the country, although the isolation may have been healthy from the point of view of keeping the people primitive and simple in their habits. Yet, once they began to mix freely with the outside world, it was bound to produce difficulties. Men found that they could earn quadruple the amount by taking positions as watchmen, and so forth, in India, that they lived in greater comfort than was possible in their own country, although in greater heat, and, therefore, there was a great diminution in the number of men who returned to their homes.

As a Gurkha, living in India, once said to me, " The whole question is this, it is one Chépti Paisa ($\frac{1}{2}$*d.*) against one rupee, and the rupee will always win." I think that that difficulty is being surmounted, but it still partially obtains, and it is a sign of the times that no matter what laws are made by a State, it is the great fundamental economic laws that will in time prevail, and it is this very same question which has brought difficulties from another quarter.

The enlistment of men in Nepal is under the strictest regulations, agreed to mutually by the Nepalese Government and our own. Safeguards of all kinds are required and given, both for the purposes of recruiting and for the well-being of the recruits. But now, due entirely to the high wages prevailing in India, and the like, illegal recruiting has become a great nuisance, and those who carry it on for their own benefit are doing an ill service, both to the British Empire and to the kingdom of Nepal. We can only hope that the excellent conditions under which Gurkhas now serve in the Indian Army may partially help to counteract this tendency, by keeping recruitment on legitimate lines, and by supplying a regular annual influx of wealth into the country.

The political history of Nepal is the political history, purely, of the reigning classes, the fights and the struggles and the massacres and revolutions that have occurred have been almost entirely affairs of the palace, and the aristocracy with the exception of such soldiery as were immediately concerned, and the support of the army was always what each faction strove to obtain. The life of the ordinary country people jogged along as usual. In consequence they have retained a simplicity of character and hardness of life which it would be a terrible pity to spoil or alter, and which also, no doubt, has been largely due to that same policy of isolation from the outside world.

It is, therefore, much to be hoped that these difficulties which I have mentioned, both economic and other, may in time settle themselves, especially as every hillman throughout the world naturally yearns for his own home. It may be said, and probably with truth, that the country is poor and over-populated, and that there has always been a leakage, but the recruitment now is far greater than in old times, and the leakage far greater. In the old days there was a distinct analogy between the Switzerland of the Middle Ages and Nepal. The Swiss were poor, and made fine soldiers, and were in request as mercenaries throughout Europe. The Nepalese the same. Did not the Maharaja Ranjit Singh, of Sikh fame, enlist them at Lahore? And it is curious to note that Gurkha recruits coming from Central Nepal and entering our army are still known familiarly as *Lahoria*, from the fact that the early men were nearly always bound for that place.

So, in a small way, there is still an analogy, though everything nowadays is on an immensely larger scale, and the danger is over-drainage and not over-population.

Although general education throughout the Nepal kingdom—even primary education—is not very widespread, there have been established, in the last thirty years or so, nearly sixty Government schools in different parts of the country. In Nepal itself there is an excellent school, which gives a much higher standard of education than that provided in the district schools, while the Nepalese are also now allowed to go to Calcutta and other universities for the purpose of vocational training, it being the distinct policy of Government to provide engineers, doctors, and so on, from among their own people.

As a matter of fact, there is in the character of the people a distinct taste for engineering. On their main roads they have excellent bridges, not only of the old cantilever type, but some of masonry, and there are many suspension bridges throughout the country. Some of these suspension bridges have been in existence for a great number of years. In fact, the ingenuity of the Nepalese in this respect has certainly been forced upon them. In a country which is so broken by deep valleys and rushing mountain rivers, which might have to be crossed without bridges, intercommunication, without such aids between different parts of the country, would be almost impossible. Even now, although communications are much improved, it frequently happens that officials travelling from Kathmandu to the western confines of the country find it more convenient to descend to the plains of India and travel by the British railways to stations on the western frontier, from whence they can easily march to their destination.

But it is, I fancy, only a question of time before internal communications will be greatly improved. The whole country largely suffers, too, from a want of general transport, which makes these internal communications often very difficult. The tracks are mostly bad, and are precipitous everywhere, and the main transport of the country is men, and men only, and fine carriers all the peasants are. It is indeed a country of carrying. All the trade between the hill villages and the great fairs and markets, all the moving of grain, or nearly all, is done on men's backs. At the junctions of rivers throughout the country weekly bazaars are held for the barter of goods, and whole families, men, women and children, carrying loads proportionate to their age and strength, may be seen coming down to exchange their produce for the necessities of life.

There is nothing more tantalizing, or more stimulating, to the traveller, especially the traveller who is conversant with the Himalayas generally, than to stand, on a clear winter morning, on the top of the Chandra Giri Pass, which overlooks the Nepal valley, and to gaze across at the vast Himalayan range dominating the valley. There are the glorious and magnificent peaks of which so little is known, Dwālāgiri, Māchha puchri (The Fish Tail), Jib Jibia and Gosain than, and of which only a distant view is granted one, while innumerable valleys and mountain ridges descend from them and their neighbours.

Then, away to the east and west, more and more unknown and glorious country: the little that one has been allowed to see only whets the appetite for more. Assuredly no part of the Himalayan range, not even the prodigious vision of Kinchin Junga from Senchal, is more wonderful than this great panorama.

And then the pleasure of travelling in a country where all appear to be smiling and laughing, where there is an evident and keen sense of humour, especially of the ludicrous, amongst the people. Really the Government cannot be a bad Government when the people all appear to be so happy.

Finally, if in any way the results of this book help to arouse an interest and an appreciation in this country of Nepal, and its difficulties, and of the services which it has rendered to the British Empire, the authors will feel that they have not laboured in vain.

CONTENTS

PART I

HISTORY

PART II

GENERAL

PART III

WESTERN NEPAL

CONTENTS

PART IV

CENTRAL NEPAL

PART V

EASTERN NEPAL

PART VI

NEPAL AND THE GREAT WAR

APPENDICES

LIST OF ILLUSTRATIONS

THE GURKHAS

PART I

HISTORY

THE GURKHAS

CHAPTER I

INTRODUCTORY

ON the southern slopes of the Himalaya there is a small and, as far as Europeans are concerned, practically unknown and unexplored tract of country—the kingdom of Nepal. It is bounded on the north by Tibet; on the south by the Indian provinces of Bihar, Orissa and Oudh; on the east by Sikkim and Bengal; and on the west by the Kali river. Thus, lying between the 80th and 88th degrees of east longitude, it is 520 miles long and nowhere more than 140 miles broad, but averaging between 90 and 100 miles.

The country as a whole may be roughly divided into four distinct zones: the Terai, lying but little above the level of the sea; the Duns, or valleys at the foot of the hill country; the hills proper, averaging from 4,000 to 10,000 feet in height above sea-level; and lastly the Alpine region extending from the hills up to and including the main range of the Himalaya.

It can thus be seen that within the boundaries of this small state is to be found every variety of climate and scenery, for on its northern frontier are situated some of the highest mountains in the world, whilst in the southern part of the country lies the much-dreaded area of forest and swamp known as the Terai. This latter, although justly famed for the wonderful sport it provides—being the haunt of swarms of tiger and rhinoceros—is, perhaps, one of the most malarious spots on the face of the earth.

Besides this division into differing zones of country, the territory of Nepal can be further divided, from west to east, by the series of ridges which are given off respectively by the mountains Nanda Devi (25,700 feet), Dhaulagiri (26,826 feet), Gosainthan (26,305 feet), and Kinchinjunga (28,156 feet). Mount Everest, the highest mountain in the world, lying partly in Nepal and partly in Tibet, and situated roughly midway between the last two named mountains, but somewhat behind the main range, gives off no main ridges, and so does not affect the divisions of the country in this respect. It can thus be seen how each of these districts, enclosed as they are by mountain barriers, forms a mountain basin sloping gradually down to the south, and cut up by numerous streams which rise in the surrounding hills. All these rivers flow in the direction of the plains of India, and tend to converge towards one another. The districts thus formed are classified as follows:

1. The Western Division, or basin of the Karnali.
2. The Central Division, or basin of the Gandak.
3. The Eastern Division, or basin of the Kosi.

In addition to these three main geographical divisions there are two others:

4. The Nepal Valley, in which lies Kathmandu, the capital.
5. The Terai.

The Nepal Valley is formed by the bifurcation of the ridge which runs south from Gosainthan, and thus forms an isolated triangle.

The main rivers of Nepal, from west to east, are the Kali, Karnali, Rapti, Gandak, Baghmati, Kosi and Mechi.

No further description of the natural features of the country is given at this point, for each of the above divisions, together with the manners and customs of its inhabitants, will be described in detail.

CHAPTER II

THE HISTORY OF NEPAL

THE early history of Nepal is shrouded in doubt and uncertainty. Dynasty succeeded dynasty, an occasional monarch leaving his mark upon the country. It is not, however, until the year A.D. 1769, with the rise to power of Prithwi Narayan, that we commence to get an accurate picture of past events in Nepal. Before dealing with the period following on that king's accession it is first necessary to survey briefly what little is known of the early history of the country.

Nepal enters into authentic and positive history in the fourth century of the Christian Era. The first known document which contains any mention of the country is the panygyric of the Emperor Samudra Gupta on the pillar of Allahabad. In the enumeration on it of the various peoples who were, at that time, either vassals or direct subjects of the powerful sovereign then dominating India, the King of Nepal is mentioned as being one of those who "paid tribute to and obeyed the orders of the Imperial Master." His name is found between those of two other princes: the kings of Katrapura and Kamarupa. Of these, the former name is untraceable elsewhere, and remains enigmatical; but the latter occurs frequently in ancient literature in connection with that of Nepal, and refers to the tract of country in North-West Assam bordering on the little independent state of Bhutan.

Early literature, whether Hindu or Buddhist, is extremely vague where Nepal is concerned, and according to various scholars, the name of the country does not occur in either of the great Epic poems, the *Mahabharat* and the *Ramayana*, although the Himalaya occupies a prominent part, and is frequently mentioned in the legends and stories of those times. It appears that while Kamarupa is specifically mentioned in those religious narratives, the existence of Nepal is merely suggested as the legendary home of certain barbarians, inaccessible in their mountain fastnesses and much dreaded by the people of the plains. Buddhist literature is equally vague, for though the word Nepal is not infrequently mentioned, it is difficult to place any reliance on the dates which are given concerning it. It is placed on record, however, that at some time during the fifth or sixth century B.C. a celebrated ascetic, named Vasubandhu, visited Nepal accompanied by some five hundred disciples, and that he founded in this country religious schools, whose members, as they increased in numbers, spread religion throughout the country. To this man may be ascribed the rôle of having been the first authentic person to have got into touch with that mysterious land.

Although the early history of Nepal is so veiled in mystery there appears little doubt, not only from the ancient Hindu writings but also from certain geological remains, that the valley was at one time a huge lake. Its subsequent transformation into a fertile valley is accounted for in the early legends of the Hindus and the Buddhists by the story that Vishnu, according to the Hindus, or Manjusri, according to the Buddhists, cut a pass through the mountains which encircled the valley and thus allowed the water to escape. In any case, ancient legend attributes to this Manjusri—which word does not imply any specific person but merely " The venerable one from Manchuria "—the establishment of the first known king of Nepal, one Dharmakara. Manjusri, whoever he may have been, is presumed to have come from China on a pilgrimage, and he was accompanied by Dharmakara, known at that time, on account of his virtue and extreme piety, as the " Treasure of the Law."

It can readily be understood how Dharmakara, on his subsequently becoming king, infused the influence of the country of his birth into the land over which he was now destined to rule, for it is stated that he organized it entirely on the Chinese model, the traces of which influence are not only discernible in the knowledge, commerce and culture, but even in the buildings which were constructed in several stages in the form now well known as the Pagoda style.

On the death of Dharmakara many kings and rajas succeeded one another in assuming the reins of government. They came from many countries, such as Bengal and Madras, whence came the Raja Dharma Datta of Conjevedram with a conquering army. He it was who peopled the country with the four castes of Hindus, and who further is said to have built the most famous and venerated of all the Hindu shrines in the valley—the temple of Pasupati.

The famous Buddhist temple of Bodhnath, in the valley of Nepal, is said to owe its existence to the son of a king who succeeded to the throne at no very great period after Raja Dharma Datta, and so it may be seen how far back in ancient history some of the more important of the temples to be seen in Nepal to this day are said to date, though tradition may have exaggerated the antiquity not a little.

The first of any recognized dynasty, however, is said to have been established by one Ne Muni, the patron saint of Nepal. Living at the confluence of the Baghmati and Bishnumati rivers, where he

BUDDHIST TEMPLE OF SWAYAMBHUNATH

LOOKING OVER THE NEPAL VALLEY FROM KAKANI

expounded his doctrines, Ne Muni was looked up to as an oracle in all things, and it was he who, by common consent, selected a pious cowherd to be the first of the long line of kings known as the Gopala, or Cowherd dynasty. It was a matter of pastoral dispute arising over the question of better grazing lands, rather than any political rivalry, that caused the downfall of the last of the eight kings who formed the Cowherd dynasty. They, in their turn, were supplanted by yet another race of shepherds, known as the Ahirs, also strangers from Hindustan. Both of these names remain in modern times, and the Ahirs are now merely a subdivision of the Gowalas, both names being frequently substituted one for the other according to the localities in which they are employed, though the term Gowala is more common in Bengal, and that of Ahir in Bihar.

The country was not, however, destined to enjoy a reign of peace for long, for the valley, occupied as it was by a sedentary and unwarlike population, offered an easy prey to the barbarians of the neighbouring mountains. Hence, we learn that after a dynasty consisting of but three kings, the country was overrun by a race known as the Kirantis, who inhabited the wild and mountainous districts to the east of the valley. A more detailed description of the rise of the Kirantis will be found in the chapters dealing with Eastern Nepal, and they are discussed here only in so far as they affect the general history of the country. According to Professor Sylvain Levi, the names of the original Kiranti kings are clearly barbarian, but the same scholar lays stress on the fact that there is no doubt that they were a real people —however shadowy and mythical their predecessors may have been—and that they, in common with most of the Himalayan peoples, had, without doubt, their royal genealogies. The name of the first of their kings, Yalambar, is said to be connected with the legend which places the foundation of the Tibetan race, and the sojourn of its first king, on the banks of the river Yalung, in North-Eastern Nepal.

In 249 or 250 B.C., during the reign of Stunko, the fourteenth king of this dynasty, Asoka, whose capital was at Pataliputra, or the modern Patna, came to Nepal, where his daughter subsequently settled and founded Devapatan, near Pasupati. Asoka's dominion comprised, at that time, the whole of Northern India, including Kashmir. He was a zealous Buddhist and is celebrated for his edicts engraved on rocks and pillars in various parts of India, one at least of which was set up within the boundaries of modern Nepal at Rummin-dei, the ancient Lumbini, to mark the birthplace of the Buddha.

The Kirantis, however, were not to be spared the fate which had overtaken the many previous rulers of Nepal, for they, in their turn, failed to stem the tide of another Hindu invasion from the south, and were forced to abandon the country to the invaders, who, led by a Hindu named Numikha, founded what is known as the Somavansa dynasty. There were but five generations of these, but the last of their kings, by name Bhaskara Varman, became a powerful and wealthy potentate, whose name is further handed down to tradition as the conqueror of the whole of India. On his death yet another dynasty came into existence, for, having no son, he appointed as his successor a Chettri of the Surajvansi, or Solar race of the Rajputs, and this man founded a line of kings with the style of Surajvansi, which lasted for thirty-one generations.

In this dynasty, which produced no other figure of outstanding personality, Mahadeva, the twenty-first king of the line, stood out conspicuously for the wisdom of his rule and magnanimity of his character. Endowed with considerable personal charm and admirably brought up by his mother, Rajyavati, who, on the death of her royal spouse, ensured his accession to the now vacant throne, Mahadeva did much to raise the standard of culture and literature throughout his kingdom. Besides these moral and intellectual improvements, however, commerce flourished as it had never done before, and the interchange of trade between such countries as India and Tibet was the means of enriching the country and instituting a fresh field for development.

The kingdom of the Surajvansis extended at the time of Mahadeva outside the valley, both to the east and to the west, where it extended beyond the Gandak river and included the fortresses of the Mallas, a sect of which there will be more to say later on in this chapter. The thirty-first, and last, king of this line, Vishvadeva Varman, had no male issue, and so gave his daughter in marriage to a Vaisya Thakur of pure Rajput descent named Amsu Varman, who was destined later to found the Thakur dynasty. A period of distress and internal trouble followed the close of the Surajvansi dynasty, but the events of that time cannot now be accurately followed, for the Nepalese historian, anxious to trace Nepalese ancestors to a famous and far more ancient origin, has introduced the appearance of a personage who, according to the Hindu chronologists, reigned at a period some seven hundred years before the time of which we are writing. This person, Vikramaditya, is represented by the Nepalese historians as having overrun the country at this time and established his own era, but it appears from more accurate history that he was actually crowned king of Ujjain in the year 57 B.C. The real conqueror of Nepal was probably a powerful Indian king named Sriharsa, who forced the adoption of his era on to the Nepalese princes, humbled by recent events in their country. The date of this era, which is generally supposed to have begun in the year A.D. 606 or 607, certainly coincides much better with the date of the period under discussion than that of Vikramaditya, who existed at a period seven hundred years before this time.

It is generally supposed that Sriharsha returned to India after invading the country, but that he left some one to rule in his stead, and that this ruler was, in his turn, himself driven out of the country and Amsu Varman made king. The doubt regarding the dates and actual names of the Indian invaders was, not unnaturally, extended to the date of the reign of Amsu Varman, but despite the intentional inaccuracies of the Nepalese chroniclers it is proved by the frequent mention of his name in the chronicles of the well-known Chinese traveller Hiuen Tsang, who is known as the best and most reliable of those foreigners who visited Nepal about the year A.D. 637, that this king ascended the throne in the first part of the seventh century.

Nepalese chronicles have given the name of Vaisya Thakur to the dynasty of Amsu Varman. The Thakurs, even to the present day, are all members of the "Royal" class, and in view of their exalted birth are granted certain exemptions from taxes, and certain privileges which include even the right to intervene in the affairs of the State, should the kingdom appear to be in peril. Vaisya, on the other hand, is the name of the Rajput clan from which Amsu Varman owed his descent. The great Emperor of India, referred to later in this chapter, was a member of the same clan, and their descendants were to be found in comparatively recent times amongst the Rajputs who were to be found living in the south of the province of Oudh.

Amsu Varman, who founded the dynasty of eighteen kings known as the Thakur dynasty, was a vigorous and active man, and indefatigable in the pursuit of his own ends. He was, amongst the ancient kings of Nepal, the spoiled child of fortune, for he ascended the throne without any hereditary rights. He founded a new dynasty and a new era, and both the Chinese and Tibetans have immortalized his name in the histories and legends of their countries. Ancient manuscripts and inscriptions record the fact that Amsu Varman interested himself in science and literature, the publication of the first Sanskrit grammar in Nepal being generally assigned to his reign. In addition to these achievements the discovery of certain coins struck during his reign are a further testimony of his power. The outstanding feature, however, of Amsu Varman's reign was the appearance of Tibet in the history of Nepal. While the Emperor of Hindustan, Harsa Vardhana, was, at the beginning of the seventh century, laying the foundation of an empire which was to extend from Gujarat to Bengal—but which was in point of fact destined not to survive him—a new nation had arisen on the high plateaus to the north of the Himalaya.

In these snowy solitudes lay the country known as Tibet, or, in the vernacular, Bod. From the rough untutored people who formed its inhabitants an army was formed, numbering, it is said, in the early part of the seventh century 100,000 men, which threatened the peace of India and China. The first king of Tibet, to whom the traditions of his country had given the name Namri Srong Btsan, was a man of energy and determination. He had received from China the rudiments of medicine and astrology, and his power extended towards the south-west as far as the country of the Brahmans, or India, as we now know it. The glory of this king, the founder of the Tibetan Empire, however, was eclipsed by his son, Srong Btsan Sgam Po, who was destined to become the Alexander of Tibet. Although the exact dates of his reign are disputed by Tibetan and Chinese historians, the most reliable information available gives the date of his death as A.D. 650. Eager from the outset to acquire a knowledge of reading and writing, at that time practically unknown in his barbaric kingdom, he had, at the beginning of his reign, sent a mission to India to study the secrets of these arts. The mission brought back, as a result of their investigations, an alphabet which was, at that time, in use in Northern India, and which was adapted to suit the sounds of the Tibetan language. Once master of these newly acquired arts, the ambitious monarch applied his whole energy to further expanding his empire, which in course of time covered the whole of present-day Tibet, while his ministers entered into relations with the Chinese on the east, Hindustan to the south, and Nepal to the west. Not content with the mere extent of his power, he determined to consolidate it with a suitable alliance, and it is recorded that he despatched an emissary to the Court of Nepal to demand the hand of a princess of that country. Not daring to refuse any demand from so powerful a neighbour, Amsu Varman —for there exists conclusive evidence that it was he— granted him his daughter in marriage, and subsequent history records that from this period Nepal passed, for a time, into a sphere of influence under Tibet, and, according to the writings of Chinese historians, was, at the beginning of the eighth century, merely a vassal of that country.

As far as can be ascertained, Amsu Varman died about the year A.D. 640. His successors can be passed over as having done little or nothing of historical interest, but mention should be made of the seventh king of the dynasty, Narendra Dasa, for his name is ever after inseparably linked with that of Machendra, the patron saint of the valley, whom, accompanied by one Bandhidatta, he was said to have fetched from afar, to become the patron of the valley.

Although no authentic information, either in the form of coins, inscriptions, or ancient documents, has been handed down to posterity about this king, yet his name, connected as it was with that of the patron saint, figures prominently in the legends and history of Nepal. From all that was known of him he appears to have been a wise and benign ruler, much beloved and respected by all. His grandson, Jaya Deva, is said to have described him thus: " Narendra Deva had an exalted idea of honour and all the kings prostrated themselves before him."

It was during the reign of Narendra Deva that a Chinese mission visited Nepal for the first time, in A.D. 643. This was hospitably received by the ruler, and in 647 a second mission, under the leadership of Wang Hiuen Tse, was despatched. This was, however, subjected to such rough treatment and almost cut to pieces at the hands of the usurper then occupying the throne of Harsha, the Emperor of India, through whose dominions it had to pass, that the help of China's allies, Nepal and Tibet, was sought. This was promptly granted, and the mountain contingent inflicted a severe defeat on the aggressors and captured their monarch.

In later years, however, not only did Wang Hiuen Tse again return to Nepal, but a mission was sent to China by the ruler of Nepal, taking with it presents and messages of good will to the Celestial monarch. Further, it is said that throughout the reign of Narendra the country was continually visited by Chinese pilgrims, attracted perhaps by the reputation for piety that it enjoyed at this epoch.

From evidence available in Chinese documents it appears that the rule of Narendra Deva was marked by a great wave of prosperity and an advance of civilization throughout Nepal. Commerce flourished, religious edifices and convents, whether Buddhist or Hindu, were sumptuously restored, canals and fountains were erected, and a judicious system of taxation was introduced, with the result that in the year 650 Nepal could be compared with the best administered states of India at that time.

Shortly after the death of Narendra, and during the reign of his successor, Vara Deva, a bigoted Brahman, by name Sankara Acharya, is stated to have entered Nepal and commenced a bitter persecution of all people, of whatever age or sex, who professed, or attempted to practise, the religion of Buddhism. He destroyed their literature, burned their temples, and massacred their priests ; but Buddhism was too firmly rooted in the country to be destroyed by even such violent treatment as this. To commemorate so important an event, however, in the annals of his reign, the king, Vara Deva, is said to have given the name Sankara to his son, who succeeded him. The exact date of Sankara Acharya's arrival upon the scene affords yet another point for controversy, for mention is made of a man of the same name who also inaugurated the persecution of the Buddhists, but in the reign of Rudra Deva Varman, the seventeenth king of the preceding dynasty.

The fifteenth king of the Thakur dynasty is represented only in legend, for no manuscripts nor inscriptions relating to his reign have yet been discovered. Guna Kama Deva, however, is believed to have been a powerful and wealthy potentate, and he is said to have built, at the junction of the Baghmati and Bishnumati rivers, a town named Kantipura, destined to be known in modern times under the name of Kathmandu. The ancient chronicles also attribute the foundation of the city of Patan to this time, and the birth of these two large towns corresponds logically with the transformation which was now being effected in the economic life of Nepal. Prior to this time the population, living in small houses scattered about amongst the fields, existed on the produce of their cultivation, and Deva Patan, adjoining the temple of Pasupati, was the only town. Gradually, however, as trade with India began to expand and develop and the constitution of the Tibetan kingdom offered new fields for market, the cultivation of the land began to be superseded by an eagerness on the part of all and sundry to enter into trade. The manual arts, in which the Newars found full scope for their skill and natural ability, entered upon a new era of prosperity, and to accommodate the ever-increasing number of those who had adopted these and similar professions new towns were constantly arising. The death of Jayakama, the last of his line, was the signal for another change, for, having no child, a new raja was elected from amongst the Thakurs of the mountains of Nawakot, a small town some twenty miles to the west of Kathmandu, who invaded the valley at this time. Their triumph, however, was short lived, for during the reign of the fifth king of this, known as the Nawakot Thakur, dynasty, a descendant of Amsu Varman, by name Vama Deva, drove the invaders back to their original homes and founded the second Thakur dynasty, of which there were twelve kings.

The reign of the ninth king of this dynasty, Ari Deva, is interesting for the fact that it introduces us to a sect of Chetris, of whom nothing has been mentioned hitherto. These were known as the Mallas. The story relates that while Ari Deva was engaged in his favourite pastime of wrestling, a son was born to him to whom he gave the name of Malla, or "the wrestler." The word "malla" appears, in Sanskrit, to have the meaning of boxer, or athlete, and frequent allusions found in ancient legends and traditions give prominence to the fact that the idea of sport was invariably connected with the name. To quote but one example: the small principality of Malebum, situated at the foot of the mountain of Dhaulagiri, at the confluence of the Marsiangdi and Narayani rivers, is said to have owed its name to the legend that the Raja of the country, Nag Bamba, once defeated, by his superior courage and strength, a champion from Delhi, who had been reputed as invincible. The King was so delighted at the defeat of the professional wrestler that he conferred the title of Malla upon the victor. This was handed down to his descendants, with the consequence that the country acquired the name of Malebum, or "the land of the wrestler."

It is chiefly in connection with the Surajvansis that the name Malla is mentioned in the history of Nepal. From the early days of the Buddhist epoch the Mallas are said to have formed a colony in the neighbourhood of Vaishali, the city of the Surajvansis. Again, on the pillar of Changu Narayan, to the east of the valley of Nepal, an inscription is to be found which commemorates the triumphant campaign conducted by the Surajvansi, Mana Deva, against Mallapuri, the city of the Mallas, which is situated to the west of the valley and on the far side of the Gandak river.

As far as can be gathered from ancient history, it appears that the Surajvansis and Mallas were clans possessed of similar tastes and a like passion for adventure, which caused them both to covet the same mountain territory. In this struggle for land the Surajvansis subsequently came to occupy the central valley—now known as the valley of Nepal—the possession of which was ever destined to be a subject of dispute between themselves and their less fortunate rivals. Prior to its adoption by the sovereigns of Nepal, the title of Malla had already been applied to some of the kings of India, and by a curious coincidence the first of these latter to take the name appears to have been one of the rulers of Conjeveram, in the very south of India; hence Nepalese tradition has proclaimed it as the home of one of the first-known kings of Nepal, King Dharmadatta.

Abhara Malla, the successor of Ari Deva, who was responsible for the introduction of the new title, was the father of two sons, Jaya Deva Malla and Ananda Malla, of whom the former ruled over Patan, while the other is said to have been the founder of Bhatgaon, a town destined in later years to play a prominent part in the history of the country. He was, in addition, the founder of the Nepal era, the opening year of which corresponds with A.D. 1257.

At this period we have the first mention of the Khas in the history of Nepal, for during the reign of Ananda many men of that race came from the west and settled in the country. It was also during the reign of Ananda that a Rajput from the Dekkhan, Nanda Deva, is said, by many authorities, to have entered Nepal, and after defeating the present rulers, established a dynasty of his own, known as the Karnataki dynasty. Much doubt, however, exists about this line of kings, as there is no positive trace of them in history, and the most ancient of the Vanshavalis passes over the dynasty in silence. A certain amount of confusion regarding the various dynasties which apparently arose on the death of Ananda Malla may, however, be attributed to the fact that there were possibly several kingdoms in Nepal at this time. The King of Bhatgaon seems to have been the most powerful of these, and hence it is not improbable that this monarch may have been styled the King of Nepal. It is equally possible that the Karnataki or Vaisya Thakuri dynasty—another vague dynasty mentioned as being in existence at this time—was from some period or other, co-existent with the second Thakur dynasty of Amsu

Varman, and that after the death of Ananda Malla, either the Karnataki or the Vaisya Thakuri dynasty arrogated to itself the title of King of Nepal. While their exact history remains, at the present time, shrouded in mystery, these dynasties are worthy of mention for the fact that the advent of Nanda Deva, and later the Magar chieftain, Makunda Sen, introduced new and outside elements into the already varied history of the times.

Nanda Deva—whose Rajput ancestry, assigned to him by tradition, has now been generally accepted—has been represented as having conquered the whole of Nepal, and after driving the two Mallas, Jaya Deva and Ananda, to seek refuge in the plains near Tirhut, is said to have established his court at Bhatgaon, from which place he ruled over the three capital cities of the valley, Bhatgaon, Patan and Kathmandu. In Nepal he established a colony of soldiers who had accompanied him from the Nair country, in the Malabar district of Southern India, and from these the present race of Newars is supposed to have sprung. In this connection it is interesting to note that the word Karnataki, by which the dynasty of Nanda Deva was known, still survives to-day in the modern name Carnatic, by which name the country in the vicinity of Bangalore and Coimbatore is still known.

The reign of Hari Deva, the last of Nanda Deva's line, was brought to a premature conclusion by the sudden appearance of a powerful chief from the country to the west of the Nepal valley, and already alluded to here as Makunda Sen. Dr. D. Wright, in his *History of Nepal*, published in 1887, referring to this event, relates that "during the reign of the sixth and last king of the Karnataki dynasty, Hari Deva by name, a Magar attached to the court, was, through the machinations of some ministers, dismissed. This man returned to his home, and

ENTRANCE GATEWAY, BHATGAON

ENTRANCE TO BHATGAON DURBAR

spread the news that Nepal was a country where the roofs of the houses and the gutters through which the water ran were of pure gold. When the Magar Raja, by name Makunda Sen, a powerful and valiant potentate, heard of this, he came to Nepal from the country to the west, where he ruled, and defeated Hari Deva, who was then king. Many of the Nepalese troops were slain, and many fled, while the greatest confusion is said to have reigned in the three capitals. The conquerors broke and disfigured the images of the gods, and sent the Bhairava, in front of the temple of Machendra Nath, to their own country (the Palpa of to-day)."

There is a further legend to the effect that on the day on which Makunda Sen arrived at Patan the priests were about to celebrate the festival of Machendra Nath. At the sight of the invaders they fled, leaving the god to their tender mercies. At this moment the five *Nagas*, or serpents, forming the gilt canopy over his head, spouted out five jets of water upon the head of the god, and Makunda Sen, seized with respect, threw over the image the golden chain which adorned the neck of his horse. Machendra took it himself and placed it round his neck, and it is said to have remained there to this day.

The troops who came to Nepal in the conquering army of Makunda Sen are said to have comprised many Khas and Magars, two races of which up to that time little or nothing had been heard. These committed the most terrible excesses, and the southern face of Pasupati showed its formidable teeth, and sent a deity named Mahamari, the goddess of pestilence, who cleared the country of the troops of Makunda in fourteen days. Makunda himself escaped to the east in the disguise of a religious ascetic, but on arriving at Devighat, at the junction of the Tadi and Tirsuli rivers in the valley of Nawakot, to the west of Nepal, he died. Wright's account of the

Palpa monarch ends here, but it is interesting from the fact that it is the first occasion on which the Khas and Magar races—afterwards to be known as two of the most prominent of the fighting tribes—appear in the history of Nepal.

The country was completely devastated by the invasion from the west, and for seven or eight years complete anarchy reigned, until the Vaisya Thakurs from Nawakot, who had previously figured in history at the close of the Thakur dynasty of Amsu Varman, returned to Nepal and occupied the country. Their régime was marked by a system of complete decentralization, for in Patan each ward of the city had its own king, while no less than twelve ruled at the same time in Kathmandu and Bhatgaon. The Vaisya Thakurs dominated the country for 225 years, after which Harisinha Deva, King of Simraun, conquered Nepal and founded what was known as the Ajodhya dynasty. Simraun was the name of the old and strongly fortified capital of the powerful Hindu kingdom of Mithila, now known as Tirhut, which extended at that time from the Gandak to the river Kosi, and from the Ganges to the hills of Nepal.

Simraun had, so far, stood out alone against the tide of the great Mohammedan invasion, which had swept away or submerged the great Brahmanical empire which surrounded Tirhut; but in 1321 Harsinha found himself unable, in his turn, to resist the advance of the new Emperor of Delhi, Gheyas udin Tughlak. His kingdom was annexed and his capital destroyed, but rather than submit to the domination of a Mohammedan, Harsinha sought refuge in Nepal, where his descendants continued on the throne until they were displaced by Prithwi Narayan.

It was during the reign of Matisinha Deva, the second king of the new line, and about the year 1387, that relations were once more resumed between

China and Nepal. It appears that on this occasion China had taken the first step, for a letter came from the Emperor with a seal bearing an inscription which conferred an official distinction on the Nepalese monarch.

The interior history of Nepal becomes more and more involved and obscure during the closing stages of this, the Ajodhya, dynasty, but most chroniclers seem to agree that the daughter of the last king, Shyama Sinha Deva, was given in marriage to a daughter of one of the Mallas, who had fled to Tibet on the invasion of Nanda Deva, and that after the king's death there arose the third Thakur dynasty, which lasted until finally displaced by Prithwi Narayan in the middle of the eighteenth century.

Amongst the kings who comprised this dynasty the name of Yaksha Malla, the date of whose reign is given as 1429–1460, stands out prominently. Originally entrusted by his father with the government of Bhatgaon, Yaksha Malla became, in course of time, the most powerful of all the Thakur kings. According to Kirkpatrick, he annexed Morang, Tirhut and Gaya to his dominions, while he conquered Gurkha to the west and Shekkar Dzong in Tibet to the north. In addition to these fresh conquests, he completely subdued the refractory Rajas of Patan and Kathmandu. Before his death Yaksha Malla divided up his empire into four kingdoms—Bhatgaon, Kathmandu, Banepa and Patan. Of these, his elder son, Rava, or Rama Malla, was given the rule of Bhatgaon, and his younger son Kathmandu, to which was later added the rule of Banepa. Patan was said to have been destined for his daughter. This last town, however, was again to come under the sway of the royal house of Kathmandu, and did not form a separate kingdom until the beginning of the seventeenth century, when, in 1639, Harihara Sinha, the younger son of the seventh king of Kathmandu, established himself there and founded yet another dynasty, now known as the Patan dynasty.

It is important to note that after the death of Yaksha Malla there were no further kings of Nepal as a whole, but only a king of Bhatgaon, and another of Kathmandu. One of these kings, Bhupatindra Malla, was responsible for the erection of the two most striking and beautiful buildings which survive in Bhatgaon up to this day: the Durbar Hall, celebrated for its door of shining gilt, and the famous Nyat Pola, or temple of the five stages. His successor, Ranjit Malla, was defeated by Prithwi Narayan, the Gurkha, in 1769, and since that time Bhatgaon has ceased to have a separate ruler.

It is recorded that Ratna Malla, who had been appointed to rule over the kingdom of Kathmandu, was a man of great ambition, active and unscrupulous. Although destined to occupy the throne of Kathmandu, he still had to take possession of his capital by force and drive out the Thakurs who were, in reality, its proper masters. Shortly after this he declared war on the Thakurs of Nawakot, who were seeking to affirm their independence by their presumptuous and overbearing conduct, and utterly defeated them. Later on, Ratna Malla was himself hard pressed by the Tibetans and Bhutias, but the timely arrival of troops sent by the Magar king of Palpa, whom four Brahmans had persuaded to take action, enabled him to turn the tables on his new foes, who were heavily defeated. It was under the reign of this king that Mohammedans were seen for the first time in Nepal. These came for the purpose of trade. Another innovation was introduced by this monarch who, by the importation of copper from Tamba Khani, in the Chitlung valley, succeeded in creating a new type of currency.

Mahendra Malla, the fifth king of this dynasty,

SWAYAMBHUNATH TEMPLE

ENTRANCE GATEWAY, PATAN

was even more celebrated than his predecessors, for he it was who introduced into the country the coins known as *Mahendra Malli*, which exist in name in Nepal to this day.

On the death of the seventh king, Shiva Sinha, to whom, according to an existing inscription, was attributed the reparation of the temple of Swayambunath in 1594, his two sons divided the kingdom of Kathmandu into two portions, the elder, Lakshmi, retaining the city itself, while the younger, Harihara, founded a dynasty at Patan. There was already, at this period, a separate king of Bhatgaon, so that there were now three separate and distinct kingdoms in the valley of Nepal.

The elder son, Lakshmi, although subsequently becoming insane and kept in confinement for sixteen years, attained some distinction by building the wooden temple of Gorakhnath, also called Kath-Mandir, or the temple of wood; and it was not until this event that the town of Kathmandu, which had up to this time been known as Kantipura, was called by its present name, which means much the same as Kath-Mandir. Lakshmi was fortunate in possessing amongst his ministers a man of undoubted intelligence and devotion named Bhima Malla. This man, by personal visits to the country, had done much towards strengthening and consolidating relations with Tibet, and had eventually prevailed upon the Lama to conclude a sort of treaty of commerce with Nepal. Legends, however, associate him as having, presumably at some date later than that of which we are writing, himself led an army against Tibet, and Dr. Oldfield, in his *Sketches from Nepal*, relates how, near the village of Taria, on the road leading from Nawakot to Gosainthan, the following incident is said to have occurred.

A Tibetan Lama detached, by means of a powerful charm, a large rock from off the mountain-side and let it roll down on to the Nepalese army, but upon Bhima merely raising his hand the passage of the rock was checked and the blow averted.

His numerous acts of heroism and devotion, however, were powerless in the end to prevent Bhima from falling a victim to his own master's vacillating and capricious will, for shortly before that monarch's affliction he was condemned to death and executed.

Pratap Malla, who succeeded to the throne of Kathmandu on the death of his father, reigned for fifty years. His reign was distinguished by the foundation of innumerable religious edifices and monuments, amongst which the handsome square tank erected in honour of some Rani, and now known as the Rani Pokhra, situated at one end of the big Kathmandu parade ground, occupies a prominent place. His religious and literary activities—for there are many inscriptions that bear testimony to his ability as a poet—did not, however, prevent him from occasionally engaging in the usual petty warfare which was a feature in the lives of most of the early Nepalese potentates. He is said to have waged war with the King of Patan, and by some historians he is credited with having checked the aggressions of the Tibetans, who were encroaching on the north-west boundary of Nepal. During his lifetime Pratap Malla allowed each of his sons to reign in turn for a year, and after his death in 1689, he was succeeded by his third son, Mahindra Malla.

When the eleventh king of the line, Bhaskara Malla, died childless, a distant relative, Jagat Jaya Malla, was placed on the throne. In 1736 Jagat Jaya drove the King of Gurkha, who had extended his conquests even as far as Nawakot, back to his own country. Upon reaching Gurkha again the defeated monarch was deposed by Prithwi Narayan, perhaps the most dominating personality in all

Nepalese history, who was later to conquer the whole valley.

The Patan dynasty founded by the younger son of Shiva Sinha, the seventh king of Kathmandu, produced no ruler worthy of mention in this chapter. There were, in all, twelve kings of this line. The majority of them ruled for very short periods, when they either fell victims to the executioner's arm, or were robbed of their powers by various invaders. The dynasty came to an end in 1769, when Patan, in common with the other two kingdoms in the valley, fell a victim to the all-conquering Prithwi Narayan.

Before proceeding further with this narrative it should be pointed out that the events so far described have been almost entirely confined to the actual valley of Nepal, which consisted of the three small principalities of Kathmandu, Patan and Bhatgaon. The advent of Prithwi Narayan, however, a foreign king who hailed from beyond the boundaries of the valley, introduces a new historic element into the story, and it will be necessary, in the next few pages, to describe briefly the origin and early history of the Gurkhas, the new nation which, from now on, was to dominate the whole of Nepal.

Little is known of the Gurkhas as a nation previous to their invasion of the valley of Nepal, but ancient traditions and legends point to the fact that their royal family was lineally descended from the Rajput princes of Udaipur, their connection with this place being traceable from the following extract from the ancient history of India.

The two most powerful monarchs of the Surajvansi and Chandrabansi Rajas, who are said to have ruled over India in early days until they were defeated by the Mohammedans, were Vikramaditya and Salivahana. The former is generally said, by Hindu authorities, to have been installed about the year

57 B.C., and the latter is represented as having reigned about the year A.D. 80. These two monarchs selected a large number of rajas from amongst the remnants of the two dynasties mentioned above and divided the country up into various small principalities. Amongst these was Rishi Raja Rana, who was made Raja of Chotogarh, over which country his descendants ruled for thirteen generations. The last raja of this line, Deva Sarma Bhattarak, was defeated by the Mohammedans, who left the country after establishing their authority. On the loss of his independence, the son of Deva Sarma, by name Ayutaban, gave up the title of Bhattarak, and retained only the caste surname of Rana, a name which occupies a prominent place in the Khas and Magar castes to this day. A descendant of this line, to whose title of Rana was subsequently added the further title of Rava, or Rao, Bhupati Rana, had three sons, Udayabam Ranaji Rava, Fatthe Sing Ranaji Rava and Manmath Ranaji Rava. The unrivalled beauty of the daughter of Fatthe Sing, Sadal by name, attracted the attention of the Mohammedan Emperor of that day, who demanded that she should be given to him. When this was refused he attacked Chitor, and in the battle which ensued King Bhupati, Fatthe Sing and a great many Rajputs were killed. After this the beautiful daughter, the cause of the trouble, committed suicide by jumping into a pan of boiling oil.

Of the two remaining sons of King Bhupati, Udayabam Rana Rava founded Udaipur, where he settled with those of his followers who had escaped from the battle. The other brother, Manmath, went to Ujjain. This last had two sons, but in course of time they quarrelled and agreed to separate, the elder remaining at Ujjain, while the younger turned his steps towards the great mountains to the north of India, and, after many days of wandering, eventually reached the country now known as Nepal. The first

Photo. by Nepal Darbar

POKHRA BAZAAR

Photo. by Nepal Darbar

LAMJUNG DARBA

place of any importance in Nepal mentioned by him was Riri, a small town in the province of Palpa. From here he proceeded to Bhirkot, to the east of Riri, where he bought land and made himself a home, and it was here that, later on, his two sons were born. These two boys, Khancha and Mincha, were destined to become the first known rulers of that part of Central Nepal which is known as the home of the fighting tribes of the Magars and Gurungs of to-day. Khancha conquered the country of Mangranth, which lies to the west of the Gandak river, and comprises such districts as Gulmi, Dhor, Gaerhung and Bhirkot—all names connected, since time immemorial, with the Magar race. Mincha, although already chief of Nawakot, extended his rule in course of time to Kaski, Lamjung and Tannhu—equally well known as the stronghold of the Gurungs. According to Hamilton both Khancha and Mincha were of Magar descent, for in his account of Nepal, published over a hundred years ago, he writes: "The first two persons of the Gurkha family, of whom I have heard, were two brothers named Khancha and Mincha, words altogether barbarous, denoting their descent from a Magar family, and not from the Pamirs, as they pretend."

Although Khancha was, in reality, the founder of the imperial branch of the Gurkha family, he and his descendants remained for the time being Magars by faith and customs. Mincha, on the other hand, adopted the Hindu religion, and his descendants intermarried with the best families, although this was looked upon with disfavour by many of their kith and kin.

It will be necessary to leave the Magars, and the subsequent history of Khancha and his descendants, and, proceeding eastwards, to trace the career of that branch of the Mincha family who ruled at Kaski, where the subsequent constant quarrelling and warring between that chief and his neighbours, the Rajas of Lamjung and Tanhu, led to the capture of the town of Gurkha, from which place the modern inhabitants of Nepal take their name.

The chief of Lamjung, a small town to the north of Gurkha, was descended from the family who were in power at Kaski, and was a powerful and influential chief, whose word, not only the Kaski ruler, but also the Raja of Tanhu, another Gurung stronghold, was only too ready to obey.

The rulers of Nawakot have survived only in name, but the son of the forty-third, Jagdeva, who obtained the power at Kaski, had seven sons, of which the eldest succeeded him, and the second, Kalu Sah, became King of Lamjung. Kalu Sah was murdered, and for some time there was no raja at Lamjung, but eventually the inhabitants petitioned Kulmandan to send them another son as their ruler. On the undertaking that he should not suffer the same fate as his unfortunate brother, Kulmandan Sah allowed them to choose any one of the remaining six sons, and the choice fell on the youngest, Yasobam, who thereupon became King of Lamjung. Yasobam had two sons, of which the elder ruled over Lamjung; but the younger, Drabva Sah, deciding to cut himself adrift from his family, seized the city of Gurkha, and, after killing the raja, who belonged to the Khas race, with his own hand, occupied the throne and proclaimed himself king. This was in 1559. The kings who followed after Drabva Sah have left no mark on the history of their times, although the fourth, Sri Rama Sah, achieved some fame as a legislator, and introduced weights and measures, some of which are in use to this day.

In 1736 the ninth king of the house of Gurkha, Narbhupal Sah, hoping to profit by the numerous petty quarrels and dissensions in which, as he was fully aware, the three principalities of Kathmandu,

Photo. by Nepal Darbar

THE VILLAGES OF TANHU AND BANDIPUR

Patan and Bhatgaon were constantly involved, invaded the valley of Nepal. The raid, however, proved unsuccessful, for Jayaprakasa Malla, the thirteenth king of the Kathmandu dynasty, proved a courageous and skilful adversary, and the invaders had to beat an ignominious retreat. On the death of Narbhupal in 1742, his son, Prithwi Narayan Sah, became King of Gurkha, at the very early age of twelve.

With the accession of Prithwi Narayan to the throne of Gurkha, the history of Nepal may be said to have entered upon yet another phase, and it is deemed advisable, at this point, to review the situation and describe the main divisions into which the country was now divided, and the system of government existing in each.

To the west of the kingdom of Nepal—which, as has already been explained, consisted in those days of the three principalities whose jurisdiction extended beyond the confines of the actual valley itself as far as the Dudh Kosi river in the east and the river Trisulganga to the west—lay the kingdom of Gurkha, its eastern and western boundaries being the Trisulganga and Marsiangdi rivers. To the west of this again, and extending as far as the Kali river—now the actual western boundary of the country—the country was divided into forty-six principalities, each under a separate ruler. These last were composed of two groups. Firstly, a group of twenty-four small states, known as the Chaubisia Raj, or country of the twenty-four kings, and which comprised the main districts of Central Nepal, such as Palpa, Bhirkot, Lamjung, Kaski and Tanhu ; and secondly, the group of twenty-two dependencies, known as the Baisia Raj. These last were situated to the west of the Chaubisia Raj, and included such places as Daelekh, Jumla and Doti, the last named bordering on what is now the British district of Kumaon. All of these were nominally tributary to the Raja of Jumla, a petty chieftain whose territory lay in the high country to the north-west of Nepal.

To the east of the valley of Nepal, and beyond the Dudh Kosi river, lay the country of the Kirantis, at this time a quite independent state. It is, however, with the kingdom of Gurkha that we are, for the present, chiefly concerned, and it is to the history of that place that we must again return.

CHAPTER III

THE HISTORY OF NEPAL—*continued*

IN the year 1742, when Prithwi Narayan came to the throne, the main support of the Gurkha Government was afforded by the tribes of the Brahman and Kshettriya orders, then, as to-day, enjoying an authority and a prestige denied to members of the other classes. These were, for the most part, of the Khas and Magar tribes, the latter being such Magars as had been converted by the Brahmans and invested with the sacred thread; but men of other races, such as Gurungs, Newars, and the various menial classes, were also to be found. While there seemed to be no immediate cause calculated to disturb the peace that reigned for the moment in Gurkha, dark clouds were already beginning to form over the valley of Nepal, and there were evident signs that the three kingdoms of the Mallas were doomed to fall before long. The kings of both Bhatgaon and Kathmandu were men of ability and energy, and appeared genuinely eager to improve the conditions of their subjects and to embellish the seats of their Government by the erection of numerous religious monuments and edifices. Petty jealousies and dissensions, however, arising from such trivial matters as a quarrel over the erection of a certain stone pillar, or the arrest of subjects belonging to the rival kingdom, were commencing, slowly but surely, to sap the strength and security of both these kingdoms, while at the same time, as is often the case, a sort of religious upheaval, stirred into being by a Buddhist fanatic named Shodhana, who was trying to effect a religious revolution, added to the political troubles. While these conditions prevailed in Bhatgaon and Kathmandu, at Patan there existed a state of affairs bordering on anarchy. Many kings had occupied the throne since the accession of the first ruler, Harihara Sinha, in 1693; but on the death of the seventh king, Vishnu Malla, murders and expulsions followed each other in rapid succession, until the Sardars, or Nobles, who constituted the Government, sent an emissary to Prithwi Narayan. Prithwi's reputation was already beginning to expand outside his own territory, and the people of Patan asked him to accept the throne and restore order in the kingdom where, at that time, revolution and anarchy held sway.

Prithwi Narayan refused the offer of the people of Patan, but he deputed his youngest brother, Dalmadan Sah, to rule the kingdom for him, and this last reigned for four years, when he was deposed, and Tej Narsing Malla, a poor man, but of royal blood, was elected by the leaders of the principality to occupy the throne. It was the feud, however—ever increasing in magnitude—between the kingdoms of Bhatgaon and Kathmandu that nearly caused the direct intervention of Prithwi Narayan in the affairs of the Nepal valley, for in 1749 the King of Bhatgaon, exasperated by the aggressive and insulting attitude of Jayaprakasa, King of Kathmandu, asked Prithwi to come to his aid. Before any definite answer to this request had been received, however, Ranjit Malla, the Bhatgaon ruler, discovered that Prithwi Narayan had been secretly collecting an army of Gurkhas, and was even now intriguing with the chiefs of various neighbouring principalities, and scheming to seize the whole country of Nepal. His powers of persuasion were successful in gaining the support of many of the petty chieftains, who were further seduced by the promises of reward and increased power and authority held out to them. Prithwi's army gained possession of all the mountains surrounding the Nepal valley and built a chain of small forts on their summits, which gave them command of all the approaches as well. Realizing the danger which now threatened them, the three rulers of the Valley Kingdom agreed to cease their differences, and to make cause against the common enemy.

Before his actual invasion of the valley, Prithwi Narayan had had some experience of warfare, for soon after his accession to the throne he had attempted to lay hands on Nawakot, the key to the road leading to the valley of Nepal, but the unexpected arrival of the troops of the King of Kathmandu had frustrated his attempt. Thwarted, for the time being, close to home, he then turned his attention to the more distant regions that lay to the east of Kathmandu, where he seized the territory of his brother-in-law, situated on the borders of the Kiranti country, and took him back to Gurkha as a captive.

It was during the year 1749 that Prithwi Narayan entered on the first definite phase of the four years' war which was to end in the downfall of the triple kingdoms of the valley, and the transfer of the seat of power from Gurkha to Kathmandu. The town selected as the first object of attack, and which was destined to live in the history of Nepal by reason of the bravery of its inhabitants and the sufferings they underwent, was Kirtipur, situated upon a small rise some 300 feet above the surrounding plain in the south-west corner of the valley. Although under the suzerainty of Patan, to whose king the inhabitants looked in vain for support, the town was saved, for a time, by the personal bravery and gallant leadership of Jayaprakasa, the deposed King of Patan, who, arriving in the nick of time, repulsed the Gurkhas with great slaughter. The leader escaped with his life through the bravery and devotion of two men of low caste, who carried him away under cover of darkness to Nawakot. After this preliminary failure to achieve his object, Prithwi attempted to starve the country into submission, and with this object in view posted troops at all the passes in the mountains, in order to prevent the passage of supplies into the beleagured valley. Not content with this scheme, in the furtherance of which he employed brutal and tyrannical methods—hanging many persons of both sexes, whom he suspected of violating his orders—Prithwi resorted to his former policy of intrigue, and by means of flattery persuaded the Brahmans, then as now possessed of vast power and influence, to foment dissension amongst the nobles of the valley, many of whom were, in consequence, induced to accord him their moral, if not material, support.

In 1765 Prithwi Narayan, thinking the time was ripe for a renewed attack, invaded the valley and laid siege, for a second time, to Kirtipur, only to be again repulsed with heavy losses and driven back in ignominious flight to the hills. During the second attempt to seize Kirtipur, the brother of Prithwi, Suru Pratap by name, suffered the loss of an eye from an arrow, and this misfortune was subsequently made the occasion for a vengeance on the inhabitants of the city that was as barbarous as it was unprecedented. After a few months' respite, during which he was collecting a force for the third and final assault, Prithwi sent an army to invest the heroic city, and though the three kings of Patan, Bhatgaon and Kathmandu united their forces in an effort, borne of despair, to keep the dreaded foe at bay, this time he was successful, for a traitor from within went over to the enemy camp and led his forces, by a secret passage, into the lower part of the city. After this final act of treachery, in which a general amnesty was proclaimed, though never granted, the gallant inhabitants were forced to surrender, Jayaprakasa himself being fortunate enough to escape, with a handful of followers, to Patan. Finding those whom he had for so long been unable to subdue now at his mercy, the Gurkha king proceeded to wreak vengeance on them for the harm they had caused his brother, and shortly after their submission, ordered the noses and lips of all the inhabitants, even of infants who were not actually in arms, to be cut off, a few who could play on wind instruments only escaping this terrible fate. As a further reminder—if that should be necessary—he changed the name of the city to Naskatipur, or the City of Cut Noses.

Immediately after raising the siege of Kirtipur, Prithwi Narayan turned his attention to Patan, and by threatening the inhabitants of that city with a fate similar to that which had already befallen Kirtipur—with the additional loss of the right wrist as well—was on the point of bringing this town also to a speedy subjection. At this juncture, however, a totally unexpected and unforeseen event occurred, which was to draw the invading army away from Patan and enable the inhabitants to strengthen their preparations.

During the third and last assault on Kirtipur, the leader of the defence, Jayaprakasa, had sought the aid of the British in order to expel the Gurkha king and to maintain the not inconsiderable trade which existed at that time between Nepal and India. The British Government thereupon despatched a small force to the aid of the people of Nepal, but, with his ranks decimated by malaria, and finding the streams swollen and impassable, it being in the rainy season, Captain Kinloch, seeing himself in danger of being cut off from his provisions, decided to retire. This action, though somewhat damaging to the prestige of the British Army, afforded a welcome respite to the sore-pressed inhabitants of Patan, and postponed the fall of the city for nearly a year. The departure of Kinloch left the way open once more for Prithwi Narayan, but for the time being he paid no more attention to the place, but instead withdrew his army to Kathmandu, where he made all preparations for a long and protracted siege. It was during the early stages of this siege, which lasted for many months, that Prithwi, leaving a force before the city sufficient to deal with any situation, engaged in further operations in the country that lay to the east of the valley of Nepal. Here, near the town of Chaukot, close to the place now known as Dhulikhel, the Gurkha king found his way barred by a brave and skilful opponent, by name Mohindra Rai, who for six months offered a stout resistance, until paucity of numbers caused his eventual downfall in a hard-fought battle on June 21, 1768. Prithwi Narayan, with a clemency but rarely shown in his cruel, tyrannical nature, not only spared the life of his vanquished foe, but took his family under his protection and maintained them.

Kathmandu capitulated on September 29 of the same year, when entrance to the city was effected without any resistance, owing to the fact that the Newar festival of the *Indrajatra* was then in full swing, and the majority of the troops and inhabitants, sad to relate, were in a state of intoxication. Jayaprakasa, who had now become king, escaped to Patan, taking with him Tejnarsing, the ruler of that city. Kathmandu being now in his hands, Prithwi Narayan laid siege to Patan once more, and although Jayaprakasa and Tejnarsing did all they could to keep up the spirits and maintain the courage of their troops, their efforts were of no avail, for, cajoled by the false promises of the Brahmans, and with the example of Kirtipur before them, neither the soldiery nor the citizens would offer any resistance, and the city

DARBAR SQUARE, BHATGAON

GOLDEN GATEWAY, BHATGAON

surrendered without a struggle. All the fury of Prithwi's savage and cruel nature was turned upon the unfortunate town, which bears marks of the ravage inflicted upon it to this day.

Bhatgaon was now the only town that had survived the onslaught of the Gurkhas, and in the spring of 1769 the garrison of this place too succumbed a prey to the treachery and intrigue that had caused the downfall and ruin of Patan and Kathmandu.

The ruler of Bhatgaon, now an old and infirm man, from whom Prithwi Narayan had received much kindness and hospitality in his earlier days, was not molested, but, on the contrary, received kind and respectful treatment. Although asked by his vanquishers to continue his rule of the city, he asked permission to retire to Benares, where he died not long afterwards. Tejnarsing, the King of Patan, was confined in irons until he died, and Jayaprakasa, late King of Kathmandu, who had been wounded in the foot in an attempt to escape from Patan, was given permission to retire to Pasupati, where he died.

With the fall of the three kingdoms in the valley, the two countries of Gurkha and Nepal were united into one kingdom and under one ruler. Prithwi Narayan elected thenceforth to be known as the King of Nepal, a title which his descendants retain to the present day. From this time onwards the capital of the new ruler was transferred to Kathmandu, but he himself was not destined to remain idle for long, for almost directly after the submission of Bhatgaon, he proceeded to attack those states of the Chaubisia Raj which had not assisted him in his invasion of Nepal. Insatiable in his desire for fresh conquests he sent an army towards the east, in order to invade the country of the Kirantis, even menacing Sikkim, while other troops, under the command of a Thakur general, Kaji Kahar Sing, subdued the country towards the north as far as the passes of Kuti and Kirong, and to the south as far as the Terai. Of the twenty states of the Chaubisia Raj, Tanhu offered such a brave resistance that in 1772 Prithwi Narayan was forced to abandon these conquests, owing to the severe handling that his army had received. Although now master of the whole of Nepal, Prithwi did not live long enough to reap the full benefit of his triumphant career, for he died in 1775 at Mohan Tirtha, on the Gandak river, leaving behind him two sons, Pratab Sinha Sahi and Bahadur Sahi.

Pratab Sinha succeeded to the throne; and his first act was to imprison his brother, of whom he was extremely jealous. He reigned but for three years, in the course of which he waged war with Sikkim with varying success, though he did not succeed in forcing submission upon that country. After his death in 1778, his son, Ranbahadur, became king; but as he was as yet in his infancy, his uncle, Bahadur, immediately returned from his place of exile and appointed himself Regent. The death of their great leader had not brought the victorious advance of the Gurkhas to an end, for finding himself lacking in neither troops nor the sinews of war, the new ruler entered upon a campaign, with the object of extending his dominions to the west. In order to secure his assistance against the last few chiefs of the Chaubisia Raj who still retained their independence, he contracted a matrimonial alliance with the daughter of Mahadatta, the King of Palpa, and thereupon proposed a united campaign, with an equal share of the spoils. The Palpa king fell into the snare so cleverly laid, and a gallant and clever officer, Damodar Pande, a Khas by birth, was sent in charge of the Regent's forces to undertake the campaign. Betrayed by the King of Palpa, who alone might have saved them, the chiefs, not only of the Chaubisia Raj, but also of the twenty-two kingdoms away to the west, fell, one by one, before the well-trained and skilfully led troops of the invaders, and the long-sought-after prize was at last in the hands of the Gurkhas.

The greater part of the spoils Damodar took for his master, but he allowed Mahadatta to retain the states of Gulmi, Argha and Khachi. Following on his triumphant march, which was sweeping all before him, Damodar is said to have crossed the western boundary of modern Nepal, the river Kali, and invaded the province of Kumaon, which he annexed to the kingdom of Nepal. In the meantime the Regent was encountering difficulties in Kathmandu, for the infant's mother, a woman of great energy and talents, resented the presence of the intruder, and her influence and power were such that she contrived to secure his imprisonment and banished him once more, this time to Bettiah, where he remained until her death.

With the submission of the principalities in the west safely accomplished, the Gurkhas now turned their attention again to the east, and about the year 1787 an army penetrated Sikkim and occupied the capital. Seeing their frontiers menaced, the Tibetans moved a force to check the forward onslaught of the Gurkhas, but the attempt was ineffectual, and in 1789 Sikkim was annexed to Nepal. Finding Tibet an easy prey, the Gurkhas crossed the passes into that country and plundered Shekkar Dzong. Their activities in this direction, however, attracted the attention of the Chinese, who, tiring of the ceaseless and barefaced acts of aggression of the Nepalese, and their encroachment beyond the Himalaya into the plains of Tibet, despatched in 1792 an army of 70,000 men to punish the offenders. The Chinese, after desperate fighting, advanced into Nepal as far as Nawakot, only twenty miles from Kathmandu, where they forced the Darbar of the capital to submit to their terms.

On March 1, 1793, Colonel Kirkpatrick entered Nepal, the first Englishman to visit the country. He was sent at the instigation of Lord Cornwallis, who, on behalf of the British Government, had entered into a treaty with the King of Nepal acknowledging the independence and rights of that country. The articles of this treaty, which was purely commercial, regulated the duties on exports and imports between the territory of the old East India Company and that of Nepal. They had not been satisfactorily observed by the Nepalese, and with the object of placing the treaty on a more satisfactory footing, as well as the further promotion of friendship between the two nations, Colonel Kirkpatrick was instructed to try and induce the Nepalese to allow the establishment of a British Resident at Kathmandu. All efforts at effecting any agreement or compromise on this subject, however, proved unavailing, and Colonel Kirkpatrick left Nepal the same year, finding the Nepalese unwilling to embark upon any alliance of a closer or more binding nature.

In the meantime, undeterred by happenings in the east, where the campaign had ended in complete disaster, the brother of Damodar Pande, Jagakit, was extending the Gurkha conquests in the west. In 1794 the Garhwalis were heavily defeated in the valley of the Dun; the Garhwali Raja was killed and the Dun territory, and subsequently the whole of Garhwal, annexed by the all-conquering Gurkhas. With the conquest of Garhwal, the Gurkha kingdom now extended from Bhutan to Kashmir, and from the high mountains of Tibet to the border of the British provinces of Agra and Oudh, now the United Provinces, and Bihar to the south.

In 1795, on the death of the Queen Regent, Bahadur Sahi returned from his exile in Bettiah and immediately assumed the office of Regent. His triumph, however, was short-lived, for after a few months he was imprisoned by the king, Ranbahadur, now a young man of twenty years of age, and remained in confinement until his death, some two years later.

Ranbahadur now assumed the reins of government, but the profligacy and ignorance in which he had been kept during his minority by the cunning designs of his uncle had made him a dissolute and unprincipled man, and he practised excesses and outrages to an extent that even Nepal had hardly seen before. The king had two wives, the first and senior of whom was the daughter of a Gulmi Raja, named Lalita Tripari Sundari. She was a woman of great intelligence and a faithful and devoted wife, but bore her husband no children. The second was the daughter of a Parbatia Chetri, who bore him a son, the legitimate heir to the throne, although, as she was not of Rajput descent, the legitimacy was open to doubt. Both these wives, however, were subsequently discarded in favour of the daughter of a Brahman, who bore the king a son, by name Girbhan Juddha Vikram Sahi, who, though illegitimate—the law forbidding marriage between a Chetri and a woman of Brahman blood—was afterwards adopted as the heir. In 1800, in consequence of his excesses, Ranbahadur was compelled to abdicate, and accompanied by the senior Rani, retired to Benares while Girbhan Juddha, his bastard son, was put on the throne, and the able and prudent Damodar Pande, the successful leader of Bahadur Sahi's army, was appointed Prime Minister.

Amongst the retinue of Ranbahadur at Benares was a man named Bhim Sen, who, although occupying but a humble post in the household, was afterwards to rule his country's destinies for a period of nearly thirty years. The sudden change of Government led to the reintroduction of British policy into the affairs of Nepal, for the people, fearing that the presence of Ranbahadur in their territory might induce the British to intervene and reinstate the former ruler, formed a treaty, styled the "Treaty of Commerce and Alliance," with the British Government. This, as in the former case, was framed chiefly on a commercial basis, its main clauses being devoted to the encouragement and protection of the trade between Tibet and India which passed through Nepal, and by its terms the Darbar agreed to receive a permanent British Resident at Kathmandu.

At this time petticoat influence was playing an important part in the politics of Nepal, and the younger Rani, who, in compensation for the supersession of her own son, had been appointed Regent for the present king, fearing the return to power of her rivals, lost no time in ratifying the treaty with the British; but on the return of Lalita Tripari from Bettiah, whence she had been driven from Benares by the insults and persecution of her husband, a determined opposition to the treaty soon became manifest. As a result of this, Captain Knox, the newly appointed British Resident, finding that the Nepalese were becoming more and more averse to the idea of any closer relations with the British Government, and that their repugnance to his continuance as Resident was increasing, left Nepal and returned to India in March 1803. In the following year Lord Wellesley formally dissolved the alliance with the Nepal Durbar, and relations between the two countries were restored to the former negative state that obtained prior to the treaty of 1792. On the departure of Captain Knox, Ranbahadur Sahi, feeling that he could still depend on the devotion and loyal support of his former Ranis in Kathmandu, seized the first opportunity to leave his place of exile and return to Nepal. On nearing the capital he was met by a large body of troops under Damodar, who on hearing of his approach had set forth with the idea of opposing his advance.

The very troops sent to resist him, however, acclaimed Ranbahadur as their master, and shortly afterwards the gallant Damodar Pande was put to death, chiefly, it is said, at the instigation of Bhim Sen, a man whose influence with his royal master was increasing daily.

Ranbahadur now assumed the chief position in the land, and again committed excesses and outrages such as had tarnished his name on his first accession to power in 1795, devoting his time to a systematic persecution of the Brahmans, whose land, conferred upon them in perpetuity, he confiscated. The unhappy state of affairs in which Nepal now found itself continued for some three years, when Ranbahadur, in 1807, met his death at the hands of Sherbahadur, his illegitimate brother, who cut him down with his sword during a quarrel between the two. On the death of Ranbahadur, Girbhan Juddha, who although endowed with no real power had continued on the throne during all this time of storm and stress, and who, in fact, continued to occupy the throne until his death in 1816, appointed Bhim Sen as Prime Minister. It is generally considered to be about this time that Palpa, the last of the kingdoms of the Chaubisia Raj which had hitherto maintained its independence, fell into the hands of the all-powerful kingdom of Nepal, for General Amar Sing Thapa, the father of Bhim Sen, had marched there with a considerable force and the kingdom had surrendered without opposition. Turning his face again to the west, Amar Sing, advancing through Garhwal, threatened Kangra, in the Punjab, where the ruined fort still stands to this day. Here, however, he found himself confronted by an adversary as redoubtable as himself in the person of Ranjit Singh, the famous Sikh leader, who, embroiled in the war through personal quarrels with the Mohammedans, was at that time engaged in the conquest of the Punjab and Kashmir. Kangra, therefore, escaped the clutches of Amar Sing but came under the power of the Sikhs instead.

After the dissolution of the alliance in 1804, and for the next ten years or so after this date, the relations between the British Government and Nepal were of an unsatisfactory character. Ever since 1787 the Nepalese had been constantly seizing villages near or encroaching on the British frontier, and these constant acts of aggression, culminating in the seizure of some territory in the British district of Ramnagar and the murder of some police near Batoli, led to a declaration of war against Nepal in 1814.

At this time the Gurkha army consisted of 12,000 men who were equipped and disciplined after the pattern of the East India Company's army. The British troops which had been collected to oppose this force mustered some 30,000 men, including some irregulars, with sixty guns, and was told off into four divisions. Great as was the disparity in numbers, the war, which commenced on November 1, 1814, was not brought to a conclusion until March 4, 1816, chiefly owing to the bad leadership of the British generals who had been entrusted with the carrying out of the campaign. Although discreditable in the highest degree to the military capabilities of those in command, the war reflected the greatest credit on the troops, as the campaign proved to be one of the most arduous in which the Company's army had as yet engaged.

Operations commenced by the advance of a division from Meerut, under General Gillespie, over the Sewalik hills upon Dehra Dun, which was captured without opposition. Further progress, however, was impeded for a whole month by the heroic behaviour of the Gurkha garrison of the fort of Kalanga, or Nalapani, situated on a hill 500 to 600 feet high and five miles from Dehra Dun. Here, Balbahadur, the Gurkha commander, whose force consisted of 600 men, largely composed, it is said, of soldiers of the Purana Gorakh, a regiment composed entirely of Magars, resisted two attacks of General Gillespie's division. Three days' incessant shelling, however, compelled the eventual withdrawal of the heroic garrison, and the survivors, ninety in number, escaped through the British lines, but not before the British commander had been killed and 31 officers and 750 men killed and wounded.

General Martindell was appointed to succeed General Gillespie, and he, passing through Nahan, proceeded to attack Jythak, to which place Colonel Kesar Sing, with 2,000 of the pick of the Nepalese army, had retired from Nahan. Majors Ludlow and Richards were sent to occupy two ridges on the flanks of the Gurkha position, but here again the attackers met with the same stubborn resistance which had held up the British advance at Nalapani. Although the detachment under Richards achieved its object, Major Ludlow advanced too far, and his men, becoming panic-stricken at the ferocity of the counter-attack, in spite of the gallant efforts of their commander to rally them, would not stand, and the columns were obliged to retreat with the loss of 12 officers and 450 men wounded and killed.

For the British disaster now followed disaster, and again in February 1815 a force of 2,000 irregulars under Lieutenant Young suffered defeat at the hands of 200 Gurkhas, who were commanded by Ranjit Sing. In the meanwhile an advance was made by General Wood, commanding the division at Gorakhpur, in the direction of Batoli. In this his ill-success was only due to his own incompetence, for, at the very moment when the enemy, thinking the day was lost, were retiring from the position they were occupying in a Sal forest near Batoli, he himself ordered the retreat to be sounded, and the force retired without achieving its object. No better fortune attended the Company's other troops in the field, for on January 1, 1815, two posts belonging to the army of General Marley, who had been instructed to advance straight on Kathmandu through the Bichiakoh and Hetowra passes, were surprised in the Terai and completely cut up. General Marley was himself superseded for incompetence, but although a fine individual effort is recorded to the credit of Lieutenant Pickersgill, who surprised and cut up a force of 500 Gurkhas with a body of cavalry, the ensuing month brought no victory to the sorely tried army, for the new commander, General G. Wood, fearing the malaria of the Terai, would not risk a further advance, and the troops accordingly remained inactive.

So far the campaign could not be said to have progressed favourably for the British arms, but in December 1814 Lord Hastings gave orders for the raising of two corps of Kumaon levies under Colonel Gardiner and Major Hearsey, as he considered that a diversion from a new direction might have a good effect. Heavy fighting subsequently took place round Almora, where, although Hearsey had been defeated on his advance and been taken prisoner, Colonel Gardiner, supported by 2,000 men and 10 guns, proved successful. The whole of the province of Kumaon was surrendered on April 27, and the tide of evil fortune that had so far dogged the Company's army was stemmed. It was left to General Ochterlony, however, to administer the final blow, and retrieve the prestige that the many failures had lost to the British arms. Taking command in the middle of October, he conducted operations with the greatest perseverance and skill, and out-manœuvring General Amar Sing from position to position, he gradually forced him to withdraw to Malaun, where he was forced to capitulate, on the most honourable terms.

On the fall of Malaon the campaign of 1814–15

came to an end, but when peace negotiations were opened it was found impossible for the two Governments to come to terms, and the subsequent refusal of the Nepal Durbar to submit to the conditions imposed by Lord Hastings led to the resumption of hostilities in February 1816. General Ochterlony, who had been so successful in the previous campaign, advanced towards Kathmandu by the main route through the Terai, but found himself checked at the pass of Bichia Koh. Finding the position impregnable he gave up any further idea of carrying the position by means of a frontal attack; but the fates were once more propitious, and he discovered a secret path unknown to the enemy by which he was able to turn the position without any great difficulty. This turning movement, however, now brought him in front of Hariharpur, and the two actions which finally decided the issue of the campaign were both fought in the wooded and undulating country in the neighbourhood of that place.

On the night of February 28, a post, known as Sekha Khattri, situated on a hill to the left of the British position, was attacked by a large force of Gurkhas, but the successful resistance of the garrison gained the day. Although greatly outnumbered they resisted all the enemy attempts to dislodge them, and, on the arrival of strong reinforcements, were able to beat off the attackers, whose losses amounted to 800 killed and wounded.

The other operation took place, on March 1, some half a mile from Hariharpur, where the Gurkhas made desperate efforts to recover a strong point from which a picquet had been dislodged. The nature of the ground made hand-to-hand fighting—a form of warfare in which the Gurkhas particularly excelled—impossible, and with the arrival of guns on the scene the Gurkhas finally lost all chance of recapturing the position.

The news of the British victories at Sekha Khattri and Hariharpur caused the greatest consternation at Kathmandu, and the Darbar, finding that they were incapable of further resisting the efforts of their powerful neighbours, tendered an unqualified submission, and thus the second war came to an end.

On March 4 the Treaty of Segowli was signed, by the terms of which Nepal lost Sikkim, Kumaon, Garhwal and all the Terai to the west of the Gandak river, thus reducing the country to its present limits, the river Mechi on the east and the Kali on the west.

Lord Hastings had previously insisted that the appointment of a British Resident at Kathmandu was to be one of the fundamental conditions of peace, and consequently, in fulfilment of the terms, Mr. Gardner was selected to fill this post. With a view to better expressing his wish to maintain friendly relations between the two countries, Lord Hastings consented, at the end of 1816, to modify the treaty somewhat, and a portion of the Terai was restored to Nepal. A prominent feature of this treaty was the conclusion of an arrangement under which three regiments of Gurkhas were raised for service under the British Government, and which constituted the nucleus of the present establishment of ten regiments.

Immediately after the war the king, Girbhan Juddha Vikram Sahi, died, at the age of eighteen, and was succeeded by his son, Rajendra Vikram Sahi, then an infant of two years old. Girbhan Juddha had enjoyed no authority or power during his reign, but he is represented as having been pious and devout, and punctilious in his fastings and other religious observances. The persecution of the Brahmans, whom he greatly respected, by his former minister, Ranbahadur Sahi, must have caused him much distress.

The change of rulers and the accession of a king

of tender years, of whom little could be expected for some time, served to consolidate the power of Bhim Sen, the Prime Minister, as it also did, in no less degree, that of Lalita Tripari Sundari, the royal baby's grandmother. The premiership of Bhim Sen, then, as in modern days, the actual seat of authority by which the country is governed, was marked by the introduction of many acts of progress and reform. Fresh sources of revenue were found, a new and more effective system of taxation was introduced, and the efficiency and discipline of the army were increased to such an extent that Nepal became a strong military power.

For several years after the treaty of 1816 no events of any importance occurred to disturb the peace of the country, or to interfere with the fulfilment of the policy of reform introduced by the determined and persevering minister. In April 1832, however, the Queen Mother, Tripari Sundari, died, and from the date of her death the power which Bhim Sen had enjoyed for so many years began to wane. In 1833 Matbar Sing, the nephew of the Prime Minister, was appointed to the Government of Gurkha. At this time quite a young man, he was possessed of outstanding talents and energy, and his rapid rise to power had made him the object of envy and suspicion to Bhim Sen's brother, Ranbir Sing Thapa, at that time Commander-in-Chief of the Nepalese Army, a man who was doing his best to prejudice the young King against these two powerful relations.

In addition to the ill-feeling—ever tending to become greater—which existed within the family of the Prime Minister, yet another factor which foreboded evil in the future was becoming daily more apparent in the causes which appeared to be undermining the power he had hitherto enjoyed. The influence of the Pandi, or Brahman, party led by Ranjang, the son of Damodar Pandi, was now increasing daily, and from this date, 1838, the signs of a counter-revolution against the Thapas, or Bhim Sen's party, which had been supreme since the restoration of Ranbahadur Sahi, were beginning to take definite shape. The first blow against the latter fell in the following year, when some of Bhim Sen's former favourites were dismissed from office, and Matbar, on some trivial pretext, deprived of his command at Gurkha. It should be noted that petticoat influence was again, at this period, a predominating feature of the politics of Kathmandu, for the King had two wives, the first being an adherent of the Pandi faction, while the second was an equally staunch supporter of the Thapas, the party of Bhim Sen. It followed, therefore, that the positions of the two rival factions was very largely dependent on the influence and power enjoyed at the moment by their respective adherents at Court. In the middle of July 1803 the infant son of the senior Rani died suddenly. This was immediately made the pretext for undermining the authority which Bhim Sen at this time wielded, for the Pandi party, supported by the Rani herself, lost no time in spreading the report that the child's death had been instigated by Bhim Sen, some even declaring that the Prime Minister had intended to poison the lady herself. In consequence of the accusation, Bhim Sen, his nephew Matbar and several other notables were imprisoned and subjected to the greatest torture and indignity, while their properties were confiscated. Bhim Sen's political opponent, Ranjang, was appointed Prime Minister, but this time the counsels of the younger Rani prevailed, and the prisoners were subsequently released and their property returned to them. Though spared the indignities of imprisonment, Bhim Sen was fast losing his influence, and the dissension between the two Queens—the senior demanding the appointment of Ranjang, and the junior that of Bhim Sen—only served to increase the general confusion that existed.

In the spring of 1838 Matbar Sing retired into exile, for reasons never disclosed, and for the time the Pandis reigned supreme, the weak and vacillating monarch and his royal spouse both supporting that party. Ranjang was now definitely appointed Prime Minister and the persecution of the Thapas was once more renewed. All the old accusations against Bhim Sen were revived, and although that gallant old warrior loudly protested his innocence, his appeals were unheard, and driven to despair he committed suicide in the following year. With the removal of Bhim Sen the last obstacle in the path of the senior Rani and the Pandi party was removed, but their triumphant progress was to suffer a check from another quarter.

Since several years the Pandi faction had manifested a distinctly anti-British feeling, and this, supplemented by various acts of encroachment and aggression, had culminated in the forcible seizure of some territory in the Ramnagar district. The British Government replied by sending an armed force to the frontier, and this had the desired effect, for the Nepalese not only evacuated the occupied territory, but agreed to dismiss the Pandi Government as well, a type of Coalition Government being appointed in its stead.

In 1841 the senior Rani died, and in the following year, the existing rule being found unsatisfactory, a general meeting of the principal chiefs and officers of the State was called, at which the junior Rani was virtually invested with full political powers. Having been their most staunch supporter from the first, it was only natural that the new ruler should do all in her power to restore the Thapas to power. In February 1843, therefore, an invitation was sent to the exiled Matbar to return to Nepal, which, in an evil hour, he accepted, for he was to leave the peace and security of British protection for the storm and stress of a political life, in a state where but few men of authority came to a peaceful end. Amongst his followers was a young nephew, a man named Jang Bahadur, destined later to become perhaps the greatest of all the statesmen in the past history of Nepal. The tables were now turned on the Pandi party, for one of Matbar's first acts was, not unnaturally, to seek out his uncle's accusers and wreak vengeance in a way that was swift and effective, the leader of the party falling a victim to the executioner's knife.

For a while Matbar enjoyed full power, but he too was to suffer at the feminine hands which still influenced the lives of all those who were prominent in the politics of the country at this time. Disappointed in her estimate of the man she had striven to reinstate, the Queen plotted with the now almost imbecile King to bring about his downfall; and in May 1845 Matbar Sing was murdered, at the instigation, it is believed, of one Gagan Sing, her confidential attendant and paramour, who was notoriously hostile to the murdered man. Jang Bahadur was considered by many to have been a party to the murder as well, but evidence on this point is conflicting, and the extent of his participation in the crime cannot be accurately recorded.

The influence of the Queen, of whom he was now the avowed lover, secured the chief power for Gagan Sing, although he was never actually appointed Premier. At this time the great talents, daring and ability of Jang Bahadur gave him a moral position which those in power could hardly afford to ignore, although he merely retained his rank as a general and held no official post. For about a year after the death of Matbar, nothing of any great importance occurred, but the increasing intimacy between the

Queen and Gagan Sing, now Commander-in-Chief of the Army, was arousing the suspicion and jealousy of the King, who had him murdered as he was at prayer in his own house.

Of humble birth and at one time occupying the position of a menial in the palace, Gagan Sing had never been popular with the other chiefs and ministers, and there is little doubt that these latter were party to the crime, although the actual *coup de grâce* was said to have been administered by a Brahman, of known bad character, summoned for the purpose by the King. The assassination of Gagan Sing was the signal for an outburst of bloodshed and carnage, which bid fair to surpass in ferocity anything seen in Nepal for many years, for there now followed a general massacre of all those who were supposed to have been in any way connected with the crime, and thirty-one of the most influential chiefs met their death in this way.

After the massacre Jang Bahadur was appointed Prime Minister, but the Queen really exercised the supreme power, and it was not long before friction broke out anew. Becoming irritated at his ever evading the request to make her son the heir apparent, and to put the two princes, sons of the senior Rani, to death, the Queen hatched a plot to murder Jang Bahadur. Informed of her intentions by one of the generals, the Prime Minister ordered the immediate exile of the Queen, King and their two sons, the rightful heir apparent remaining in Nepal in order to act as Regent in the absence of his father. The King, profiting by the presence of several discontented exiles, now started, in his turn, a conspiracy against Jang Bahadur, but the movement found little support, either in military or civil circles, and to ease the situation and bring at any rate a semblance of security and stability to the disorganized country, on May 12 the heir apparent, Surendra Vikram Sahi, was proclaimed King. In September of this same year the deposed King made an organized attempt to recover the throne, but in an engagement with the small force sent by the Prime Minister, his followers were routed, while he himself was taken prisoner and incarcerated in Bhatgaon until the day of his death.

The rule of Jang Bahadur was distinguished by many reforms and an evident desire to use his undeniable talents and ability for the furtherance of the interests of his subjects and for the general good of the country over which he held sway. His desire to assist the British Government was manifested on several occasions, the first being in 1848, when he volunteered the service of eight regiments under his personal command, to assist the British in the war with the Sikhs, but for various reasons the offer could not be accepted.

In 1850 Jang Bahadur visited England, the object of his journey being to convey to Queen Victoria the respects of the King and the assurance of his continued friendship. It is recorded that the charm and sincerity of his manner made him at once a striking and popular figure in all circles. On his return from England a plot against the life of the Prime Minister was discovered, and it transpired that a party of notables, which included Jang Bahadur's younger brother and his cousin, on the pretext that the Premier had lost caste by eating and drinking with Europeans, had conspired to take his place and seize the powers of government. This conspiracy was frustrated, however, by General Bambahadur, the Premier's elder brother, who informed Jang Bahadur of what was about to happen. The conspirators were immediately arrested, but as Jang Bahadur was unwilling that they should be put to death, or suffer the hardly less terrible penalty of having their eyes put out, they were handed over to the British Government for confinement, and they remained in Allahabad until their death.

In 1854 the Nepalese, exasperated by the treatment which their subjects in Lhasa had been receiving at the hands of the Tibetans, entered into a war with that country. This war, which lasted for two years, was distinguished by the severity of the fighting and the unparalleled conditions of hardship under which the campaign was carried out, the scene of action being the high mountain plateau of Tibet, with its rough and inhospitable soil. The fighting raged chiefly round the passes of Kuti and Kirong, which were, in the first place, captured by the Gurkhas, then lost, and finally taken again. The bravery and energy of the father of the present Prime Minister eventually gained the day, and on March 31, 1856, the Tibetans, recognizing that the game was lost, decided to sign a peace. The terms included the surrender of the territory gained by the Nepalese as the result of the campaign, and the payment of an annual indemnity by the Tibetans of ten thousand rupees. At the same time customs duties on Nepalese goods entering Tibet were abolished, and a Nepalese representative was stationed in Lhasa, in order to protect the interests of Nepalese traders in that city.

On August 1, 1856, Jang Bahadur, to the surprise of all parties, including even his own brothers, resigned the premiership in favour of his brother Bambahadur, giving as the reason for his act the fact that he was weary of the hard work and responsibility that his office entailed. A short time after this, however, the King conferred upon him the title of Maharaja, and publicly invested him with the sovereign rights of the two principalities of Kaski and Lamjung, two states of the old twenty-two kingdoms. At the same time the succession to the premiership of the country was conferred upon Jang

Bahadur's family in perpetuity, in the first instance to his brother, and then to his sons in succession, while he himself was to assume the powers of Dictator over the foreign relations of Nepal.

The death of Bambahadur, however, in 1857 brought Jang Bahadur back again into the public eye, for, at the general wish of the King, his relations and all the leading chieftains, he assumed the office of Prime Minister once more in June of the same year. At this time the Mutiny had broken out in India, and Jang Bahadur, anxious to show his friendship for the British, offered the assistance of troops. This time the offer was gratefully accepted, and 12,000 troops, under the personal command of Jang Bahadur himself, assisted in the campaigns of 1857 and 1858, at the close of which the Prime Minister was created a Grand Commander of the Order of the Bath, and a tract of country on the Oudh frontier, ceded to the British Government in 1816, was restored to Nepal.

Sir Jang Bahadur died in 1877. The causes of his death were never correctly ascertained, some attributing it to fever, while the general opinion seemed to consider it to be due to injuries received from a wounded tiger—the pursuit of big game constituting his favourite pastime—and thus the career of one of the greatest of Nepal's sons was brought to a close.

In accordance with the laws of succession made in 1856, which obtain up to the present day, by which the office of Prime Minister falls to the nearest male relative, his elder brother, Ranodhip Sing, became Prime Minister. In 1877 the King, Surendra Vikram, died, after a reign lasting for thirty-four years, during which his power was purely nominal, and his grandson, Prithwi Viri Vikram Sahi, was appointed in his stead. To-day, as in the case of the time of which we are writing, although the Maharajadhiraj, as the King is called, is the nominal ruler of Nepal,

HIS HIGHNESS SIR CHANDRA SHAMSHER JUNG BAHADUR RANA G.C.B., G.C.M.G., G.C.S.I., G.C.V.O., D.C.L., MAHARAJA AND PRIME MINISTER OF NEPAL

and important documents of State are issued under his seal, he has no actual power, and the real government of the country is entirely in the hands of the Prime Minister, the striving for which office has been almost invariably the cause of the various political revolutions in Nepal.

Ranodhip Sing only lived to occupy his position for eight years, for in 1885 he was assassinated, and his nephew, Bir Shamsher Jang Bahadur Rana, was appointed to succeed him. On the latter's accession he at once proceeded to exile such of his relations as were likely to prove a source of danger to him, amongst whom figured the son of Sir Jang Bahadur. Despite two attempts to assassinate him, Bir Shamsher lived until 1901, when he died as the result of a burst blood vessel. His regime had been marked by moderation, liberality, and impartiality, and he was loved and respected by all. Sir Bir Shamsher—for he was knighted in 1893—was succeeded by his brother, Deb Shamsher, but in June of the same year, the new Premier was dismissed from office for misconduct, and exiled. He was succeeded by his brother, General Sir Chandra Shamsher, the then Commander-in-Chief, who still holds office at the present day.

PART II

GENERAL

CHAPTER IV

THE PEOPLE AND THEIR LANGUAGES

By Professor R. L. Turner

TO the Western European nothing could be more astonishing than the diversity of language which he would find in Nepal. In a population of under six millions in all there are spoken at least a score, if not indeed a still greater number, of languages, all mutually unintelligible, and some broken up again into numerous and often very different dialects. Even within the limits of a single valley there may be a village the inhabitants of which speak a language completely unintelligible to their neighbours in the next village a mile or two away.

The origin of this diversity is to be found firstly in the various migrations which have brought the present population into the country, and secondly in the difficulties of intercommunication imposed by the geographical features.

All observers have agreed that the bulk of the population display physical features which justify us in classing them as a whole as belonging to Mongolian or Mongoloid stock.

But it is likely that the Mongolians, whose advance down the southern slopes of the Himalaya appears to have taken place at a comparatively late period, may have overlaid an earlier population. What this was we cannot say with certainty. But recent researches have shown that in all probability the earlier inhabitants of North India belonged to the Austro-Asiatic race, or at least spoke Austro-Asiatic languages. As will be seen later, some authorities also include in this family certain of the many languages of Nepal. It is therefore probable that the speakers of these are the descendants, however much mingled in blood with the subsequent Mongolian invaders, of the original inhabitants whom those invaders found already in the country.

Tribes of Mongoloid stock are found along the whole length of the Himalaya with languages closely akin to those of the Tibetans on the northern side, while farther east similar peoples have driven the older Austro-Asiatic-speaking populations out of most of Burma and Siam.

This immigration of Mongolians is still to some extent proceeding, since there is a certain influx of people from Tibet into the higher valleys of Nepal. But the beginnings of the process probably go back to an early period and may well have preceded the first flow into the country of the third main component of the population.

These are the Aryan speakers from India proper, who, as we shall see, entered Nepal probably both from the west, along the hills, and from the plains on the south. Although certainly much less in number than the Mongolian element, they have yet affected the physical type to an appreciable degree, and among certain classes, such as Chetris, men and women may be seen of a type approximating to that usually found on the Gangetic plain.

It is doubtful what credence should be placed in the tradition that the Newārs, a race of Mongoloid appearance, and, as we shall see, with a language akin to that of Tibet, are of Dravidian stock and came originally to the valley from South India. But it must be remembered that the Dravidian languages once extended farther to the north, and that even to-day isolated representatives of this family reach up through Orissa into Bihar as far north as the Ganges itself.

Amidst this number of tribes of different speech and often of diverse origin there are to-day generally recognized eleven main divisions, arranged here in a descending order of social standing :

Brāhmans
Thākurs
Ċhetris or Khas
Gurungs
Magars
Newārs
Limbus
Rais
Sunwārs
Murmis
Thārus.

More detailed descriptions of these will be found in subsequent chapters. But it may be noted that the conquest of Nepal by the house of Gurkhā,* and the subsequent consolidation and extension of a central Government, has resulted in the name of Gurkhā being generally applied to all the inhabitants of Nepal.

We can now consider the distribution of the languages spoken by the different sections of the populations ; and in so doing make clear the origin of that one which, as the language of administration, has become the *lingua franca* of the whole country, and is destined eventually to exterminate all the others.

It has already been suggested that these multifarious languages belong to at least three distinct families of speech—(*a*) Muṇḍā, a division of Austro-

* Older Gōrkhā.

Asiatic; (*b*) Tibeto-Burman; (*c*) Indo-Aryan. It may be well to add here a note of warning: identity of language does not necessarily connote identity of race; and, as we have seen, in Nepal itself the aborigines, of whatsoever race, largely changed their language for that of the Mongolian invaders, while we may to-day observe the same process as the language of the latter is gradually replaced by the Aryan.

To the earliest or Muṇḍā stratum, J. Przyluski * ascribes the following:

Dārmiyā
Byāṅgsi
Caudāṅgsi
Khambu
Yākhā
Vāyu
Limbu
Thāmi

The Austro-Asiatic is a diverse family of languages spoken from Annam in the east to the plateau of Chhota Nagpur in the west. Of this family the Muṇḍā group is a sub-division spoken at one time over the whole of Northern India, but now confined to the plateau of Chhota Nagpur and possibly a few isolated dialects, on the southern face of the Himalaya, not only in Nepal itself, as noted above, but also further to the west. These languages are, however, so much mixed with elements from those which have for long been supplanting them, namely, Indo-Aryan and especially Tibeto-Burman, that some scholars † have classified them as belonging, not to the Muṇḍā, but to the Tibeto-Burman family.

* *Les Langues du Monde* (ed. Meillet and Cohen. Champion, Paris, 1924), p. 399.

† *E.g.* Prof. Sten Konow, in *Linguistic Survey of India*, vol. iii., pt i., pp. 179 ff. He admits, however, Muṇḍā influence.

Among the latter, in any case, the following are usually included :

Gurung
Magar
Newāri
Sunwār
Murmi.

Of these Newāri is the most important ; for it alone possesses a literature. Referring to it, Sten Konow says * : " Buddhism was introduced into Nepal at a very early date. The sacred books of the Nepalese Buddhists were written in Sanskrit, and that language became the principal vehicle of Nepalese literature. Nēwārī was, however, also used for literary purposes at a comparatively early period. Most Nēwārī books are, according to Hodgson, translations and comments from and upon the Sanskrit literature current in Nepal. We also find works on the history of the country, Sanskrit-Nēwārī dictionaries, and so forth, and in some Nepalese plays stage directions are written in Nēwārī. The oldest Nēwārī manuscript as yet known was written in the fourteenth century. It is a Vaṁśāvali, and chronicles the chief events in the history of Nepal from A.D. 1056 till 1388. We do not know how long before that time Nēwārī had been used as a literary language, and, on the whole, our knowledge about Nēwārī literature is very unsatisfactory."

The Tibeto-Burman family of languages are those spoken by some twenty millions of persons throughout Tibet and a large part of Burma, and related ultimately with Chinese. The speakers of these languages have, since an early period, gradually been overflowing on to the south side of the Himalaya, where they have overlaid the languages of the earlier Muṇḍā speakers.

* *Op. cit.*, p. 214.

In addition to the languages which have been provisionally classified as Muṇḍā or Tibeto-Burman, there are also many others, of which practically nothing is known but the names, *e.g.* Kāmkurā, and Rai, with its, at least, ten different dialects.

We come now to the third and most important family, the Indo-Aryan. At some time during the second millennium B.C. there appeared in the passes of the north-west people who called themselves Āryans. The language spoken by them had no connection with either of the two families we have been considering. On the contrary, it belongs to the great Indo-European family which comprises to-day most of the languages of Europe, including our own and, outside Europe, those of Armenia and Persia. Documents written in Indo-European languages have been found even as far east as Chinese Turkestan. The Aryans, when they appeared on the borders of India, had but recently parted company with the Iranians, from whose tongue are descended the Iranian languages spoken to-day from the Caucasus to the Pamirs, and from the Caspian to Baluchistan, including, of course, Persian itself. Both these groups —the Iranians left north of the Hindu Kush, and the Aryans, now beginning the invasion of India—spoke languages which, at that time, very closely resembled each other.

That of the Indo-Aryans is known to us first in the hymns of the Rig-Veda. Preserved as a literary language, it was eventually standardized under the name of Sanskrit. With the spread of Aryan conquest and the carrying of Aryan civilization over India, the language spoken by the conquerors, and by degrees imposed upon and learnt by the populations they conquered, underwent inevitable evolution and has developed, in the course of centuries, into the modern so-called Indo-Aryan languages of India, which, amongst innumerable dialects, include Kashmīrī, Sindhī, Panjābī, Hindī and Ūrdū, Bengali, Assamese, Oṛiyā, Gujarātī, and Marāṭhī. Later emigrations from India carried representatives of these languages in the south into Ceylon, as Singhalese, while in the north-west the wanderings of Gypsy bands have brought it back to Europe, where it still survives in the languages spoken at the present day by the Gypsies.

As the Aryans spread over the plains of India, so also they found their way south-east along the southern slopes of the Himalaya, and to-day an unbroken chain of Indo-Aryan dialects, showing certain characteristics in common and merging by almost imperceptible degrees one into the other, stretches from Chitral in the north-west, through Gilgit and Kashmir, along the whole southern slopes of the Himalaya through the Simla Hills, Garhwal and Kumaon, to Nepal.

These hill dialects, once carried into the valleys where they are now spoken, have, doubtless, been open from time to time to the influence of their relations in the plains, so that the hill dialects north of the Panjab have certain features in common with Panjābī; those north of the Hindī-speaking area have certain features in common with Hindī. Other historical accidents, such as the retreat of considerable numbers of Rajputs into the mountains under Mohammedan pressure, may have led to some further mixture of dialect. And subsequently to the extension of Aryan languages and influences over the Gangetic plain, similar forces must have been exercised by the political and cultural relations of the valley of Nepal itself with the country lying to the south. Indeed, immediately to the south, at the junction of the Ganges and the Son, was the city of Pātaliputra—the modern Patna—at one time capital of the empire of Aśoka, whose monuments have been found inside the boundaries of modern Nepal and who, according to tradition, visited that country in 249 B.C., and later founded the city of Patan to replace the older capital of Manju Patan. It follows, therefore, that the Indo-Aryan language first known to the inhabitants of the valley was probably that of the capital city of Pāṭaliputra, or of the plains lying between it and the Terai, which later developed into the group of dialects classed as Bihārī. One of these, Maithilī, immediately to the south of the eastern Nepal Terai, developed a literature dating from the fifteenth century, and traces of its influence can be seen in the dialects of the Terai and in the Valley itself. It was not from here, however, that the Indo-Aryan dialect, now the language of Government and administration throughout the kingdom of Nepal, variously called Khaskurā,* Parbatiyā, Gorkhāli, or officially and preferably, Nepāli, entered the country. For Nepāli has as its closest linguistic relation, not the Indo-Aryan dialects to its south on the plains, but that on the west, namely Kumaonī. It is thus the most easterly of those Indo-Aryan languages which made their way along the foothills of the Himalaya. It must have been brought, eventually, into the valley of Nepal by those movements of conquest and infiltration from west to east which culminated in the conquest of Kathmandu by the house of Gurkha.

Nepāli was not committed to writing until, as the language of the rulers, it reached the valley of Nepal ; and up to the present no documents in it have come to light which are very much more than

* Literally the language of the Khas. The Khas (Sanskrit *khaśa*) appear to have been a mountain tribe inhabiting the Himalaya who adopted and subsequently extended the language of the Aryan conquerors. Their traces are found in caste and place names along the whole length of the Himalaya. The popular derivation of the word *khas*, as meaning " the degraded," from the Nepāli *khasnu*, " to fall," is probably an invention on the part of the Brahmans, and is without foundation.

one hundred years old, though it may be hoped that others will still be found in the libraries of Kathmandu and elsewhere.

The direct connection of Nepāli with the Indo-Aryan languages of the western Himalaya is indicated by early sound-charges common to both but not shared by the languages of the plains. For example, in Sanskrit words containing a *t* following an *n* the *t* has been changed to *d*, while on the plains east of the Panjab it has remained unchanged : *e.g.* Sanskrit *tántuḥ*, " thread," becomes Lahndā *tand*, Nepāli *tā̃do*, " bowstring," while Hindī has *tā̃t*.

On the other hand, once these dialects had made their way along the mountains their speakers established closer relations with the people of the neighbouring plains, and it came about that the subsequent development progressed along lines similar to those of the adjoining plains. Thus, in Hindī an original short vowel followed by a double consonant was lengthened, and one of the consonants dropped ; whereas to the west, in Panjābī, such a group remained unchanged. Since this was a change which occurred at a date comparatively late, when the mountain languages had already made their way far to the east, we need not be surprised to find it in Nepāli, whereas those mountain dialects in touch with Panjābī do not show it. For example, Sanskrit *hástaḥ*, " hand," becomes in Panjābī *hatth*, but in Hindī *hāth*, and in Nepāli *hāt*.

Being brought into close contact with languages of Tibeto-Burman origin and imposed upon the speakers of these languages, Nepāli has not escaped influence from them. No doubt numerous words, and in particular idioms, in the language owe their origin to this source.

One other point must be noted. Reference was made above to the standardization of the early Indo-Aryan spoken language in a literary form called

Sanskrit. The spoken language, as we have seen, continued to change and develop, but the literary language, as far as its outward form was concerned, remained unchanged. In the same way Latin, developing as a spoken language variously into Italian, Spanish, French, and so on, as a literary language continued to be used unaltered into the Middle Ages and even to the present day in the Roman Church. A learned language, such as this, used side by side with a popular tongue, could not fail to influence it, and actually the modern Romance languages contain not only words inherited from their original Latin ancestor, such as French *frêle*, "weak," inherited from Latin *fragilis*, but also immense numbers of words borrowed from the literary, as French *fragile* borrowed, as opposed to inherited, from Latin *fragilis*.

Exactly the same state of affairs is found in India and the Indo-Aryan languages. Their basic vocabulary consists of words inherited from the original spoken Sanskrit, many of them much altered in the course of centuries. At the same time they have been filled with an ever-increasing number of words borrowed from literary Sanskrit. So in Nepāli we have common words, like those already quoted, *inherited* from Sanskrit, while others, and particularly words of religious significance since it was the Brahmans who learnt Sanskrit, have been *borrowed*. For example, words like *deutā*, "a god," *pujā*, "worship," *pavitra*, "pure," have been *borrowed* and not *inherited* from the Sanskrit *dēvatā*, *pūjā*, and *pavitra* respectively. The constant repetition of poems, often with a religious basis, and containing large numbers of such originally literary words, has led to their eventual adoption in the common speech, although not necessarily and exclusively in a religious sense. In other cases the fear of naming a dangerous animal by its proper name, or the desire to propitiate it by according it its high-sounding Sanskrit title, has led to the substitution of the popular inherited word by its Sanskrit original. Thus the snake is now no longer generally termed *sā̃p* (inherited word), but *sarpa* (borrowed Sanskrit original). And generally with the increase of printed works this incorporation of learned words is proceeding apace.

CHAPTER V

RELIGION AND FESTIVALS

AT one time Buddhism was the predominant religion of Nepal, but at the present day the great majority of the people profess the Hindu faith, although, apart from the inhabitants of the valley, they cannot be considered as very strict followers of that religion.

Buddhism, so far as it exists at the present time, has been very much modified by the adoption or retention of many Hindu doctrines and practices which have, naturally, been introduced into the country by outside influence. As is to be expected, the people living in the north and north-eastern parts of the country profess a religion which is but little removed from the Buddhism of present-day Tibet, although they too on occasion pay homage to the various Hindu deities and are classed officially as Hindus.

As an instance of this curious blending of Hinduism and Buddhism, it is interesting to note that situated in the very cloisters of Swayambhunath—the most revered Buddhist shrine in the whole of Nepal, and yearly visited by many pilgrims from Tibet and elsewhere—there is to be found a purely Hindu temple. This temple is dedicated to Devi Sitla, whose assistance is deemed necessary for recovery from smallpox, and was built at a time when that disease—at one time very common in Nepal—was rampant in the valley. The Buddhists of that time,

FIGURE OF KAL BHAIRAB, KATHMANDU

AT WORSHIP--SWAYAMBHUNATH

finding that they were no more immune from the disease than their neighbours of the Hindu persuasion, and having no appropriate deity of their own whose powers could be invoked in connection with this specific disease, had no scruples in building a new temple and dedicating it to the Hindu god. The temple is still in existence, and a visit to it is now considered an integral part of the elaborate ceremonial attendant upon a visit to this famous place of pilgrimage.

More examples of a similar nature could easily be cited, but the foregoing is sufficient to show the curious admixture of the two once rival religions which has taken place and is still continuing, but always towards the eventual extinction of Buddhism.

The rulers of Nepal are, of course, strict followers of the Hindu faith in all its details. Their example is primarily responsible for the fact that the majority of the people have adopted Hinduism as the fashionable cult, although, apart from the dwellers in the actual valley of Nepal, they cannot be said to be strict followers, either of this, the Buddhist, or any other religion.

Although somewhat lax in their religious observances, these mountain peoples are very fond of the displays of dancing, music, and general hilarity which are considered an indispensable adjunct to the majority of the Hindu festivals. It thus follows that these festivals, which differ but little from those practised in Hindustan, are celebrated throughout the length and breadth of the country with great enthusiasm.

Of these festivals, by far the most important is that known as Dasehra, which commemorates the victory of the goddess Durga over the monster Maheshur.

This festival, which lasts for ten days, usually takes place early in October, but the actual date for its commencement is determined by astrologers, and is dependent upon the position of the moon.

From the Gurkha point of view, the first six days, known technically as *Saradh*, are considered of comparatively little importance, but during this period a certain amount of ceremonial, which entails also much singing and dancing and, let it be noted, the usual libations, without which no such ceremony can be considered complete, takes place.

On the first day of the festival the Brahmans sow barley at the spot where they worship and sprinkle it daily with sacred water, but it is the last four days of this festival—known respectively as *Phulpati*, *Astami*, *Naumi* and *Dasami*—which are considered the most important in the whole Hindu calendar, and the Gurkha, however much he may neglect the remainder of his religious duties, usually contrives to be present at the almost continuous ritual which is carried on during this time.

At sunset on the seventh, or *Phulpati*, day, a big review of the Kathmandu garrison takes place. This is held on the Thuni Khel, the big grass-covered parade ground in the centre of the city. All round the Thuni Khel the people stand in dense masses awaiting the arrival of the King who, on this occasion, makes one of his rare appearances in public. Every one is dressed in gala attire, the bright dresses of the women-folk adding further touches of colour to the natural brightness of the scene. The troops are drawn up, forming three sides of a square, and the artillery is massed in the space left, with the combined bands of all the regiments in the centre. Near the middle of the parade ground is a large tree, and below this is a platform on which His Majesty, supported by a large gathering of Nepalese nobility, takes his stand. At a given signal all the troops on parade commence to fire a *feu-de-joie*, and in this the artillery presently join. The noise quickly becomes deafening and continues for some twenty minutes, when it suddenly ceases. His Majesty now takes his departure, and the enormous crowd of spectators which throng the edges of the parade ground gradually disperses to continue the festivities in their own homes, while the troops return to their quarters.

At sunset on the next, or *Astami*, day, the actual sacrificial ceremony commences and lasts throughout the night, only terminating at eight or nine the following morning.

On this occasion buffaloes and goats are sacrificed by means of decapitation with a *khukri*, the number thus offered to the goddess Durga being solely dependent on the means of those making the sacrifice. On this day the scene at the Kot, in Kathmandu, where no less than seven regiments are quartered, must be seen to be believed. The helpless animals are dragged into the arena, seemingly aware of their fate, and brought up to the post before which their executioner stands ready to administer the *coup-de-grâce*. The decapitation of a fully-grown buffalo at one stroke of the *khukri* is a feat demanding no ordinary strength and skill, and the successful performance of this operation invariably wins the applause of the crowd. Failure to sever the head from the body at one stroke is considered an occurrence of ill omen, and the onlookers are quick to express their disapproval of the performer's lack of skill by smearing his face with the still warm blood of his unfortunate victim. On the other hand, the clean, sure stroke is greeted with applause, and the performer is rewarded with the gift of a new white *pagri* or turban, which is tied round his head by the highest in rank present at the moment.

As the ceremony proceeds, both onlookers and performers become gradually worked up into a religious frenzy, stimulated by the gruesome sights taking place before them. By this time the arena is streaming with blood and the headless carcases of the recently slaughtered victims lie about on all sides. In one corner sits a Brahman, the priest officiating at the ceremony. Only he is imperturbable as he chants incessantly the appropriate verses from the Hindu sacred books. In front of him burns a small lamp ; this is the sacred flame, and around it are strewn the petals of the marigold, a flower indispensable for any Hindu religious ceremony. As each animal falls the body is dragged to one side and the dripping head is placed in front of the officiating priest, until finally he is almost obscured from view by the heap of bleeding tokens. The conclusion of the ceremony is marked by the pulling up of the young barley shoots which were planted on the first day. This is carried out by the Brahmans, who distribute small bunches in return for the gifts which are always offered to them.

A similar ceremony, but naturally on a smaller scale, takes place in every village in Nepal on this occasion, and the festival is also celebrated at the various headquarters of the Gurkha Regiments of the Indian Army.

Twenty days after the conclusion of the Dasehra, the festival known as Diwali takes place. This lasts for five days and is sacred to Lakshmi, the goddess of wealth and prosperity, and the consort of the god Vishnu. According to Hindu mythology, Vishnu is said to have killed at this time of the year Marakasur, a hitherto invincible giant, after a desperate battle, and to have entered his city in triumph early on the following morning. The people illuminated the city and received him with joy, and from this cause the festival is called " The Festival of Illumination," and is kept up to commemorate this great victory of Vishnu.

This festival, whatever its religious significance may formerly have been, is now looked upon as the

HANUMAN DHOKA (GATEWAY OF THE MONKEY GOD)
KATHMANDU

great opportunity of the year for gambling in public. Throughout Nepal gambling, normally forbidden, is for three days allowed to take place without let or hindrance, and the Gurkha, born gambler as he is, takes full advantage of the opportunity thus offered to indulge in one of his favourite pastimes.

There is no limit to which a Gurkha will not go when in gambling mood, and many are the stories relating to the heavy and curious stakes for which the Nepalese have, on occasion, played. It is stated, for instance, that men have staked their wives on a throw of the dice, and one man is even said to have cut off his left hand and placed it under a cloth as a stake. On finding himself the winner it is related of him that he demanded his opponent's hand, or the refund of the money he had previously lost.

Although gambling plays a very important part in this festival, the five days during which it takes place are dedicated to the worship of certain animals and people, who are looked upon as sacred during this period. There appears to be a slight variation in the objects worshipped, but, generally speaking, a day is devoted to the worship of each of the following: The crow; the dog; the cow; the bull; and the brother; but of these, only the last three appear to be worshipped throughout Nepal.

On the fifth, or last, day the daughters of the household regard their brothers in the light of deities, and the ceremonial on this occasion includes the placing by the sister of the caste mark on her brother's forehead.

During the whole period of Diwali every house is nightly illuminated by as many little lamps as the householders can produce; and in the case of a large city like Kathmandu this illumination is most effective. On every window are to be seen rows of little earthenware lamps, and even the streets are filled with brightly illuminated booths which, on closer inspection, prove to be gambling dens in miniature.

The third, and remaining, major festival celebrated throughout Nepal is that known as the Holi. This is held in honour of the god Krishna, and takes place eight days before the full moon of the month of *Phagun*, or early in March.

The ceremony consists in the erection of a wooden post, or pine tree, decorated with streamers of red-and-white cloth. On the last day of the festival this is burnt with much ceremony, and the rite is believed to represent the burning of the body of the old year.

During these eight days it is the fashion to perambulate the streets armed with a bag of bright-red powder, known as *golal*, with which passers-by are plentifully bombarded. Little regard is paid to the clothes, and towards the latter part of the festival most people exhibit traces of their active participation in it.

In former days this festival was the occasion for much obscene behaviour, but latterly this practice has become modified.

The remaining, purely Hindu, festivals are not of sufficient interest to merit detailed description, but for the benefit of those interested in the subject they are tabulated at the end of the book. Generally speaking they are similar in their detail to those of which a description may be found in the standard works on Hindu customs.

CHAPTER VI

THE GOVERNMENT AND ADMINISTRATION OF NEPAL

NEPAL enjoys complete political independence, and her relations with the British Government are regulated by the Treaty of Friendship. This was concluded in 1923, and its most important clauses accord to Nepal permission to import arms, ammunition, and other stores from and through British India. Each country has a minister accredited at the Court of the other. On the British side the minister is styled British Envoy at the Court of Nepal, and resides in Kathmandu. The Nepalese representative is accredited to the Government of India, with whom he deals direct.

It can thus be seen that the position of Nepal in no way resembles that of the Native States of India, whose policy is directed by Government, but is rather that of an ally with whom we are on particularly friendly terms.

Under the treaty of A.D. 1856 Nepal receives an annual tribute of ten thousand rupees from Tibet, but except in the way of trade, there is little intercourse between the two countries. A Nepalese representative is in residence at Lhasa, the capital of Tibet, but his duties are simply to safeguard the trade interests of his countrymen.

Nepal had, at one time, friendly relations with China, but since the Sino-Tibetan imbroglio the road from China to Nepal has remained blocked, and no effort has been made to reopen political relations with that country.

Landlocked as the country is, its external relations have, up to date, been confined to the above.

His Majesty the Maharajadhiraj, as the King is called, is the sovereign of this independent Hindu kingdom, but His Highness the Maharaja, as the Prime Minister is styled, is the virtual ruler of the country, and is, to all intents and purposes, supreme in all matters affecting government, whether political, administrative, executive, or military. He is advised, in all matters of importance, by ordinary and extraordinary councils, composed of Bharadars, or Nobles, and certain officers of the State, according as the nature and gravity of the matter under consideration may require.

For ordinary administrative purposes the country is divided into circles, each under a separate official known as Bara Hakim, or principal district officer, who is the local representative of the Government in all matters, both civil and military. His position is somewhat analagous to that of a district commissioner in India under the old regime, when civil and military duties were combined under one official.

A circle consists of a number of *jillas* (districts) or *thums*, in the hills, and of two *jillas* only in the Terai, and at the headquarters of each there are collectorates for revenue and also judicial courts.

The bulk of the revenue of the country is derived from land dues. The average rent per bigha (a measure of land equal to about half an acre) of land in the Terai varies, according to the class of land and locality, from two to nine rupees, and in the hills from a half to one rupee. The reason for the difference in rates is due to the fact that the Terai land is more productive than that in the hills.

Other sources of revenue are customs duty, fines levied at courts of justice, sale of timber, hides and skins. There is, however, no system of direct taxation in Nepal. The total amount of revenue is said, by the Nepal Government, to amount to about one and a half crores of rupees per annum.

For the collection and payment of land revenue each village has an officer known as a *Mukhiya* (head-man). These men collect rent from tenants of Government land and are provided with rent rolls for this purpose, the amounts so collected being paid into the nearest *jilla*. The Mukhiyas are remunerated with five per cent. of their collections, and are also entitled to one day's service a year from each man in their village. The office is hereditary, but in the event of a vacancy occurring by reason of there being no heir, or of a change necessitated by misconduct, the post is filled either by popular vote or by a nominee of the nearest Government official.

The chief crop of the Terai is rice, but oil seed and jute pulse are frequently grown as a second crop. In the lower hills rice, again, is the staple crop, while higher up its place is taken by maize, or Indian corn. After these, barley, wheat and millet are the other crops most usually seen.

Copper, iron and lead are to be found in various parts of Nepal, but the mines are worked on primitive lines and no attempt has been made to use modern scientific methods, it being left to the local inhabitants to extract what they can of the minerals on payment of certain royalties to Government.

Explorations made in what were considered promising areas in the Nepal valley have, so far, resulted in the finding of deposits of only lignite coal which, too inferior in quality for domestic purposes, is used only in brick kilns.

Nepal is fortunate in the possession of much valuable forest land, most of which is situated in the Terai area, but it is only of recent years that steps have been taken to exploit this to its fullest extent. Regarded as a timber-producing area, the Terai can be divided into four different forest zones. Firstly, the forests of Sal (*Shorea Robusta*), the most important tree in the country; secondly, the riveraine forests of Shisham (*Dalbergia Sissoo*) and Khair (*Acacia*); thirdly, mixed deciduous forests, in which the predominant trees are Asna (*Terminalia tomentosa*), the Simal (*Bombax Malabaricum*), and the Toon (*Cedrela Toona*); lastly, the moist Savannah forests, consisting of areas of tall grasses.

Above the Terai, in the temperate zone, where live a large part of the population, forest areas may again be divided. Firstly, a belt situated between 4,000 and 8,500 feet above sea-level, containing such trees as oaks, maples and pines; secondly, the forest above 8,500 feet, in which spruces, firs and larches are the chief species. Although the temperate zone is of comparatively little commercial importance, it fulfils a purpose even more important than that of a source of revenue, in that it supplies the dense population of this area with fuel, timber and grazing.

In the Alpine zones we find only the rhododendrons and juniper—trees of no commercial importance, although useful as fuel.

External trade is practically confined to British India. In former times a considerable amount of commerce was carried on with Tibet, but since the opening of the trade route between that country and Kalimpong, in North-Eastern Bengal, it has dwindled to a negligible quantity, and the trade with Tibet now consists mainly of bartering Nepalese foodstuffs and utensils for salt, wool, woollen blankets and sheep. Rice and other food grains, ghi, oil seeds, jute, animals, timber and dye-stuffs are the main constituents of the export trade with British India, piece goods, cotton twist and yarn, metals, spices, salt and sugar of the import trade.

Nepal has its own coinage, which is struck at the Government Mint at Kathmandu. It comprises gold, silver and copper coins, the first-named being used principally as ceremonial gifts. Of the silver coins there are pieces of various value, but those in current use are a rupee and a half-rupee piece, called *mohur*. The Nepali rupee stands at a discount of twenty-five per cent. compared with the rupee of British India. Copper coins are also manufactured at various places in the vicinity of the mines, and this accounts for the very crude appearance and design of many of the examples met with.

Owing to the absence throughout the country of roads, as we know them, the conveyance of mails is no easy problem, and this is carried out entirely by runners. Post offices are few and far between, and posts infrequent. As, however, the bulk of the people are practically illiterate, this is not such a hardship as might otherwise appear.

The laws are based on the Hindu *Shastras*, modified to suit the customs and spirit of the times. They may be roughly divided into civil, revenue and criminal, and do not differ greatly from the code in force in British India. It may be noted, however, that Brahmans and women are exempt from capital punishment, no matter what the nature of their crime. Prisoners undergoing sentence appear to be well cared for, and can often be seen in the streets of Kathmandu, where they are employed on various public works. They are allowed great latitude in the matter of leaving their prisons, and are easily recognizable by the tight-fitting steel bands which are riveted on to either leg.

In Kathmandu there is stationed a considerable police force, conspicuous by their blue cotton uniforms and scarlet *pagris*. Outside the valley of Nepal, the duties of the police are performed, to a great extent, by the soldiers forming the various local garrisons, their duties, in fact, consist of little else.

Nepal is essentially a military country, and the few Europeans who have from time to time been permitted to visit the valley have all remarked on the signs of military dominance met with at every turn. As has been pointed out, the local police work is almost entirely in the hands of the military, and the power thus obtained, together with their military rank, gives them almost complete dominance over the country people. A military party arriving in a small village has only to make known its wants to have them attended to immediately. The position is somewhat analogous to that obtaining in Prussia before the war, save that the soldiery of Nepal cannot be said to be on bad terms with the civil population. The profession of arms has, from time immemorial, been looked upon as the highest to which a man not of noble birth can attain, and it is this fact which is probably responsible for the respect with which members of the military profession are everywhere regarded.

The army, including the irregulars, or militia, stands at a total of slightly over 44,000, on a peace footing ; a large percentage for a country whose total population is but five and a half millions.

Recruits are obtained by voluntary enlistment, and in normal circumstances no difficulty is experienced in obtaining the requisite numbers.

The army is drawn from the so-called fighting classes of Nepal. These are all dwellers in the hill country, and consist of Thakurs, Chetris, Gurungs, Magars, Rais, Limbus and Sunwars. In a country where aristocratic birth is considered of paramount importance it naturally follows that the bulk of the army should be composed of the two first-named classes, the Chetris greatly predominating.

The army is divided into 31 regiments, which include two of artillery, and a regiment of cavalry, consisting of but 120 sabres. These latter are used mostly as orderlies and as outriders in attendance upon members of the royal family.

COLOUR PARTY OF A NEPALESE REGIMENT

NEPALESE TROOPS ON PARADE, KATHMANDU

In the majority of the regiments men of all the above-mentioned classes are to be found serving side by side. There are, however, a few regiments whose members consist entirely of one caste. Amongst these latter are the Kali Bahadur and the Kali Parshad Regiments, composed entirely of Gurungs, and the Purana Gorakh, whose ranks are only open to Magars.

The *corps d'élite*, however, is composed of men of all classes, and is known as the Rifle Regiment. The men in it are of magnificent physique, and none of them is less than six feet in height. They are almost entirely employed in guarding the royal person, and may be regarded in a similar light to our own Household Troops.

In addition to the regular army, the greater part of which is permanently stationed in the capital, there is a further body of troops, known as the militia. These are raised locally, and do not usually leave the districts in which they live. They enrol for a period of five years, and are trained for three months every other year.

Until quite recently the army was mostly paid by means of grants of land. Of recent years, however, these land payments have been gradually replaced by monthly payments in cash, and before long the whole army will be paid on this system.

The regulars are armed with short Lee-Enfield and Martini-Henry rifles, together with a few Lewis and machine guns; while the militia have only muskets. The artillery is equipped with light mountain guns, and has in addition a few mortars, or howitzers, of very old pattern. Firearms and ammunition are manufactured at the Government arsenal, but their make and quality are greatly inferior to the modern weapons of precision with which the army is now armed, and which are, in the main, the gift of the British Government.

One curious custom in connection with the army needs to be mentioned. This is the system of service by rotation. Thus, if after a time a man desires to proceed to his home, he first arranges for a friend to take the place he will leave vacant in the regiment. These men, known as Dhakre, after spending a few years at home, may again enter the ranks and take the place of others who, in turn, lie by for a year or two. This system, particularly adapted to the country, affords much scope for the gratification of the Gurkhas' innate yearning for military service, and in addition provides a large body of partially trained men which would be available in any time of emergency.

The regiments stationed at the capital are not provided with quarters, but make their own arrangements. This system, whilst undoubtedly unsatisfactory from many points of view, is well enough adapted to the present needs of the army. It is reasonable to predict, however, that as the country progresses barracks will eventually be provided, and the discipline of the army will, in consequence, improve.

Before the War the whole army was clothed in bright-blue cotton uniform, with a very distinctive headdress, consisting of a kind of skull cap with a tightly rolled brim all round, adorned with silver or brass wire, according to rank, and finished off with the regimental emblem in front. Though still worn in the country districts, this picturesque dress is gradually giving way to the more serviceable khaki.

Although the material of which the Nepalese Army is composed is undoubtedly good, and admirably adapted to the defence of the country, for which it is primarily intended, yet it can in no way be compared with modern regular troops. Perhaps the chief weakness in the army is due to the fact that the majority of its officers are chosen by reason of their social position, rather than for their military efficiency; but, even so, the army would undoubtedly constitute a formidable foe if ever called upon to fight in its own hill country.

CHAPTER VII

GENERAL CUSTOMS OF THE NEPALESE

IN appearance the Gurkha is decidedly Mongolian, and possesses the high cheek-bones and narrow almond-shaped eyes common to that race. Small in stature—the average height is about 5 feet 2 inches—and fair of complexion, they may be said to bear a strong facial resemblance to the Japanese or Chinese.

Generally speaking the Gurkha is sturdy and thick-set, and he is the possessor of splendidly formed nether limbs, admirably adapted for the rough and pathless mountain country which is his home.

Owing to the fact that there are few roads in the country and, outside the valley of Nepal and the main Raksal-Kathmandu high road, no facilities for transport, the boys and girls of the country are accustomed from their earliest youth to walk great distances carrying loads on their backs, with the result that, as they mature, they are often able to lift the most incredible weights. Their stamina and physique, however, naturally vary according to whether the particular district in which they live is healthy or not. As has already been pointed out, the country comprises every type of climate, from the tropical heat of the Terai to the snow and ice of the higher mountains, and it naturally follows that the standard of physical fitness must vary accordingly. Thus it is often noticeable that the physique of tribes such as the Limbus, who live in the higher temperate climate of the Eastern Himalaya, is superior to that of some of the people who inhabit the lower valleys of the centre. Food supply is another thing which has great effect on the physique of the people, and it is very noticeable that men from certain notably fertile districts are far stronger and more muscular than those from parts where the crops are known to be poor.

Although the simple fare and life in the open air often ensure a stamina and state of health that are denied to many who live in the plains, yet the physique of Gurkhas as a whole cannot be said to attain to a standard any higher than—if as high as—that of some of the hardy races of the north-west frontier of India. Susceptible to chills, and the ordinary minor ailments, they are particularly prone to tuberculosis, due possibly to the fact that many of them have a habit, not only of sleeping in a room devoid of all ventilation, but of covering their heads during sleep. Although under the regime of the present Prime Minister great progress has been made in the spread of hygiene and medical knowledge in Nepal, yet in the country districts qualified medical officers are few and far between, and the sick have perforce to be entrusted to the care of the local Baidyas, a race of itinerant quacks.

The occupation of the bulk of the people of Nepal is either agricultural or pastoral. Of industry, there is little to be said, for beyond homespun cloths, paper made from the bark of trees, brass, copper, iron and wooden utensils for personal use, but little else is manufactured.

Arts and crafts, such as they are, are almost entirely in the hands of the Newars, who, on account of their superior intelligence, fill most of the civil posts under Government.

The dress of the poorer classes throughout Nepal consists in the case of a man of the following: a langoti, or strip of cloth round the loins; a thin piece of cloth wound round and round the waist, into which the khukri is tucked, and which, coming down to just above the knees, may be compared to a kind of thin kilt; a thin cotton waistcoat, either of European pattern, or made to fold across the chest and tied outside and inside by tapes and known as a cholo; a small, usually black, round cap, high on one side and low on the other; and finally a pair of stout country-made shoes sewn with strips of raw hide. In addition to the above, Gurungs, and a few other tribes living in the higher elevations, wear a thick rough sheet known as a khadi. This is worn over the top part of the body, knotted about the centre of the chest in such a way as to leave the arms bare and to form a large bag, in the small of the back, in which pots and pans and other odds and ends can be carried. This, however, is never worn in Eastern Nepal, and constitutes one of the few small points in which the dress varies slightly in different districts. The Limbus, Rais, and races inhabiting the eastern districts in their turn usually dispense with the kilt-like cloth round the waist, and wear, in its place, loose-fitting trousers. This is probably due to the fact that they live in a colder climate and so require more protection for the legs.

The national dress of the upper classes of Nepal, and of the people who live in the larger towns, is somewhat different from the above. It consists of the following: a double-breasted garment, known as a chaubandi, fitting tight over the waist, and fastened inside and outside at the shoulders, and at the waist, by tapes. The chaubandi is often made of a double layer of thin shiny cloth padded with cotton wool and forms a warm and comfortable coat. Loose trousers of the same material as the coat and a long length of thin white cloth wound round the waist complete the outfit. The cap is as already described, and shoes of European pattern are preferred to the ordinary Nepali shoe.

STONE FIGURE IN THE DARBAR SQUARE, KATHMANDU

BHOTIYA GIRLS FROM CENTRAL NEPAL

Nearly every one in Nepal, no matter what his station, wears a khukri. The khukri is the national weapon of the Gurkhas, and is a short, heavy knife with a broad and very curved blade. It is worn, sheathed in a leather scabbard, tucked into the cloth round the waist. The uses to which a khukri is put are many and various. By frequent practice from their early youth upwards the Gurkhas become remarkably proficient in its use, and competitions are frequently held in which the competitors display their skill in slicing branches of trees and in other feats which demand a strong arm and clear eye.

The dress of the women consists of a bodice (cholo), a skirt (phariya or guniu) formed of many lengths of cloth wound round the waist, and a shawl or veil worn over the head, but leaving the face uncovered. This last is known as the majetro, and is usually of a very bright colour, and the presence of a number of Gurkha women at some public festival or entertainment rarely fails to add a picturesque touch to the scene.

Like their sisters in other parts of the world, the Gurkha women delight in jewellery. Besides being mere articles of adornment, however, jewellery serves a much more practical purpose, for into it are put all the savings of the family, and it may even be said to represent the family savings bank. The jewellery consists, in the main, of large gold earrings (sun), bracelets (balo), anklets (chura and kalli), nose ring (bulaki), and necklaces of various types and designs, prominent amongst them being that known as the tilhari, a heavy ornament composed of alternate reels of gilt and coloured thread.

Up to the age of fifteen or so the young men also wear silver bracelets and plain gold earrings. Every one in Nepal has his or her ears pierced soon after birth, and although the men discontinue the wearing of their earrings as they grow up they take particular care that the holes in their ears shall remain open, and usually place cloves, or small splinters of wood, in them for this purpose.

Rice forms the staple food of the Gurkhas when they can get it, but in view of the fact that it is not procurable everywhere in the hill country, the crop being confined to the larger and more fertile valleys of the lower elevations, dwellers in the higher parts of the country have to content themselves with Indian corn, buckwheat, or millet, from which they make a rough kind of bread, and also a type of porridge, known as dhenro.

The rice, when cooked, is rarely eaten alone, but is usually supplemented with meat, spices, vegetables and, most common of all, the split pulse known as dal. The addition of the last is the means of introducing the vexed question of caste prejudices into their food, from which, on the whole, it is singularly free, for, with this one exception, all Gurkhas will eat everything in common. This prejudice in the case of dal and rice is only applicable to men after they have married, but even this dish may be taken in common if it has been prepared by a Brahman of the Opaddhia class.

Gurkhas will eat every kind of meat with the exception of cows and female goats. They are especially partial to every form of game, such as pheasant, pigeon, pea-fowl and wild pig, while chickens are eaten by all castes save the Brahman and Chetri. Whilst dealing with the question of food it should be pointed out that there are, of course, cases in which certain articles of food are eschewed by certain sects and tribes. To mention a few examples: the Gurungs of Central Nepal make no secret of the fact that they eat buffalo's meat in their own homes, but, on the other hand, they must not even touch domestic pig; while the Ghales will not touch chickens, eggs, or hares. Again, in Eastern Nepal, the Bantuwa, Kulung and Nechali clans of the Rai tribe do not eat goat's flesh; while certain other tribes draw the line even at fish, otherwise generally regarded by the Nepalese as the greatest delicacy of all. Where women are present the food is cooked by them, and, when ready, set before the men-folk of the house. The women do not eat with the men, however, and their share consists of what is left over after the men have finished. As is the prevailing custom all over the East, both men and women invariably squat on their heels to eat. Cutlery is quite unknown, the fingers of the right hand taking the place of knife and fork.

In the matter of what they drink, Gurkhas, again, save Brahmans and Chetris, have no scruples whatsoever, and they have no hesitation in sampling any kind of ordinary European stimulant, such as wine, beer, or any sort of spirits. In their own homes they brew a kind of beer, made from fermented rice, millet, or Indian corn, known as *ianr*, of which they are very fond, but while they also drink a kind of spirit known as raksi, the ordinary commissariat rum, such as is procurable in the canteen of Gurkha regiments, is perhaps their favourite beverage.

The houses of the poorer classes are made of stone and mud bricks, and, outside the valley of Nepal, the roofs are usually made of thatch. Usually single-storied, they contain but few rooms, one for sleeping and one more for cooking being generally considered sufficient. In the front of the house there is usually a large veranda. This is used as a sitting-room, and forms an indispensable adjunct to a home where inside accommodation is so limited. Humble as is their exterior, the conditions that prevail within are of an equally simple nature, for of furniture there is little or none, and it is usual for the inmates to sleep on the floor. Though from a European point of view they appear to be lacking in what may be regarded as almost the essentials of comfort, houses in Nepal are clean and well kept. Surrounded as they often are by gay patches of brightly coloured flowers, they present a pleasing, homely appearance, and one that is in keeping with the cheerful and simple character of the people who live in them.

Although the cottages of the humbler folk take this simple form, the occasional residences of local officials, and such buildings as Government store-houses, to be met with in the hills, are built on much more imposing lines, and with their high white-washed walls and—too often, alas—shining tin roofs form conspicuous landmarks in the quiet, unassuming landscape.

The Gurkha differs from the people of India as much in appearance as he does in character. His Mongolian origin is responsible for a vein of humour and bonhomie that is not found in the more solemn and austere races of Aryan descent, and his frank and open character permits an intimacy in his intercourse with Europeans rarely to be found in the East. Shy and somewhat reserved at first, he attaches himself very closely to those under whom he takes service, and the devotion and loyalty of the Gurkhas who enlist in our service to their British officers often tend to become what might almost be termed a fault. Coming from a strange country, which, though bordering on India, is so far removed from it in matters of language, customs, and even thought, the young Gurkha, naturally, feels himself to be a stranger in a strange land when first he sets foot in India. His ignorance of the language, which though naturally lessening in course of time, serves to accentuate his awkwardness and seeming inability to understand what is required of him, occasionally gives people who are unfamiliar with him and his ways the impression that he is inclined to be somewhat surly and aloof. Many years' service, even, often seem to fail to create any desire in the Gurkha to interest himself in people, European or otherwise, with whom he is not directly concerned, or who are unable to speak or understand his language. Once his confidence is gained, however, he reveals, little by little, his true character and proves himself a staunch and faithful friend.

Gurkhas are passionately fond of flowers, with which they delight to adorn their caps and persons. They take a great pride in their appearance, and the gay stockings and mufflers affected by our soldiers when in mufti bear a testimony to their love of bright colours. These last are usually knitted by the women, who enter whole-heartedly into the domestic side of married life, and who take a great interest in administering to the needs and whims of their men-folk. Unhampered by any trammels of caste, the Gurkha women of the hill districts enjoy a greater measure of freedom than is allowed to their sisters in the Indian plains, and they are, accordingly, able to take an interest in life and what is going on around them in a manner more approximating to that of the women of Europe. They are, as a rule, bright and intelligent, and have the same gift of humour and repartee as the men, while those who obtain employment in such occupation as picking tea in the Darjeeling and other tea districts almost invariably prove to be capable and industrious workers. Like their men-folk, they are great smokers, and also share their predilection for rice beer raksi, or any other intoxicating liquor that may come their way.

Life in a hill village is, of necessity, lacking in the amusements open to dwellers in cities, and it falls to the lot of the people themselves to make it cheerful or depressing as the case may be. Fortunately, the Gurkha is in this respect fully up to the occasion, and his cheery, buoyant nature comes quickly to the fore in the production of pastimes and amusements of his own with which to compensate for the lack of other more worldly distractions. A born soldier, the game he perhaps delights in the most during his childhood is that of playing at soldiers, and little groups of children can often be seen drilling each other, or taking part in the mimic battles dear to the youth of most European countries.

It is in the matter of sport, however, that the Gurkha chiefly excels. Living, as he does, in a country where game is abundant and the game laws lax, he has ample opportunity of indulging his favourite hobby, and this love of sport, fostered in his boyhood days, seems to increase rather than diminish with advancing years. The methods they adopt when out shooting cannot be said even to approximate to those of English sportsmen, but they are very effective none the less. They usually stalk their prey until it is within a few yards of the muzzle of their weapon and then fire, with the result in some cases that the animal or bird is practically blown to pieces. In all cases, however, the guiding principle is to get full value for the amount of ammunition expended, and in order to bring this about they usually reserve their fire until they have manœuvred themselves into such a position as to get three or four birds in one line.

Neither guns nor ammunition are easily procurable in Nepal, and a licence is required in order to keep them. There are, however, muzzle-loading weapons of a somewhat primitive design which are obtainable in the country, and with these and the weapons purchased in India by soldiers before their retirement, there are but few families in the hills where at least one of its members does not possess a weapon of some kind or another.

Besides guns, which even if not altogether unprocurable at any rate involve a certain amount of expense in their purchase and upkeep, there is another weapon which is much used by the country people of Nepal, the pellet bow. Visitors to certain parts of India, where large numbers of Gurkhas are either stationed or domiciled, may often see them, bow in hand, walking slowly along by the side of some road or stream, their faces turned upward with anxious eyes, in the hope that some unsuspecting bird may shortly offer a target on which they may try their skill. Although his implements are often primitive, and his manner of shooting somewhat unorthodox, yet the fact remains that the Gurkha is a plucky and enterprising sportsman, and when the opportunity of securing good targets, large or small, presents itself, no danger is too great for him, no labour too severe.

Dancing and singing play another very important part in the lives of the Nepalese. In camp, in the lines of the regiments, even when working in the fields, their songs are almost always heard, while on the occasion of any important festival, such as the Dasehra or Holi, they appear to sing continuously throughout the night and day while the celebration lasts. A Gurkha sing-song is both pleasant and inspiriting, and the most downcast individual present cannot fail to be infected with a little of the cheerful and lighthearted spirit which prevails. Seated on the ground—if it be night, round a big log fire blazing on the ground—accompanied by one or two of their number, who beat out the time on their long oval drums, they sing innumerable choruses, clapping their hands in time as they sing, while in the centre the principal dancer slowly gyrates, his feet beating time to the throbbing of the drums. Amongst the Magars and Gurungs of Central Nepal, where, even if they are permitted to join in the singing, the women, except on very rare occasions, are not allowed to dance, it is customary for some of the men to be dressed in female attire. Decked out with the jewellery dear to the Gurkha maiden's heart, with their smooth Mongolian faces and graceful, stately movements, they are not easily distinguishable from the other sex, whose rôle they are adopting. Nepalese songs, by reason of the constant and irritating repetition of the short refrain, appear somewhat monotonous to European ears, but some of them are by no means devoid of melody. This is particularly the case in Eastern Nepal, where the harvesting songs of the Limbus and Rais have often a tuneful and fascinating lilt, rarely found in Oriental music.

Pasturage and cultivation form the chief occupations of the people. Trade is almost entirely in the hands of the Newars, who are also mainly responsible for the carvings in wood and brass which adorn the houses and temples in the valley. While there is nothing derogatory to caste in following the professions of cultivator or shepherd, there are certain occupations which can only be practised by men of the menial classes. These are the lowest of all in social status in the country, and in their ranks are found such people as tailors, goldsmiths, carpenters, miners, musicians, butchers and scavengers. These form a separate class of the community, and live a life apart from the rest. In all matters pertaining to food and drink they are considered as untouchable, and no man of a caste superior to their own would ever dream of even setting foot inside their houses.

There are but few barbers in Nepal, and the class of washermen or dhobis, well known in the East for their remorseless treatment of clothes, are also unrepresented, for the Gurkha washes his own clothes in the nearest convenient stream.

Life in a Gurkha village is simple but strenuous. After the habit of nearly all Eastern races, the Nepalese rise early, and, as a rule, the countryside is astir by cock-crow. The women take their share in the field work, with the result that very often the whole family sets out in the early morning, the baby, carried in a basket slung on its mother's back, accompanying the party.

During the summer season those who possess cattle and sheep send them up into the higher elevations, sometimes only just below the snow line, for grazing. Here the shepherds erect rough shelters of hurdles and leaves, known as *Goths*, as temporary dwelling places, and here it is that they pass their days, until the monsoon is over, when they return to their villages, often many marches away. Wandering on the hillside one may hear, from time to time, the soft notes of some neatherd's flute, as he drives his flocks slowly across the grassy slopes, and the sounds seem to enhance the unbroken solitude of the scene.

Musical instruments — beyond those of the simplest form, and roughly fashioned out of materials at hand, such as the shepherd's flute and drums used in accompanying the songs and dances—are rarely seen. But such as do exist are played only by the professional musicians of the country, a race known as the Damais, who besides being hereditary musicians are also the tailors of the country. These supply the music on the occasion of the many ceremonies at which music, feasting and dancing play an all-important part. It is from this class that the bulk of the bandsmen and buglers in the Nepalese Army are principally drawn. There is also a class of professional singing women, known as *Gainis*, in Nepal. These are probably few in proportion to their counterparts in India, and are chiefly found in the lower hill districts such as Dang Salyana. They wander from village to village, together with a few musicians, who accompany their songs, and with their display of tawdry jewellery, semi-Indian dress, and bold, painted faces, bear a close resemblance to the nautch girls of the plains.

One of the Gurkha's great failings is his passion—amounting in many cases to almost a vice—for gambling. This is strictly forbidden in Nepal except on such special occasions as the Diwali Festival. Ordinarily well behaved and extremely amenable to discipline, the Gurkha will lose no opportunity of indulging surreptitiously in his favourite pastime, and the stakes for which he will, on occasions, play are as varied as they are high.

All Gurkhas, from the Brahmans to the lowest classes, may contract what is known as a *mit* relationship with any friends of whom they are particularly fond. The meaning of the word *mit* is friend, and to make a *mit* relationship may be compared with making a " blood brotherhood " in other parts of the world. This relationship can be contracted between men of different classes, tribes and castes, and between people who are already related to one another. Once contracted, the new relationship thus formed holds good where marriage and similar ceremonies are concerned.

Civilization has advanced in Nepal no less than in other countries all over the world, and many of the old customs, relics almost of barbarism, have been altered and adapted to meet the new conditions imposed by a more progressive age. Hence, it follows that certain punishments, which in old days involved the summary execution of the guilty person by the injured one, have been superseded by more humane sentences, usually passed in courts of justice. In former times it was the custom for a husband, whose wife had been found unfaithful, to cut down the seducer with a *khukri*. The latter could save his life by passing under the uplifted leg of the outraged husband, but this was considered so ignominious that in nearly every case death was preferred. Nowadays, however, all this is changed, and, although to this day there are occasional cases

TYPICAL STREET SCENE—A QUIET GAME OF CARDS

A STREET IN KATHMANDU

where the seducer claims the right to pass under the uplifted leg of the husband, this is merely done in cases where he cannot, or is unwilling, to meet the damages mulcted of him. The summary *khukri* execution, however, is not now allowed. In modern times cases of infidelity are dealt with either through the medium of the Law Courts, or by a local village court of arbitration. This latter consists, as a rule, of eight or ten notables of the village, before whom the parties are summoned. In nearly every case the husband is merely awarded his original marriage expenses, a popular award which is considered to be more than ample compensation for the loss of a fickle spouse.

The laws of inheritance do not, on the whole, differ very much from those in force in India, under which the eldest son obtains the largest share of the property, while provision is also made for the widow and the other children. They vary slightly, however, amongst certain tribes. In the case of the Gurungs, for instance, the eldest son is entitled to the best of the livestock, such as the buffaloes and cows, while the land is divided equally amongst the next-of-kin. Again, amongst the Limbus and Rais of Eastern Nepal, the distribution of the property of a dead man is usually made by a small committee formed of six or seven of the elders of the village. Here, the largest share again is usually given to the eldest son, or should there be no offspring, then to the eldest surviving brother of the deceased. Amongst the last-named tribes a pretence is usually made of apportioning shares to the sisters and daughters of the dead man, but in actual practice they invariably receive nothing at all, whereas amongst the Gurungs, daughters and sisters, provided they are not of marriageable age, are awarded equal shares.

Gurkhas who, in the performance of their military duties, are compelled to cross the sea, must be granted a dispensation known as Pani Patiya on their return. This restores to them all the privileges of caste and rights, which they are presumed to have forfeited in consequence of crossing the sea. Failure to obtain the dispensation renders a man not only liable to heavy punishment, but also places others, who may have unwittingly taken food and water with him, under the same ban as the transgressor himself.

Nepalese, as is common with all Mongolian tribes, are intensely superstitious, and wizards, witches and witchcraft play an important part in the private lives of many, although the subject is one that is as a rule not discussed with the foreigner, and its symptoms are, in consequence, not very apparent. There are, however, innumerable customs that date back to very early animistic worship, and the prevalence of the belief in ghosts or *bhuts*, as they are called, which haunt rivers and streams, and are known by different names such as *masan*, *pichas*, and the *mathkata* (ghost with its head under its arms), is another proof of this.

Although Gurungs themselves are loth to admit it, there is no doubt that on the death of a male Gurung, a ceremony and dance, in which a gilded bull's head plays a prominent part, often takes place. This ceremony is probably of northern origin, and is probably a relic of the pre-lamaistic religion of Tibet brought down by the Gurungs from the north at the time of their immigration to Nepal. Again, in the month of Kartik (October 15 to November 15), the word *sanp* must never be used for snake, but only the word *ghasarne*, "the creeping one."

The customs and institutions described in the foregoing pages are common throughout Nepal, and are applicable to all the various races inhabiting the country. Manners and customs peculiar to separate tribes will be found described in their appropriate chapters.

CHAPTER VIII

SLAVERY AND THE LABOUR PROBLEM

AMONGST the many reforms introduced into the country under the beneficent and far-seeing rule of the present Prime Minister, the abolition of slavery occupies a prominent place.

It will come as a surprise to many that until quite recently slavery existed in a nation so fiercely jealous of its own independence as Nepal. Although differing in form to an extent that admitted no comparison with that which prevailed in other countries in bygone days, the fact remains that the system did exist, and the Prime Minister never relaxed his unceasing efforts to abolish an institution which, according to the standards of the civilized world, inflicted a grave stigma on the fair name of Nepal.

It can well be imagined that the introduction of a reform destined to uproot a custom so firmly planted in the social life of the country, and sanctioned by religion, was a matter that called for unusual judgment and discernment. By his tact and personality, however, the Prime Minister proved fully equal to handling so difficult a task, and in the winter of 1924 a decree was passed in which the abolition of slavery throughout Nepal was promulgated.

In view of the fact that Nepal was one of the few countries in which this institution existed at so recent a date, we have considered it a matter of interest to describe the form under which slavery existed here, and the events which led up to its gradual limitation and final abolition.

Slavery existed in Nepal from time immemorial, and, indeed, was claimed to be as old as the traditions of the country. It found a mention in the *Smritis* and *Tantras*, ancient books in which, among other things, the whole system of dealing with slaves was expounded and various details regarding their treatment in certain circumstances laid down. The institution of slavery had, in fact, been so fused into the everyday life of the Nepalese that it had gradually become a national custom.

The Government of Nepal had for a long time been considering the best means of ameliorating conditions in an institution so fraught with evil. As far back as 1896 a *Lal Mohur*, or Commission, was promulgated in which all the four *Varnas* or castes were emphatically prohibited from enslaving any free man, woman or child. This decree subsequently became law, and was re-enacted under every successive Government since that date. This was followed by further legislation, which had as its object the amelioration of the condition of the slaves, and included a clause under which offences against slaves were punishable in a like manner to those against free men. With the object of inducing them to settle in such parts of the country as Naya Mulk and Morang, in the Terai, further enactments were introduced exempting runaway slaves who were discovered living in these districts from being captured and restored to their owners. A considerable time elapsed before any improvement was visible in the slaves' condition in spite of the sincere intentions of the Nepal Government, as these decrees were not widely promulgated. With the spread of education, however, and the advent of a more progressive age, knowledge of what constituted their rights could no longer be withheld from the slaves, and it gradually came to be known that a slave who availed himself to the fullest extent of the new legislation became, in everything but name, a free man.

In a population numbering some five and a half millions, the total number of persons affected by the abolition of the system was not very large. According to returns specially prepared the number of slave-owners was 15,719, and those held in slavery 51,419, from which it will be seen that roughly only 1 per cent. of the entire population was concerned. Although the owners, being as a rule possessed of large estates and employing much labour, were, for the most part, men who enjoyed a certain prominence and social status in their own sphere, yet their numerical inferiority rendered the task of abolishing the system easier; pointing, as it did, to the obvious inference that the employment of slaves appeared not only inacceptable, but unnecessary, in the eyes of the bulk of the population.

The men owning slaves could be grouped broadly into three classes. There were those who found themselves the possessors of slaves as the result of the inheritance of a large estate of which they formed part and parcel. To these men the abolition of slavery was hailed with appreciation, for detesting, for the most part, a system under which human beings—in appearance, feelings and sensibilities the same as themselves—had been, by an evil destiny, subjected to the degrading conditions that slavery imposed, they were, in consequence, kindly disposed towards their unfortunate fellow beings, and treated them in a humane manner, often assisting them in the upbringing of their children and in the support of their parents. Next came those owners who maintained slaves purely for labour. Living chiefly in isolated places and depending entirely on their slaves to carry on their household and farm work, it was but natural that these men looked with apprehension on a proposal that appeared to them to threaten their very existence. Lastly, there were those owners, few in number, who maintained slaves in order to carry out a nefarious trade in human beings. These men did not scruple to separate husband from wife, or mother from child. They did not hesitate to resort to any method, however base, to circumvent the law, their only aim and object being to become rich as quickly as possible by the most reprehensible and revolting means.

With the exception of the last-mentioned class, the treatment of slaves, as the ancient statutes had recommended, had always been humane, and it is clear that the cruelty and oppression which existed in other countries where slavery was practised were, to a large extent, lacking in Nepal. Cases were by no means infrequent where slaves who had served long and faithfully in one family took an active interest in its welfare, in some cases even assuming entire control during the minority of an heir. There were households where, during the absence of the master on business or pleasure, the slaves could be trusted to ensure that no dislocation or interruption of the daily routine occurred, while in others the distinction between master and slave was practically non-existent.

Although the slaves' lot was, in many cases, not an unhappy one, yet kind treatment could do but little to mitigate the thought of the hopeless bondage into which they had been born and which branded them with the mark of servitude before all their fellow men. As can be easily realized, it was in the matter of the slaves' marriage and family that many evil practices and abuses of the existing regulations began to creep in, and the exposure of many of the worst cases, opening the eyes of people to the existence of a state of affairs which had been, up to then, a sealed book, doubtless played a large part in winning the support of the country for the Prime Minister in his humane proposals.

Realizing the importance of increasing the supply of labour on their estates, the slave-owners took the earliest opportunities of finding mates for their unfortunate bond servants. Under the laws of the country which obtained prior to the abolition of slavery, the father of a child by a slave girl, if he were a free man other than the owner, could emancipate it by payment of a certain stipulated sum to the master of the girl. Many cases, however, were found to exist where slave girls were given as concubines to men who were in too straitened circumstances to emancipate any offspring that ensued. In cases such as these the children remained the property of the slave-owner, who was at liberty to dispose of them as he pleased. Where the children were the result of union between a slave girl and her owner they were automatically set free under the law. The unscrupulous slave-owner therefore evaded the provisions of the law by handing over his slave women to the embraces of impoverished strangers. It can easily be understood what suffering and hardship ensued in families brought up under these conditions. Cases were bound to occur where the master found himself unable to afford to keep the slave's increasing family, and when this occurred, it was, as might be expected, on the slaves that the burden of additional hardship or separation fell. The natural consequence of such a state of affairs was that no ambition or qualities, such as prudence and thrift, could be expected to take shape in the minds of beings brought up, from their earliest infancy, to regard themselves as mere goods and chattels, and that their normal impulse was to do the least possible amount of work that would ensure them a bare existence.

The evils accruing from such a state of things

were clearly recognized by the ruling authorities, and in 1921 a law was passed investing the slaves with the right to own and inherit property. Even this was found to produce little amelioration of the slaves' condition; for owing to the fact that the slaves had little or no time of their own, opportunities for them to earn money were exceedingly limited, and property, in most cases, was confined to personal belongings.

The arguments urged by the slave-owners against the proposals to abolish an institution which formed part of their livelihood were varied. It was urged that in such matters as the guarding of their property a greater reliability could be placed on slaves, as by virtue of their being the personal property of their master they would be easier of arrest should they, by any chance, violate the trust which had been placed in them. Another argument that was frequently produced was that with the abolition of slavery the slaves themselves might leave the country. Fears such as these might, with reason, have been entertained by slave-owners in such countries as the West Indies and Mauritius, where the population, in those days, consisted of aliens forcibly taken away from their homes and retained in bondage. In Zanzibar, when slavery flourished, there were 200,000 slaves to less than 100,000 free men, and in the West Indies again slaves reached a total of 700,000. In countries such as these, where the land under slave cultivation comprised an enormous area, and where such a large number of skilled labourers was difficult to replace, the possibility of a general exodus might, with reason, be regarded with apprehension. In the case of the slaves of Nepal, however, the danger was not apparent, for the majority were born and bred in the country, and their family ties and occupations—involving, generally, employment on domestic and farm work in the home land—were such as to preclude any idea of their leaving the country altogether.

In addition to those provided by slaves, there were other reserves of labour which could be called up at certain seasons of the year when agricultural operations were at their heaviest. Under one of these, a system of co-operative labour, known as *Parma*, every household furnishes what labour it can in times of transplantation or gathering in of crops, to other households, subsequently receiving similar help in return. Again, in cases where estates are large and many labourers are required, when help available under the *Parma* system is insufficient, hired labourers, known as *Bani* or *Darmahadars*, are often employed. These are engaged for periods of varying duration—on occasions even for a single day—and are provided with food and a small remuneration either in kind or in money. A special feature of this custom is that the contract for service may extend to a month, or to several months, or even to a year, and it may be renewed on expiry. In certain of the hill districts the total monthly expenditure involved under this system was found to work out at about six rupees (nine shillings) per man. Careful inquiries have shown that, given an equal number of slaves and *Bani* labourers, the output from cultivation worked under the *Bani* system amounted to nearly twice as much as that worked by slaves, while the expense involved was very little more.

Another argument against the abolition of slavery was that slaves, when well treated, were in a less unfavourable position than the *Bandas*. These are persons who have become hopelessly indebted, or who are compelled by urgent reasons to raise sums of money which they can only repay by their personal labour. The *Banda* will enter into a legal contract to work solely for his creditor until his debt is paid off. Consequently a *Banda* may be in a worse plight than an actual slave, as the creditor has less interest in the *Banda's* physical well-being than a humane slave-owner would have. This, however, is an argument against the *Banda* system rather than a valid point in favour of slavery.

It was not until November 28, 1924, that the Prime Minister, in an eloquent speech at Kathmandu, disclosed the details of his proposals, which were subsequently adopted, for the complete emancipation of slaves and the abolition of slavery. The proposals comprised three main clauses, which were as follows :—

Firstly, that from a certain date, to be fixed as early as possible, having regard to the state of public opinion, the legal status of slavery should cease throughout Nepal. Secondly, that the owners be paid a statutory price for each slave whose claim had been fully established. Lastly, that the slaves, after receiving their freedom, should be apprenticed to their former owners for a period of seven years, during which time they would have to work for them and would in return be provided with food and clothing. The last clause was introduced in the hope that the freed slaves would, by performing, as free men, the same duties which they had previously carried out as slaves, gradually accustom themselves to the new order of things, and would accordingly eventually settle down as ordinary hired labourers in the localities where they had been living. It was evident that during the process of readjustment the onus of maintaining the old and infirm as well as the very young, which had been borne up to now by the slave-owners, would be transferred to the slaves themselves, and the owners were accordingly asked gradually to substitute wages in kind or money for the food and clothing they had been in the habit of giving, to enable the slaves to bear the burden which the maintenance of their dependants would lay upon them.

Although slavery has been definitely abolished throughout Nepal, there still exists a kind of forced labour, which is divided into three classes, known respectively as *Begari*, *Jhara* and *Beti*. Of these, the first two are in force in order to supply official requirements, and are enforced under the orders of the local authorities, through the village headmen. *Begari* applies solely to questions of transport work, which, owing to the absence of roads passable for vehicles, is performed almost entirely by coolies. This form of labour is put into force on such occasions as the tour of a Governor, or other important official, for the transport of whose baggage a large number of porters may be required.

The second form, *Jhara*, is confined to such labour as may be required in connection with the building of bridges and roads, the roofing of houses, and clearing of forests. It may be enforced for a period of several days, and in some cases may even extend to a month.

The last form of forced labour is known as *Bethi*. It consists in the carrying out of work, of a purely private nature, for the headman of a village, such as thatching of a roof or working in the fields, and constitutes part of his pay. Every one is liable for this for one day in the year, and exemption can be obtained on the payment of the small sum of four annas.

Although not strictly speaking a labour question, the method of obtaining Gurkha recruits for the twenty battalions of the Indian Army may perhaps be mentioned here. As has been explained, Nepal is closed to Europeans, so that the recruiting officers are not themselves able to take an active part in the work. The system adopted is for each regiment to send a small party to Gorakhpur in India, and not far from the Nepal frontier. From this place these recruiters are sent out into the Nepalese hills, and return as soon as they have been able to pick up a few likely lads whom they bring in to the recruiting headquarters. This work is only carried on during the winter, as at other times of the year the Terai, through which all must pass on their way to and from the hills, is very unhealthy.

PART III

WESTERN NEPAL

CHAPTER IX

THE COUNTRY OF WESTERN NEPAL

WESTERN NEPAL comprises all the country lying between the Kauriala river and the Kali, the western frontier of the country. In general appearance the western districts are much less beautiful than the other parts of Nepal, being dry and somewhat barren, and producing crops of a very inferior quality, and only barely sufficient for the needs of the people. The people, too, bear but little resemblance to the real Nepalese living farther to the east, but as they are subjects of the Gurkha king we must consider them as belonging to that race, although it will be unnecessary to describe them in any great detail.

The farther one goes towards the east of Nepal, the more does one find the races becoming influenced by Mongolian ideas, not only in the matter of religion and customs, but still more so in appearance, until, finally all traces of Hinduism disappear in the races that are to be found in the country lying to the east of Nepal's eastern frontier.

In a like manner, as one progresses in a westerly direction the races inhabiting Central Nepal become more and more prone to Hinduism until they gradually lose every trace of any Mongolian influence in anything pertaining to them, and finally become pure Hindu in culture, differing in name only from the Aryan-speaking tribes to be found in the British districts adjacent to the western frontier of Nepal.

In connection with the above, it should be remembered that prior to the Treaty of Segowli in 1816, the Nepalese were not only masters of Sikkim to the east and part of the Terai in the south, but also of the important hill country lying due west of the river Kali—the western boundary of modern Nepal—known as Kumaon and Garhwal.

It can therefore be readily understood how the races living on either side of the western boundary of Nepal have been, for many years, so merging into each other by intermarriage and from other causes, that the difference between those living within Nepalese territory and their neighbours in the states of Kumaon and Garhwal is now but slight. Hence it follows that it is common to describe those races which inhabit the extreme western districts of Nepal, such as Doti, Baetadi, Bajhang, Jumla, Thalahra and Accham, as not being Gurkhas at all.

Whatever their exact racial definition, they bear, with very few exceptions, no resemblance to their sturdier neighbours of Central and Eastern Nepal. In appearance, customs, and even speech they differ but little, if at all, from the Kumaonis, who are to be found in the country lying immediately to the west of the river Kali, but it should be mentioned that, apart from their tribal languages, they speak Nepali whenever it becomes necessary for them to employ a *lingua franca*.

In physique they are, for the most part, far inferior to the other races of Nepal, a fact which might reasonably be attributed to the barrenness of their country, which mitigates against the production of good crops.

Although members of most of the tribes inhabiting Central Nepal—such as Magars, Gurungs and Thakurs—are to be found living in the western districts, Chetris, on the whole, predominate, but they are, for the most part, Chetris of somewhat inferior caste and breeding.

As has already been explained, the people of Western Nepal are decidedly non-Mongolian in appearance, being of dark complexion and possessing the loose-limbed type of frame more characteristic of the inhabitants of India. Those living on the extreme western border speak a dialect but little removed from Kumaoni, and they conform to the ordinary Hindu ceremonial with such modifications as may be, from time to time, necessitated by local conditions and situations.

There are in Nepal many local feudal chiefs, or rajas, successors of the old Baisia and Chaubisia rajas, and amongst these are to be numbered those of Bajhang, Jumla and Accham, the three western districts already referred to.

Concerning these feudal chiefs the Nepal Durbar has given us to understand that the descendants of those rajas of former days, who were dispossessed of their lands by the conquering Gurkhas, are now following the various walks of life that are open to every one else—agriculture, petty trade, and so on; whereas those who still enjoy their original titles and position pay certain fixed dues or tributes to the central Government at Kathmandu. Neither of the above classes of feudatory chiefs, however, has now the slightest influence or even position in the country, and they are rajas only in name.

There are three main approaches into Western Nepal from British India. Firstly, there is the large frontier town, in British territory, of Tanakpur, lying on the western bank of the Kali river, the terminus of a small branch railway line. Secondly, the bridge over the Kali at Jhula Ghat, a village some miles to the east of the big Gurkha settlement of Pithoragarh in the Almora district. Lastly, there is the bridge at Dharchula, a three days' march above Jhula Ghat.

It was to the first two of these three places that His Highness the Maharaja kindly granted us permission to cross the river and penetrate a few miles into the country on the other side.

Tanakpur lies in the Terai at the foot of the hills, and here the Kali, in its lower reaches known as the Sarda, is a broad and beautiful stream, its water icy cold from the masses of melted snow brought down from the great mountains at its source. There is no bridge, but a ford which is crossed in curious boats consisting merely of a hollowed tree trunk.

On the Nepalese side of the river is a small village containing a guardhouse and a few buildings, which comprise the customs house, *adda*, and forest offices. The village is known by the name of Simalghat, and in the hot and rainy season is deserted, except by the few Government officials whose duties keep them there throughout the year. In the winter, however, the place presents quite a different aspect, for the enterprising Marwari shopkeepers from the plains erect many temporary booths, and it has all the appearance of a busy thriving bazaar.

Our escort consisted of two *Subadars*, both Brahmans, and two sturdy Magars. One of the Subadars was in charge of the local gaol house, and the other belonged to the forest service. The faces of these men bore signs of the ravages of malaria—man's most dreaded enemy in these parts—but they neither grumbled nor complained, and seemed to bear their lot with the calm stoicism which is one of the chief characteristics of their race. They talked in loving terms of the river, and, indeed, without it life would be depressing and dull in such a place, for the country here is typical of the forest country of the Terai, an endless wilderness of big trees. The river, though, is full of fish, and in the forest on its banks small game is plentiful. The Gurkha is a keen sportsman, so for him there are compensations in a life at Simalghat.

It did not take long to exhaust the sights of

TEMPLE OF BARAMDEO—WESTERN NEPAL

SIMALGHAT—A VILLAGE IN THE WESTERN NEPAL TERAI

the small bazaar, and we were then taken to see the temple of Baramdeo, some two miles distant in the forest. The path lay along the banks of the river, and on our way we passed many Dotials and Bajhangis, as the inhabitants of these districts are known. They were, for the most part, of the Chetri tribe, and the coarseness of their clothes, and their rough, uncouth appearance seemed to betoken an existence harder than that known to the races of Central and Eastern Nepal.

Our escort spoke of the temple with bated breath, but to us it presented no very imposing appearance—a rough, small shrine set in a clearing of the dense forest—but the obvious veneration in which it is held, and its situation, gave the place a certain air of romance and charm.

Some four marches up the river, at Jhula Ghat, the scenery changes, and the river, now known as the Kali, runs, deep and swift, between steep banks of rock and trees. Here it is spanned by a suspension bridge, on the far side of which is a Nepalese guard-house, with its alert sentries ever ready to deny passage to him who fails to produce a Nepalese Government permit. On the Nepal side the path ascends steeply to the village and fort of Baetadi, garrisoned by a company of infantry. Here, also, lives the captain commanding, a relation of the ruling house. The country here does not differ from that of contiguous Kumaon, and the soil is barren, rocky and dry.

CHAPTER X

THE BRAHMANS, THAKURS AND CHETRIS

THE Brahmans of Nepal occupy the same high social standing that they do in all parts of India, and it is from their ranks that the official priesthood of the country is entirely drawn. Not as a rule enlisted in the fighting ranks of the Nepalese Army, they are to be found occupying posts in civil and military non-combatant offices, while of the humbler members of their caste some take service in the police and kindred services. Others, in consequence of their exalted caste, are employed as cooks, for food cooked by a Brahman may be taken—without danger to caste prejudice—by all races in Nepal.

The Brahmans are divided into two main classes, the Upaddhe and the Jaisi, of which the latter, distinctly of lower social standing, are the offspring of a Upaddhe and a Brahman widow,* and cannot eat with members of the higher class.

In view of the fact that the customs and manners of the Nepalese Brahmans differ but little, if at all, from those of the Brahmans in India, concerning whom countless books have been written, it is not proposed to discuss them in this book, which deals solely with customs not found outside Nepal.

* A Hindu widow cannot remarry according to the strict tenets of the faith. Should she, however, contract an unofficial alliance with a Brahman, the children of such alliance would be termed Jaisi, and the second class of Brahman has come about in this way.

The Brahmans first found their way into Nepal amongst the multitudes of Indians, fleeing before the Mohammedan invasion in the twelfth century. They were the first to convert the local peoples to Hinduism, and are to-day held in the greatest respect and veneration, being consulted in all matters by high and low alike.

To the earliest and most distinguished of their original converts they are said to have given the rank and honour of the Chetri order. This order they subsequently further bestowed on the offspring of Brahmans and the local hill women. It is from this mixture of the two races that the present powerful tribe of the Khas, now more generally known as Chetris, has sprung.

With regard to the words Khas, Chetri and Kshatriya, it should be explained that Chetris were formerly known as Khas, but the latter word is now rapidly falling into disuse. Hereafter only the word Chetri will be employed in this book. Chetri is a corrupt form of the Sanskrit word *kshatriya*, and means literally a fighting man, or one of the fighting caste.

Apart from the most modern theories as to the probable origin of the Khas, mention of them as a race is frequently found in ancient legends and tradition.

To take only a few examples. Ancient Hindu writings show that a nation known as Khas existed during the reign of Narendra Deva of Nepal in the earliest portion of the twelfth century ; again, other old traditions refer to a country between Kashmir and the Nepal valley as " the land of the Khas," while a race of Hindus called Khas were known to have inhabited the country lying round Palpa and the southern part of Nepal.

No particular importance need be attached to the fact that their original seat was Gurkha. This idea is founded merely on the fact that it was from Gurkha that they sallied forth under Prithwi Narayan on their victorious march into Nepal, and we learn from Brian Hodgson that the Khas had been spread over the whole of the Chaubisia long before the age of Prithwi Narayan.

This last-named scholar gives perhaps the best and most lucid explanation of how the social standing given to the race formed from the mixture of Chetris has been built up, and the following extract from his writings throws much light on the subject :

"The Brahmans found the natives illiterate, and without faith, but fierce and proud. They saw that the barbarians had vacant minds, ready to receive their doctrines, but spirits not apt to stoop to degradation, and they acted accordingly. To the earliest and most distinguished of their converts they communicated, in defiance of the creed they taught, the lofty rank and honour of the *Kshatriya* order.

"But the Brahman's had sensual passions to gratify as well as ambition. They found the native females—even the most distinguished—nothing loth, but still of a temper like that of the males, prompt to resent indignities.

"These females would indeed welcome the polished Brahmans to their embraces, but their offspring must not be stigmatized as the infamous progeny of a Brahman and a *Mleccha* (infidel). To this progeny, also, then, the Brahmans, in still greater defiance of their creed, communicated the rank of the second order of Hinduism ; and from these two roots (convert and illegitimate progeny) mainly spring the now numerous predominant and extensively ramified tribe of Khas, originally the name of a small clan of creedless barbarians, now bearing the proud title of *Kshatriya*, or the military order of the kingdom of Nepal.

"The offspring of the original Khas females and

THE KALI RIVER—THE FRONTIER BETWEEN WESTERN NEPAL AND INDIA

THE POPTI LA—A PASS BETWEEN TIBET AND NEPAL

of Brahmans, with the honours and rank of the second order of Hinduism, got the patronymic titles of the first order; and hence the key to the anomalous nomenclature of so many branches of the military tribes of Nepal is to be sought in the nomenclature of the sacred thread."

It is clear that the Brahmans found in their new mountain homes many willing converts, yet a large number refused to adopt the new faith. To the former the Brahmans granted the sacred thread, but to the latter they denied it; hence there sprang up such tribes as Thapas, Ranas and Ghartis, names which are to-day found amongst the clans of both the Chetris and Magars, but only those belonging to the former are allowed to wear the thread.

Most of the races inhabiting the country of Nepal are to be found within fairly closely defined tribal boundaries. The Chetris, however, are found all over the country, with a slight preponderance in the extreme western districts.

The Chetris, who were from the first the dominating influence in the country, have retained this hold over the other tribes right up to the present day. Few things, indeed, impress the visitor to Nepal more forcibly than the extent to which the country is dominated by the soldier caste. It is they who hold all the chief appointments in the Government offices, whether civil or military, and their very name proclaims the fact that they rank higher than the Magar, Gurung, Rai, Limbu and Sunwar, who are officially classified as *Sudras*, a term denoting a menial in the Hindu social code.

The bulk of the Nepalese Army is recruited from the Chetris, and a large proportion of the officers, even in the purely class regiments composed only of Magars and Gurungs, are of the same caste, it being almost impossible for officers drawn from the other classes to attain a rank higher than that of captain.

Endowed with the same military qualities possessed by the other fighting classes, they are more intelligent and quick to learn, and thus make excellent soldiers.

In physique the Chetris are taller, and of slightly different build, being generally slighter and more active than the other Nepalese races, while in features they incline towards the Aryan rather than the Mongolian type of countenance.

They never allow their superior caste to interfere in any way with the performance of their military duties, but it stands to reason that they are more subject to caste prejudices than the other tribes, who have adopted the Hindu faith more as an outward manifestation of piety than as a religion. This tendency, never very great, becomes slightly more evident after they have adopted the sacred thread, a practice which imposes certain restrictions with regard to eating certain foods.

There are some twenty clans in the Chetri caste, bearing such names as Bandari, Karki, Khatri, Adhikari, Bisht and Khandka, amongst which the Khatri, although accorded the privilege of wearing the sacred thread, is said to rank below the others.

Amongst these clans there are also the names Burathoki, Gharti, Rana and Thapa, incidentally the names of four prominent Magar clans. This anomaly is due to the fact, already referred to, that the Brahmans, at the time of their first arrival in the country, granted the sacred thread to certain of their Magar converts, while the others remained merely Magars. Hence, the existence to this day of the names Burathoki, Gharti, Rana and Thapa in both races.

In character and general outlook on life, it is also to be expected, from their Aryan blood, that the manners and customs of the Chetris tend occasionally to lean more towards the Aryan point of view than the others, whose ancestry was more Mongolian ;

but this is a small point, and in actual fact the Chetris differ but little from the other races.

On the occasion of the birth of a Chetri, the period of the mother's uncleanliness lasts for thirteen days in the case of a boy, and for eleven in the case of a girl. During this period she has to remain at home and may only see her nearest relations. During this period no one may drink water which the mother may by any chance have touched.

The ceremonial weaning of the child takes place six months after the birth of a boy, and five after the birth of a girl. At this a big feast takes place, during the course of which each guest puts a caste mark on the forehead of the child, and also places a little rice in its mouth. This is followed by each guest, according to his means, dropping a coin into a brass plate which has been placed specially for this purpose.

As is the case with the majority of the Nepalese, there appears to be no very definite rule laid down as to the age at which the young Chetri should marry. According to the custom which formerly prevailed, marriage could take place at any time after the age of seven, and it was generally considered advisable for the girl to be married before the age of thirteen. In modern days, however, public opinion against child marriages is growing in Nepal no less than in other eastern countries, and nowadays the age at which most Nepalese are married is much more normal, being usually between the ages of seventeen and twenty-one.

The betrothal is generally arranged by the parents of the contracting parties. In the case of people of good birth and of means, the preliminary negotiations are usually conducted by emissaries, known as *Lame*, who act on behalf of their respective families. In other cases, however, where the means necessary to bear the expense of these representatives is insufficient, it is the custom for the father of the youth who is contemplating matrimony to repair to the girl's house, and there discuss matters with her father. On this first occasion he brings no present with him, and only very general subjects are discussed. He usually receives an invitation to come again a little later, when the marriage may then be talked about quite openly, and the details arranged. At this second meeting the boy's father does not come empty handed, for he brings with him a bowl of curds, and usually some ten or twelve fish in a wicker basket. These he presents to the father of his prospective daughter-in-law. In the course of the discussion which follows, a Brahman is summoned and consulted as to the most auspicious day on which the ceremony should take place.

Here it is advisable to point out that the presentation of curds will be seen to figure very frequently, not only in the case of Chetris, but in the case of all the other races whose ceremonies are described in this book. This is due to the fact that in the opinion of the Hindus, curds are regarded as having some auspicious significance attached to them, and it is for this reason that in all cases of ceremonial their presentation or use in some form or other rarely fails to occupy a prominent place.

The day having been fixed, the actual wedding ceremony takes place, as a rule, in the girl's house.

For this occasion the prospective bridegroom adorns his head with a sort of paper cap, known as *mahur*, which is kept in place by a *pagri* tightly rolled round it. Thus adorned he sets forth on his way to the house of his prospective bride. In many cases he is carried in a dooly, but where means do not permit of this he either rides on horseback or even walks on foot. He is accompanied by a host of friends and relations, but these are confined entirely to the sterner sex, no women of any kind whatsoever taking part in the procession.

On arrival at his lady's house he is received by her friends and relations, who greet him and his retainers with a shower of rice. The bridegroom does not enter the house immediately, but is made to sit outside and a little way apart. With him sits a male relation or friend whose duties are to attend the bridegroom during the remainder of the ceremony.

Whilst waiting outside, the bridegroom and the whole of his party are regaled with a meal of cooked rice, the split pulse known in India as *dal*, and goat's flesh. In Chetri weddings the plentiful libations of spirits and rice beer, which play such a prominent part—one might almost say the chief part—in the ceremonial of the other Nepalese races, are absent, for, according to the laws of his caste, a Chetri is not supposed to touch anything of an alcoholic nature.

While this feast is going on, the girl is being arrayed in her bridal dress. She, too, has two or more attendants, who are at her beck and call throughout the ceremony, and who may best be described as bridesmaids. When the bride is dressed in all her finery and the men's entertainment outside is over, the bridegroom is brought into the house.

A blanket is spread on the floor and on it the happy pair are seated side by side. In the first instance the groom is made to sit on the left, but a small ceremony has here to be performed known as the changing of places. This consists in the uttering of certain exhortations by the presiding priest, during the course of which bride and bridegroom rise and change places.

This being concluded, the mother of the bride proceeds to feed the couple with milk and curds. As soon as she has completed this act the bridegroom is taken out of the house and led to a small specially prepared pavilion, known as the *jagge*.

The *jagge*, which also figures in the marriage ceremonies of the Magars and other races of Nepal whose observances conform to the Hindu ritual, is usually erected just outside the bride's house. It is formed of four posts, covered in banana leaves, and with a roof composed of red cloth. Inside the *jagge* a kind of altar is built upon which is placed the sacred fire, while beside each of the four posts a vessel of water is put.

It is here that the bridegroom is made to take his place. He is seated on a blanket spread upon the floor, and all the time the monotonous tones of the Brahmans may be heard as they chant their sacred verses.

The bridegroom now takes some sacred grass (*kuso*), sesamum and barley in one hand, and dipping the other in water he raises it aloft and lets the water drip slowly back into the vessel. During this time the Brahman is still chanting, and when he comes to a certain passage in his book, he orders the bridegroom to open his hand and let the remaining water fall back into the vessel. Directly after this the bride is brought in and seated beside the boy. The most important part of the ceremony is now about to commence.

First of all, both take up a little water in their right hand and let it fall back into the vessel again. They then put their hands together in a devotional attitude and let them fall again, while they offer prayers supplicating the supreme deity to propitiate the various other gods whom they worship. This is necessary for the reason that although the Chetris worship a supreme deity (*Parmesur*), yet this deity can appear in many different forms. Each of these forms bears a different name, such as Shiva, Kali, Vishnu, or Hanuman, the monkey god, and each is venerated and worshipped for some specific purpose.

The various gods having been propitiated, bride and bridegroom rise and make obeisance to the officiating priest.

This over, the bridegroom presents the lady with new clothes and jewellery. The bridesmaids dress her in these, while the bridegroom proceeds to adorn her with earrings, nose-ring, bracelet, anklets and necklaces. His father-in-law and mother-in-law then inform him that henceforth he has become their son-in-law, and that the ceremony of circumambulating the sacred fire must now take place.

The bride's father hoists the boy on to his back, and another man, preferably her brother, lifts the girl on to his. Both are now carried round the fire three times and then set down in their former places. This, as other parts of the ceremony, is apt to vary in detail, for on occasions the bride is followed by the groom, and sometimes both parties walk round the fire instead of being carried.

The bridegroom now places an ornament round the girl's neck, and then sprinkles her head, down the parting of the hair, with red powder, known as *sindhur*. Now, the bride, taking hold of the long waist cloth which adorns the youth's person, leads him round the fire again three times, after which, seizing him by the coat, she bids him be seated by her side. The ceremony now comes to an end for the time being, and the happy pair are granted a few hours' rest, but they must not yet leave the altar precincts.

Before they are finally allowed to enter the house the young couple's feet are washed by the bride's relations, who also drop coins into the vessels containing the water with which this office is performed. Bride and bridegroom are now formally introduced to all the assembled relations, and the shaking of hands is here conducted with much ceremony.

The newly married pair spend their first night at the house of the bride's parents. On the following morning the bride, anointed with a new caste mark, is put into a dooly, and accompanied by her swain, either mounted or on foot, is taken to his house. On their arrival a feast is held outside the house at which musicians perform and a great deal of singing and dancing takes place. The marriage ceremony is now over.

It is rare that a Chetri marries out of his own tribe, but in cases where this occurs, the offspring assume the caste of the father. For example, if a Chetri marries a woman of the Gurung race, the children from this issue will become Chetris. Before this can be effected, however, certain formalities have to be carried out, and these usually take the following form :

A Brahman is summoned to a gathering at which the parents and the relations of the child are present. At this meeting, and before all present, he invests the infant with the sacred thread, by which act the child is admitted into the Chetri caste. In a similar way, any child born of mixed parentage can be admitted into the clan of its father by the performance of a ceremony akin to that just described.

Matters affecting caste, as is well known, are so complicated and intricate that it is impossible to deal with every aspect of the subject in this book. The many cases that are constantly cropping up in the everyday life of the Nepalese often present problems that are most difficult to solve, even by Brahmans and others considered as being thoroughly qualified to deal with such matters. In cases more than usually difficult of solution it is customary to resort to the official book of the law and statutes, published in Kathmandu, and known as the *Ain*.

To show the ease with which questions regarding caste can be raised, and how varied the forms they can assume, we have thought it of interest to give a very few examples.

Suppose a man of the Chetri caste has inadvertently eaten cooked rice with a man of a lower caste, such as a Kami, or ironsmith, he at once loses his own caste, and can only be readmitted into it after performing a certain ceremony, which entails the presence of a Brahman. To this latter he makes an offering of rice, ghee, cow's urine, and a small monetary present, in return for which the priest grants him purification, and extends the same to his house, which has also, for the time being, been considered as unclean.

To take a further example, should a Chetri marry a woman of one of the menial classes, his caste is at once lost. He becomes a complete outcast, no one being allowed to enter his house or even touch his drinking water. In a case like this last, caste is irrecoverably lost, and the man sinks to the caste of his wife.

It can be seen how many and various are the contingencies capable of introducing difficulties and complications concerning matters of caste. It is difficult, especially for the enlightened people of the West, to understand fully the tremendous extent to which the question of caste enters into the lives of the upper classes. Their whole life is ordered by it and the decision to do such and such a thing, or to make such and such a journey, is based entirely on the effect such action will have upon caste.

When a Chetri of standing dies his body is invariably cremated. Should time permit, the funeral takes place on the day of death, but if this cannot be arranged, then as early as possible on the following day.

A suitable place is selected by the banks of a river, and here a pyre is erected. If the deceased be a man, this is constructed of nine tiers of logs, placed one on top of the other; in the case of a woman it is built of only seven tiers.

The attendance of a Brahman is not absolutely essential on the funeral day, but in many cases a priest is summoned to offer up prayers for the spirit of the departed. The corpse, folded in a white shroud and placed on a stretcher, is carried to the pyre, which has been already prepared. The male relations and near friends of the dead man follow the body to its last resting-place, but no women, not even the deceased's female relations, are as a rule included in the cortège.

Just before the corpse is laid upon the pyre, a piece of wick soaked in ghee is inserted between the teeth, and when the body is finally in position, this is lighted by the nearest relation present, who also sets fire to the pyre. In order to make the wood burn more quickly, ghee is poured over it, and this together with the cost incurred in the erection of the pyre, renders cremation a matter of considerable expense. In consequence of this, it follows that although cremation is the orthodox method of disposing of the body of a Chetri after death, in cases where the expense cannot be met the body is buried. In this case the body is buried in a grave after a simple ceremony, on the conclusion of which all friends or relations present throw a handful of earth upon the body.

Chetri funerals do not conclude with a feast, as is the case with certain other of the Nepalese races. On the thirteenth day after the funeral, however, which is the recognized termination of the period of mourning, a feast is given, by the next of kin of the deceased, to all those who assisted at the funeral service. This is held in the house of the deceased, and is attended by a Brahman who performs the ceremony of purification for all present.

The period of mourning in the case of near relatives, such as father, mother, son or daughter, is thirteen days. The chief mourner is, in every case, the son ; where, however, there is no son, the nearest relative assumes this duty. The duties of the chief mourner vary according to the proximity of the relationship, but the following few examples will serve to show the type of restrictions and observances entailed.

In the case of the death of a parent the son mourns for thirteen days. During this period he shaves his head, moustache and eyebrows, and must dress completely in white, his headdress being a white *pagri*. He is only allowed to eat once a day, and his meal consists only of rice, ghee and bananas, such articles of food as game, *dal*, or even salt, being strictly forbidden.

In the case of the death of a son, the father mourns for the same period. He observes the same restrictions with regard to food, but does not shave his moustache and eyebrows. Similarly a husband mourns his wife for the same period, but is not required to shave at all, while a married sister living away from home is mourned for only five days, and only by her brothers.

Apart from the Brahmans, the Chetris and Thakurs are the most orthodox Hindus in Nepal, and they may therefore be regarded as setting the standard for religious and ceremonial ritual throughout the country. The Magars have adopted this form of ritual, practically in its entirety, for all their ceremonies, and the remaining races, such as Gurungs, Limbus, Rais and Sunwars, also practise it to a large extent. In the descriptions of the ceremonies and customs of the other races, which are given in the later pages of this book, a few instances occur where the detail would seem to approximate greatly to that already described in this chapter. In view of the fact, however, that the customs of the Nepalese are becoming more and more standardized as the influence of Hinduism grows apace, we have deemed it worth while to place many small differences and divergencies on record before they finally disappear and their significance is lost.

Below the Brahmans in social standing, but superior to all the other races in Nepal, is a tribe known as the Thakurs. Stated to be originally the descendants of princes, they constitute the finest type of Gurkha to be found in the country. Very intelligent, clean in their habits and smart in appearance, they are endowed with the highest military qualities, and, in consequence, make excellent soldiers. In appearance they bear a strong resemblance to Magars and Gurungs, and although on marriage they adopt the sacred thread, their caste prejudices are but few and little in evidence.

The Thakurs are very few in number, and are to be found scattered about all over the country. Their customs, manners and ceremonies do not differ in any way from those of the Chetris. They are much looked up to by the other races, who admire them for their fine soldierly qualities, as well as for their high caste, a combination which they attain perhaps in a higher degree than any of the other races of Nepal.

PART IV

CENTRAL NEPAL

CHAPTER XI

THE TERAI AND THE NEPAL VALLEY

THE Terai extends along practically the whole length of the southern boundary of Nepal, the portion east of the Kosi river being known as the Morang.

It can be divided into two very distinct portions: firstly, the Sal forests, known also as the Bhabar, an area some five to ten miles in width; and, secondly, the open and cultivated lowlands to the north and south of this forest, to which the name Terai, in its strictest sense, should be restricted, which have an average width of from ten to fifteen miles.

In the Terai proper the soil is of black loam, clay and sand, and considered eminently suitable for the production of sugar-cane, poppy and tobacco.

The Morang, formerly distinguished by its extreme flatness and very unhealthy climate, has been gradually cleared, and, under the direction of the present Maharaja, been made much more suitable for human habitation.

The Terai is notorious for its malarial fever, which is generated by the excessive moisture and swamps, the low site and clay bottom, and the rills percolating through the gravel and sand of the Bhabar, or Sal forest area, which is as bone dry as the Terai is wet. Uninhabitable though it be, owing to its deadly climate, for human beings, this area is the home of innumerable wild animals. Writing of it, Brian Hodgson says: " In this pest house are to be found royal tiger, panther, leopard, elephant, rhino, stags of the noblest growth, also boa constrictors of the largest size." The Terai is perhaps the most celebrated big game preserve in the world, and it is here that distinguished guests are entertained on a lavish scale in the big shooting camps held in the winter season.

Despite the extreme unhealthiness of this part of the country, the forest has here and there been cleared, and one comes across occasional small hamlets standing in the midst of small patches of cultivation. These are the habitations of the Tharus, a race nowhere else to be found, whom Oldfield describes as " a puny, badly developed, and miserable-looking race, and probably belonging to the same original stock as the natives of the adjacent plains of India."

From personal observation we cannot agree with the above remarks, for of all the Tharus we have seen, very few bore anything but a very strong Mongolian appearance, and their physique could certainly not be described as badly undeveloped, although not to be compared with that of the dwellers in the hills. The Tharus are chiefly employed as *dak* runners and mahouts, and during the hot and rainy season are employed in the difficult and dangerous task of catching wild elephants.

Whilst travelling in the Terai recently we came across a large Tharu colony, and from them elicited the following story of their origin :

The Terai was formerly inhabited by a race of wild men who knew not the meaning of law and order. Some time during the twelfth century, when the Rajputs were about to be besieged in Chitor, they sent their women-folk to take refuge in the lower hills of Nepal. Later on, when Chitor had fallen, and most of its garrison had been slaughtered, the Rajput women, who, until then, had held aloof from the local inhabitants, began to take husbands from amongst the people of the Terai, and their offspring are said to be the original Tharus.

It is interesting to note that even to-day the Tharu women, who are known as *Ranis* (queens), are considered to be the leaders of the race, and this fact undoubtedly lends colour to the story of their origin. With the one exception of the Tharus, the people of the Terai do not greatly differ from those in the contiguous plains of India.

Through the Terai runs the high-road, the only one in the country, which leads from Raksal, on the Indian frontier, to Kathmandu, a distance of some seventy-five miles.

Until comparatively recently the passage through the Terai portion of the road was an unmitigated nightmare. Leaving Raksal late at night the traveller was carried, in a dooly, to the accompaniment of monotonous chanting, by unwilling bearers from adjacent Bihar, and was lucky not to be left stranded on the road. This journey was much dreaded by the poorer people owing to the lack of drinking-water along the road, until a former Rani, impressed by the suffering and discomfort to which they were subjected, caused a series of tanks containing pure drinking-water to be erected at intervals of a few miles right through this deadly area.

All this, however, is now changed, and the journey through the Terai is now performed by rail, a popular innovation introduced in 1927 as part of the progressive policy for which the present Maharaja is responsible.

Leaving Raksal early in the morning one now arrives at Amlekhganj, on the farther side of the Terai forests, in the course of a few hours, a journey which formally occupied a whole day. From here a good motor road runs to Bhimphedi, passing over the sandstone range, which divides the Terai from the Duns, or valleys at the foot of the hill country, at Churia. Up to this point the scenery does not merit detailed description, as it is in no way different from that met with in the lower foothills all along the Himalaya.

Bhimphedi is a picturesque little town of some importance, and stands at the foot of the Sisagarhi pass. Here the road ends, and in consequence are always to be seen large numbers of coolies awaiting the numerous loads of merchandise, which from here onward have to be carried by hand. Here also we are reminded, for the first time, that we have left India behind, for the older buildings show those characteristics which are considered peculiar to Newar architecture, though the cheapness of modern tin roofing is fast destroying the charm they formerly possessed.

On leaving Bhimphedi one is confronted with an ascent of over 2,000 feet, the path being merely a boulder-strewn track at the top of which stands the little fort and village of Sisagarhi, or Chisapani. As we climbed up the path we saw a sight which is perhaps to be seen nowhere else in the world. A traction-engine—not assembled, of course—was being carried up to Nepal, and for this purpose the services of some hundred coolies had been enlisted. Step by step they moved the huge mass of metal slowly forward, urged on by their leader, who led them in the singing of a rhythmical chant not dissimilar to the hauling songs sung in Russia. In this way heavy articles are moved, at the rate of a few hundred yards a day, until they reach their destination in Kathmandu. All day long one meets an almost constant stream of coolies, many of them carrying loads of incredible size and weight. Cruel as this system may seem, the people are not unhappy in their lot, for they have been accustomed to do this work since time immemorial, and are well paid for their services. It should be pointed out, however, that in

ON THE ROAD TO KATHMANDU

METHOD OF TRANSPORTING A SICK MAN

a few years this somewhat inhumane practice will cease, for a rope railway is already partially in action and efforts are being made to construct a new cart road.

At Sisagarhi, besides a small bazaar, stand the ruins of an old fort, part of that chain of defences which once bid defiance to intruders from the plains of India. Here, too, we get our first glimpse of the army of Nepal, and our passports are examined by a sentry who stands on the path.

Sisagarhi holds a garrison of some two hundred troops. Here are seen the picturesque blue uniforms and quaint silver headdresses, too soon, alas, to be replaced by the prosaic khaki. No one would wish to deny progress to a country which is striving so hard to obtain it, but one cannot but regret, for æsthetic reasons, the changing of the old order.

From the ramparts of the fort there is a fine view of the country over which we have travelled. Ridge succeeds ridge, and away in the far distance, shimmering in the evening haze, the plains of India stretch away into infinity, a truly beautiful sight.

From Sisagarhi one climbs a few hundred feet to the top of the Chisapani pass, from whence is obtained the first glimpse of the snows. The path, which in spring is bright with rhododendron and wild apple blossom, falls steeply down to the river below, and the snows are lost to view. The hills on both sides of the stream are bare and steep. At the extremity of the gorge stands a rest-house, and a small village called Markhu, after passing which the road lies over a low, bare, undulating range of hills, called the Ekdunta, till the valley of Chitlung, or little Nepal, is reached.

We now climb through groves of rhododendron until, reaching the top of the Chandragiri pass, we get our first view of the far-famed valley of Nepal.

The valley of Nepal lies to the south of the sacred

mountain of Gosainthan, and consists of a large basin in the hills, now silted up with alluvial deposits which account for its extraordinary richness. It is surrounded by hills, and lies between the Gandak and Kosi rivers.

The word "Nepal," as applied particularly to the valley, in which Kathmandu the capital town of the kingdom stands, is found in such ancient writings as the *Mahabharat* and the *Tantras*. The old *Vanshavalis* (family trees) derive the word from Ne Muni, an ascetic who introduced the Gupta dynasty into the valley. If this derivation is correct the word would mean nurtured by Ne. Scholars, however, are not quite agreed on the derivation, and Professor Sylvain Levi, deriving the word from Chinese and Tibetan sources, has taken it to mean "The land leading to Paradise."

The valley is nearly oval in shape, and is some fifteen miles in length and thirteen miles in breadth. In early days it was called *Nag Hrad*, or the Tank of the Serpent. It is not improbable that the whole valley was at one time filled with water. Of this there is geological evidence, and it would therefore appear that the Hindu legend is based on fact.

To Manjusri by the Buddhists, and to Vishnu by the Hindus, is given the credit of transforming the lake into a fertile plain, by cutting a pass through the mountains with his sword. This cleft in the mountains remains up to the present time, and is the means by which the Baghmati river leaves the valley of Nepal.

From where we stand we see the ancient city of Kirtipur, which history relates was the scene of much bloodshed on the occasion of its siege by Prithwi Narayan. The city was defended with much gallantry by its Newar populace, and gave so much trouble before it was finally overthrown that Prithwi gave orders that every male above the age of twelve

WILD APPLE BLOSSOM—SISAGARHI PASS

SISAGARHI PASS—ON THE ROAD TO KATHMANDU

should have his nose cut off. This was in the eighteenth century. The eye now rests on the capital city of Kathmandu, with Patan a little to its south. It is far away, and all we see is a mass of red-brown roofs, but we can just distinguish the tall white tower from the top of which Jangbahadur is said to have jumped. To the left, on a small mound, rises the white dome of Swayambhunath, whose gilt spire shimmers in the sunlight. Right away in the far distance, in a fold in the hills at the eastern end of the valley, can be seen the city of Bhatgaon.

The ground between the cities is given over to cultivation, and from where we stand the general impression is rather that of a chequer board of brown and green.

The sacred rivers of Nepal—the Baghmati and Bishnumati—are faintly discernible, and the giants of the Himalaya stand guardian over all. It is a scene of extraordinary beauty, this little-known land of Nepal.

The descent to Thankot is now quickly accomplished, a pleasing contrast to a few short years ago, when the weary traveller had no alternative but to toil painfully down the steep stone steps which at that time constituted the only path.

A metalled road runs from Thankot into the capital, and the journey thence is quickly accomplished.

Upon first entering the city of Kathmandu the traveller is at once struck with the complete absence of everything Indian. On all sides stand temples of every conceivable age and style, and the many pagoda-like buildings are in pleasing contrast to the architecture of the plains. The narrow streets are thronged from morn till night with cheerful Mongol people. Newars predominate, for in their hands is most of the trade of the city ; but here also are seen all types of the Gurkha race, and the haughty Brahman is jostled by the thick-set Bhotiya from Tibet. We are again reminded of the military spirit which pervades this little mountain country, for the khaki-clad soldiers are much in evidence in the city, and the people make way for an occasional Nepalese officer, conspicuous by his red-banded peaked cap and sturdy Bhotiya pony.

The infrequent foreigner is a sight not to be missed, and we are followed about the city by a large and curious crowd of spectators, making photography a matter of much difficulty.

In Kathmandu, as in all the ancient towns of the valley, the Darbar Square, in which is situated the former royal palace, is the very heart of the city. From here streets radiate in all directions, and in their course they pass through some of the many smaller squares in which the city abounds. In general form the city is, in fact, composed of a series of *tols*, or squares, connected one with the other by lanes and alleys. There appears to be no system of drainage. Open gutters run down the sides of all the streets, and in these are collected the refuse of the surrounding buildings.

In the Darbar Square are situated the majority of the most important temples. Here is the famous temple of Talijiu, and near by the colossal image of Bhairab and the much-revered Hanuman Dhoka, whose monkey janitor is swathed in a heavy coat and protected from the sun by a silk umbrella.

The extremely picturesque, and rather Chinese appearance of the Darbar Square is somewhat marred by the present Darbar Hall, a modern building of white marble, and the unsightly electric-light standards which are out of keeping with the surrounding architecture.

Near the south-western angle of the Darbar Square is a little square now used as a fruit market. In the centre of this stands the old building, known as

Kathmandu, from which the city takes its name. This is one of the most characteristic of the old Newar buildings in the city. It was built in A.D. 1596, and derives its name from *kath*, "wood," and *mandu*, "temple," thus the wooden temple.*

Most of the streets are lined with shops in whose open fronts are displayed the wares of Nepal. Here are brightly printed cotton cloths, much sought after by the ladies of the city, shining brass utensils, lamps of various kinds, cigarettes, and, most prized of all the Gurkha's few possessions, umbrellas from the plains of India. Most of the shops are presided over by Newars, whose innate business ability has placed practically the entire trade of the country in their hands.

Opposite the north-west corner of the Darbar is the Kot, or military council chamber. Here it was that, in 1846, Gagan Sing and thirty-one of the most influential chiefs were murdered, thus paving the way for the rise of Jangbahadur.

To the east of the city, and dividing it from the palaces of the royal family, is the Thuni Khel, or big parade ground. Constructed by Bhim Sen, who also built the surrounding buildings, this fine grass-covered plain is the scene of all the big reviews and religious ceremonies, whilst the roads bordering upon it form the principal promenade of the city.

To one side of the Thuni Khel is a lofty stone column, some 120 feet in height. This was erected by Bhim Sen for no other purpose than to gain notoriety, and to astonish the people. It is now aptly known as Bhim Sen's Folly.

It is to the Emperor Asoka that Nepal owes its most ancient religious monuments, and it is believed that this monarch visited the country some time during the second century B.C., and that his daughter,

* This building was erected by Raja Lachiman Sing Mal as a house of accommodation for fakirs, for which purpose it is still used.

Charumati, was married to a Kshatriya (Chetri) named Devapala, settled in Nepal, and founded the village of Devapatan, near the sacred temple of Pasupati.

Writing on this subject, Professor Sylvain Levi (*Le Népal*) says : " During his sojourn in the valley Asoka is said to have erected five *chaityas*, one in the centre of Patan, and the others at each of the cardinal points round the city. These last four *chaityas* were meant to represent the four *Yugas*, or ages of the world."

Buddhist monuments may be divided into three categories. Firstly, those temples which are dedicated to the supreme deity and intended to evoke pious thoughts. These are known as *chaityas*, or mound temples. Secondly, those which are erected as a resting-place for holy remains, and which are known technically as *stupas*. Lastly, those which contain the actual ashes of the dead, and which are normally constructed in the form of miniature *chaityas*. These last are by far the most common, and may be seen scattered about all over the valley of Nepal.

Of all the *chaitya* temples now standing the finest and most perfect specimen is that known as Swayambhunath. Situated on a small hill some half a mile west of Kathmandu its white dome and shining gilt spire are a landmark for many miles around. According to tradition the hill on which the temple stands was raised by Manjusri after he had converted the lake of Naga Vasa into the valley of Nepal. The legend records that a single lotus flower remained floating on the lake. On it was embodied the spirit of Simbhu (Swayambhu) and on the spot where this flower finally came to rest the present hill was raised.

At the foot of the hill stands a group of colossal stone Buddhas guarding, as it were, the approach to

A CORNER OF PASUPATI

ENTRANCE TO SWAYAMBHUNATH

the sacred edifice. This spot is a sanctuary for many monkeys who, heedless of the hallowed ground on which they live, play on undisturbed. It is an act of merit to feed these creatures, and they lurk near the path ready to receive such offerings as may be thrown to them.

The temple is approached by a flight of stone steps, some six hundred in number, which near the top are steep and narrow. Confronting one at the summit is the famous *Bajra*, a copper-gilt, double-headed ornament representing the thunderbolt of Indra.

This ornament is one of the most common Buddhist designs, and is found, in some form or other, in nearly every Newar temple in Nepal.

The *chaitya*, which forms the main structure of the temple, is composed of a solid hemisphere of earth and brick supporting a lofty conical spire, the top of which is capped by a pinnacle of copper gilt. On the four sides of the base of the spire are painted, in crimson, white and black, the two eyes of Buddha ; so realistic are these that they seem to follow one's every movement.

To the west of the temple is a tall stone pillar on the top of which stands a large gilt peacock, a bird sacred to Buddhist and Hindu alike. Near this is the pagoda-roofed temple sacred to the Hindu goddess Devi Sitla, the origin of which has already been described. Every available space has been filled with a miscellaneous collection of small shrines, the delight of the countless Bhotiya children who play here all day long. A constant stream of pilgrims passes slowly round the sacred mound, and many, lost in devotion, make offering to the various shrines.

One other Buddhist monument needs to be mentioned. This is known as Bodhnath, or Kasha-chait, and is said to have been erected over the tomb of an eminent Tibetan Lama, one Kasha by name, who having come to Nepal on a pilgrimage from Lhasa, died, and was either burned or interred at this spot.

The temple is situated some three miles to the east of Kathmandu, and by reason of its great bulk and isolated position forms a conspicuous landmark. This place of pilgrimage is entirely in the hands of the Buddhists, and it is here that the many Tibetans and Bhotiyas who yearly visit the valley find a place of refuge. This temple is kept in repair at the expense of the Tibetan authorities, and is rarely visited by Hindus, but is occasionally used by the Newars who recognize its sacred associations.

The most important Hindu shrine in the country is the sacred wooden temple of Pasupatinath. It is situated on the banks of the Baghmati in a picturesque gorge and bordered by *ghats* which are ever thronged by the faithful. Here the pious Hindu hopes to die, and from far and wide flock pilgrims, to end their days, if possible, with the sacred waters lapping their feet.

The principal temple is built in the Nepalese pagoda style and is surrounded by a vast collection of temples and chapels which cover a vast space. The temple is said to have been built to commemorate the flight of Shiva who, in the form of a gazelle, took refuge in the sacred wood known as Shleshmantaka, in the remains of which the temple now stands.

It is difficult to realize fully the great part that Pasupati plays in the lives of the people. The name is constantly before one, and it is to this deity that all new projects are primarily dedicated. Here the Gurkha votary, be he king or peasant, makes his prayer, for in Lord Pasupati lies enshrined the very spirit of Nepal.

A little to the south-east of Kathmandu lies the largest city in Nepal—Patan. At one time the capital of the three principalities into which Nepal was formerly divided, Patan was, at that time, the resi dence of one of the Newar kings, and a wealthy and important city. In the year 1768 the city surrendered to Prithwi Narayan, when it was given up to plunder, and the nobility and principal men of the place were murdered. The royal palace was dismantled, the dwellings of the wealthy citizens were robbed of all their valuables, and even the temples were not spared. Traces of all this may still be seen at the present day.

The importance of Patan has now completely dwindled, but the city still retains much of its ancient charm. On all sides are temples, pagodas and *chaityas;* hardly a house is without sculpture or colour, and there are numerous tall stone pillars, surmounted by shining gilt images, the effigies of departed kings. The streets are wider than those of Kathmandu, and the scene in the Darbar Square, or Street of Palaces, can, for colour and variety, hardly be surpassed, and jaded indeed is he who fails to succumb to the charm of this ancient city.

The last city of any importance which remains to be mentioned is the city of Bhatgaon. It is situated on the eastern edge of the valley and is distant about eight miles from Kathmandu.

Bhatgaon is smaller than either Kathmandu or Patan, but is much more picturesque than either. This city also fell under the sway of Prithwi Narayan, but it escaped a good deal of the plunder and maltreatment which was meted out to the other cities in the valley. In consequence the buildings and ancient monuments are in an excellent state of preservation, and the city gives one an impression of life and prosperity which is lacking in Patan.

The most conspicuous building in Bhatgaon is the temple of the five stages, known as Nyatpola Deval. This was constructed early in the eighteenth century by the King, Bhupatindra Malla, and is built in the pagoda style found in many other temples in the valley, the most popular of which being that of Matsyandra Nath, at Patan.

This temple is built on five terraces, or stages, one above the other, which are connected by a flight of steps. On either side are ranged a series of colossal images carved in stone. The first pair of these represent two giants, Jaya Malla and Phatta by name, athletes in the service of the King, and who are reputed to have had the strength of ten men. Above them are two elephants whose strength was ten times that of the giants. Then, in succession, come lions and tigers, and, finally, the goddesses Singhini and Vyagharini, each pair being ten times stronger than that immediately below it.

The upper part of the building consists of five roofs, one above the other, each being slightly smaller than that immediately beneath it. The general effect of this giant pagoda is very striking, and it is one of the most characteristic buildings in the whole valley of Nepal.

Bhatgaon has the usual Darbar Square round which are grouped numerous temples and monoliths. Entrance to the Darbar is gained by means of the so-called Golden Gate, a fine specimen of Newar craftsmanship and richly ornamented with images of hammered brass.

A few miles from Bhatgaon, on the hills to the east, is the pretty little village of Nagarkot, the summer residence of various members of the royal family. From here one obtains a magnificent view of the unexplored country to the east, and the main track to Tibet can be seen winding away into the distance. When we were in Nagarkot the snows were completely obscured by clouds, but it is said that perhaps the finest view of all can be obtained from this spot.

Continuing along this range of hills to the west, we come to the hamlet of Kakani, which is the summer

TEMPLE OF NYATPOLA AT BHATGAON

BHATGAON

residence of the British Envoy. To one who knows the people to the west this spot is of particular interest, for from it we see the mountain of Maccha Pucchar, or the "Fish-tail peak" so often mentioned in their songs.

To the east of Maccha Pucchar, amongst many other giants of the Himalaya, are Gosainthan and the Yassu peaks. At the foot of Gosainthan is a deep and sacred lake to which devotees from all parts of India, braving the long and perilous ascent, yearly make pilgrimage. The sight must be one to stir the emotions—the still, clear water, the host of pilgrims on the banks and the ice-covered mountains all around; but no unbeliever's eyes have yet beheld the scene.

A little to the west of Kakani is the peak of Kaulia. It was here that Brian Hodgson—a man to whom, perhaps more than anybody, our knowledge of early Nepal is due—lived and worked, but the few remains of his bungalow are now half hidden by weeds.

Below Kaulia is the little town of Nawakot. This consists of a single street, with two darbars and a temple of Bhairavi in the Chinese style of Kathmandu. Once the favourite residence of the Regent Bahadur Shah, and also for a long time the station of Prithwi Narayan's court, the little town has lost all the glamour and importance of its bygone days, and is now but rarely visited by any member of the ruling house, except when used as a halting-place for a journey into the western provinces. The valley of Nayakot, some 2,000 feet below the level of the valley of Nepal, is intensely malarious from March to November. It is extremely fertile, and some seventeen different kinds of rice are grown in large quantities. Of fruit, the chief is the mango, and next come the oranges, reputed to be second to none in the world. The higher ground, such as the ridge on which the town stands, being above the malaria zone, is peopled by Nepalese of the ordinary castes such as Newars, Chetris, Magars, Gurungs, and Bhotias. The town is on a spur descending south-west from Mount Dhaibiong or Jibjibia, about a mile above the Tadi river on the south and flanked on the west by the Trisul or Trisulgandaki river. This last is a beautiful deep-blue stream, and skirting the town on the west, it joins the Tadi at Devi Ghat. The scenery at Devi Ghat is of the wildest, most romantic kind, both rivers rushing over stony beds, bordered by stupendous rocks. Devi Ghat itself is a very holy spot and under the protection of the goddess Bhairavi, whose temple stands in the town of Nawakot. Three miles upstream from Devi Ghat, the river is spanned by a bridge, leading to the village of Tirsuli Bazar and on to Gurkha, some three marches distant.

From Devi Ghat, the Tirsuli flows south-east towards the plain, and is joined in its course by several feeders from the western side of Nepal proper; eventually, after joining the great Gandaki river at Deo Ghat, it flows nearly due south and quits the hills at Tribeni through a pass in the sand-stone range to the west of the Someshwar ridge near Ramnagar in Bihar.

Although the journey back to Kathmandu contains no features of absorbing interest, it rarely fails to please by reason of the charm and variety of its scenery, and the people met with on the road. On the way down, at the little village of Jitpur, we met with a cheery party of Bhotiya girls, who smilingly submitted to the ordeal of the camera. They were from Khenchat, on the farther side of the Kakani ridge, and wore the tight anklets, brass bracelets, and knotted shoulder cloths peculiar to this part of the world.

A little below Jitpur, in the hamlet of Dharmtali, is a small white chaitya, which, with its staring

DEVI GHAT—JUNCTION OF TRISUL AND TADI RIVERS

VILLAGE OF DHARMTALLI—NEPAL VALLEY

Buddha eyes and squat round form, looks strangely like a snow man.

As we near Kathmandu again we come in sight of the British Legation, which is built on a slight rise a little to the north of the city. Now one of the most salubrious spots in the valley, the Maharaja smilingly relates that it was originally selected by his predecessors as being the most unhealthy part of Kathmandu !

The area round about the British Legation may be described as the residential quarter of Kathmandu. Here are situated the numerous modern palaces belonging to members and relations of the reigning family. Surrounded, as they are, by high brick walls it is impossible to gain more than a fleeting glimpse of them. The etiquette of the country does not permit of one visiting their owners, but, from the little one sees, they give an impression of wealth and comfort.

The most important of the palaces in Kathmandu is that known as the Singha Durbar, the residence of the Prime Minister, Sir Chandra Shamsher.

Sir Chandra Shamsher assumed office in 1901, and to him is due the era of progress and prosperity which the country now enjoys. Always devoted to the welfare of his subjects, he has spared no pains to further their interests, and rightly figures as the outstanding personality of the country to-day.

CHAPTER XII

THE NEWARS

THE Newars claim to be the original inhabitants of the Nepal Valley, and certainly their customs, in many points similar to those of other Mongolian races, lend colour to the story of their original immigration from the north, and support the theory advanced by the earliest legends of Nepal that the first person to enter the country, Manjusri, came from Mahachina, or China. On the other hand, some authorities allege that the Newars originally migrated from Southern India, being identical with the Nair soldiery, who formed a part of Nanda Deva's army which invaded Nepal in the ninth century A.D. Whatever their early history, or the country of their origin, it is quite clear that the present race of Newars is a mixed one derived from both Indian and Tibetan stock, with a slight preponderance of the latter. This mixed origin is again very evident in their religion, for though Buddhism—originally inherited from their Tibetan ancestors—may be said to be the basis of their natural faith, it has been greatly modified by the adoption or retention of many Hindu doctrines, derived from the natives of India, with whom the Tibetan ancestors of the Newars undoubtedly inter-married.

The Newars are still the most numerous group of the inhabitants of the Nepal Valley, and they are responsible for such metal work, sculpture, architecture, painting and literature as the country possesses, the Gurkhas, who overran and have ever since dominated the valley, being indifferent patrons of art and letters. Besides their skill in the arts and handicrafts, the Newars are shrewd traders, while their agricultural methods are unrivalled in Nepal. The great majority of the mechanics in the country are Newars, and the few manufactures that exist, such as the making of iron and brass pots, silver and gold ornaments, coarse cotton cloth, and paper, are carried out entirely by this steady and industrious class.

As has already been pointed out, the Newars are a mixed race, and it will be of interest to examine in more detail the effects of the intermingling of Mongolian and Aryan blood on their religion, and how, as in the case of all the other tribes of Nepal, Hinduism grows apace and will, in course of time, gradually gain complete ascendancy over the fast disappearing Buddhism.

Both from ancient legends and also by reason of the geographical situation of the Valley—separated as it is by almost impassable mountain ranges and the deadly malarious swamps of the Terai from India—there is reason to believe that the aborigines were of Chinese or Tibetan origin. Whether they were men of the Newar race, as the people themselves claim, we do not now know, but it seems fairly certain that they were followers of Buddha, for they inherited their religion from Manjushri, whoever he may have been, who introduced Buddhism into Nepal. In course of time, however, with the advent of pilgrims and exiles from the plains of India, a certain amount of Hinduism began to creep into the country, and before very long there were followers of the two rival creeds. While the majority of the newcomers were Buddhists, yet many were Hindus, and these probably succeeded in converting not a few of the simple inhabitants to their own faith, so we find that the original Newars of Nepal became divided into two classes, each following a different faith. Although these two classes came originally from the same stock, they followed creeds widely differing in tenets and observances. Yet the effect and influence of the more subtle Brahmanism came, in course of time, to make itself felt, and Buddhism, in its original form, became tainted with Brahmanistic practices. In consequence of this, caste distinctions, which the Hindu Newars had retained, came to be adopted by the Buddhist Newars also, and much of the complicated mythology and tradition of the Hindus was incorporated in the latter creed. This weakening and, one might add, demoralization of the Buddhist faith was given further impetus by the conquest of Nepal by the Gurkhas, who, bigoted and illiterate as they were, spared no efforts to oppress those who professed a religion differing from their own. As a result of this, Buddhist temples were plundered and lands confiscated, while the only chance the followers of this faith had of securing the patrimony or favour of the conquerors was by laying aside their own doctrines and adopting those of the now dominant Hindus. At the present day, Newar Buddhists are in a considerable numerical superiority in the valley of Nepal, yet the influence of Brahmanism still continues as strongly as ever, and it is only a matter of time before Buddhism is entirely supplanted and the Hindu faith adopted by all members of the community.

It can be seen from the above that with the intermingling, not only of the people, but also of the religious, it is difficult to discern the exact line of difference between Hinduism and Buddhism as practised by the Newars, the one seeming to merge imperceptibly into the other. Shrines dedicated to Ganesh and Vishnu, both Hindu deities, are constantly seen in Buddhist temples, while images of

NEPALESE NOBLE'S HOUSE—TYPICAL NEWAR ARCHITECTURE

SINGHA DURBAR—RESIDENCE OF THE MAHARAJA

Buddha are equally common in purely Hindu places of worship.

It is equally difficult to define the exact religious significance of many of the Newar festivals which take place at intervals throughout the year. In many of these so-called Hindu festivals such as the Indra-jatra, Banhras—a purely Buddhist sect—officiate as priests, while, on the other hand, Hindus join heartily in the festival known as Machendrajatra, which is of an essentially Buddhist character. Having thus described the way in which the two religions have, as it were, passed insensibly one into the other, we must now describe the main divisions of the Newars as they exist to-day, and the professions and trades adopted by each.

The Newars are divided firstly into worshippers of Buddha, known as Buddhamargis, and secondly, those who worship Shiva, called Shivamargis, and who may be termed Hindus. At the present day the latter class numbers between a third and a half of the population of the Valley, and their numbers are ever growing. The organization of the Shivamargis is somewhat similar to that of the Hindus of the plains of India, though less complicated, and, as with them, the highest caste is the Brahman, who may be regarded as the spiritual guide of the upper classes. Next in rank below the Brahmans come the Kshetriyas, and it is interesting to note that within this group the former warrior class, or Srishtas, fell, for although the Newars cannot now be considered a warlike race, they occasionally produce very good soldiers, and their heroic struggles in the days of Prithwi Narayan are sufficient evidence that they are not wanting in courage when it is needed. In the next group, known as the Vaisyas, are two castes, the Joshi, or astrologers, and the Achar, or priests of local deities. These last expound the Hindu sacred scriptures and perform other religious duties. All of the above three groups are permitted to wear the sacred thread with the exception of certain sub-castes of the Srishtas. Also belonging to this third Hindu group are several castes of Newars who had formerly figured as Buddhists, but who, becoming influenced by Brahmanic ideas, separated to some extent from their former co-religionists. These are the Kou, or blacksmiths, the Nou, or barbers, the Tati, weavers of cloth used in religious ceremonies, the Bhat, whose duties are connected with funerals, and the Kathas who dress wounds and sever the umbilical cord at birth. Finally, in the last group of Newar Buddhists, come the various menial classes known as Sudras.

The Buddhamargis a e divided into three grades, of which the highest is that known as Bandya or Banra. These may be said to correspond to the Brahmans, and are said to be the descendants of Buddhists monks who were compelled to break their vows of celibacy. They still live chiefly in the *Vihars* or monasteries in the cities of the valley. Nowadays they are allowed to marry, and their wives and children usually reside with them. The orthodox Banras are again divided into various classes, the most important of which are known as Gubharju and Bikut in Newari, or Vajra Acharya and Bhikshu in the Sanskrit language. Of these, the former are regarded as the highest class of priest, and the latter, although hereditary gold and silversmiths, exercise priestly functions of a somewhat inferior sort, and not infrequently serve as assistants to the Vajra Acharya in certain forms of worship. The majority of the Banras follow secular occupations, and many follow the vocations of coppersmith, stone worker, manufacturer of cooking utensils and so forth, while their hereditary calling as workers in gold and silver leads to such employment as coiners in the Government Mint.

The next main group of the Buddhamargi is that of the Udas. These are the class of traders and merchants of Nepal, and may be said to correspond to the Hindu orders of the Vaisyas. In addition to being traders and merchants they pursue such vocations as carpentry, baking, copper and brass work, brick and tile work, and stone masonry, the stone images and effigies of gods seen so frequently in the precincts of temples throughout the valley being generally their handiwork. The Udas are, nominally, Buddhists of a very orthodox type, rarely if ever worshipping at Hindu temples, and they may be regarded as the descendants of Buddhist laymen, as the Banras are descended from Buddhist monks. They resemble the Banras closely in manners, customs and religious ideas, and will eat from their hands, although the latter will not reciprocate in this respect; similarly a Banra may be admitted into the Udas group; but an Udas Newar can never hope to become a Banra.

The third Buddhamargi group is the most comprehensive of all, and includes all who do not belong to the first or second orders. In it are included the large class of Jyapoo, or cultivators, who constitute nearly half the population of Nepal, as well as the lower class of Newars who are employed in domestic service. Besides these there are several sections of the Jyapoo class who follow different occupations, of which the most important are perhaps the Kumhals, or potters, the other members of this group being engaged in carpentry, oil pressing, dyeing and inferior handicrafts. This order corresponds closely to the Hindu order of Sudras, and shows, to a much larger extent than the other two, the influences of Brahmanism. In consequence its members, who may be described as heterodox Buddhists, are in reality, Buddhists but in name, for they contrive to combine the worship of Shiva and other Hindu deities with that of Buddha. Although the members of this third group are much inferior in rank and social status to the Banras and the Udas, yet they are all in caste, that is to say, any Hindu may drink water from their hands without in any way forfeiting his own caste. There are, however, eight classes of Newars of mixed Buddha and Shiva caste, whose occupations and professions, being looked upon as menial, have, in consequence, become outcaste. These are the butchers, musicians, tailors, woodcutters, charcoal burners, sweepers, washermen, leatherworkers and fishermen, and no Hindu or Nepali Buddhist can take water from their hands without forfeiting his caste. It is curious to note that even these, who form the lowest strata in the Newar social scale and who correspond to the "untouchables" of India, imitate the exclusive social system of their superiors, and do not eat or intermarry amongst themselves.

Although the Newars still regard Lhasa as the seat of orthodox Buddhism, the Lamas of that city do not take any active part nor interfere in the religious affairs of the Buddhists of Nepal, though they contribute to the upkeep of the great shrines of Bodh and Swyambunath in the valley. Any difficulties that may arise on religious matters are therefore, in the absence of any recognized spiritual head or adviser, settled amongst themselves in the best possible way, a convocation of priests of the highest class being usually assembled which examines the case on its merits, and comes to a decision in accordance with what they hope is the correct interpretation of the Buddhist sacred writings.

It is worthy of note that three important occupations for which there are definite castes in India—namely, the physicians, the weavers and the liquor distillers—are not to be found amongst the Newars. The former, though said to have been in the first instance reserved for the Jaisis among Hindu Newars, is followed by any one, and weaving and liquor distilling are carried out, to a certain extent, in every household, and do not, as in other parts of the East, constitute definite professions. In this connection it should be noted that amongst Newars professions and occupations are hereditary, and the members of any particular craft may not encroach upon the professional rights of another. Exception, however, is made in the case of such crafts as do not provide the worker with a living, such as the Nalli, whose sole occupation is to paint the eye of an image at certain religious festivals. People who follow vocations such as this are permitted to supplement their earnings by also working at some other trade. Amongst Hindu Newars the only definitely secular occupation, except the general ones of fighting, trade, cultivation and religious worship, is that of cowherd; all other occupations being followed by Buddhists, whether pure or mixed. Of late years the plough has become much more popular, yet from evidence at hand it appears that the employment of cattle was not known to the Newars in ancient days, and, generally speaking, but few cattle are employed even in modern days.

The favourite implement in the cultivation of land is the *kodali*, or digging-hoe, and the straight and careful furrows to be seen in the fields of the valley of Nepal are almost invariably the work of the *kodali* and not the plough. The absence of cattle on the whole, and their non-employment for purposes of cultivation, does not appear to be due to any respect felt for cows or buffaloes, as might be expected in the case of Hindus, but is probably owing to the original ignorance of their use for this purpose and an inherent aversion to change, the principal hindrance to progress all over the East. As a consequence of this, the cowherd class is numerically very weak in the Nepal valley, although their existence since time immemorial is undoubted.

As in the case of cultivation, so most of the arts of the Newars are said to have been derived from outside influence, and it will be worth while to take a retrospective view of the subject and see how the introduction of new religious ideas was originally infused into the people, thus paving the way for an elaboration of the existing social system and the development of a new material culture among the Newars. It will be seen, too, that although Tibetan and Chinese influences have, to a certain extent, left their mark upon Nepalese Buddhism, as well as upon such material matters as the arts and crafts of the country, yet the balance of the available evidence is inclined to support the theory that it is to India, rather than to Tibet or China, that the Newars owe, not only their religious and social organization, but also the greater portion of their material culture as well. Professor Levi makes no attempt to disguise the fact that the beginnings of Newar culture and civilization owed their creation to the influence of India, and according to this scholar the light of religion was introduced by Buddhist missionaries who expounded their doctrines in a way that was easily understood by the wilder peoples of Nepal. Their work, however, was sadly interrupted, if not even largely destroyed, by the onslaughts on Buddhism, led, it is said, by the Brahman fanatic, Sankara Acharya, who, in the middle of the seventh century, descended upon Nepal and instituted a relentless persecution of all who professed or protected the Buddhist religion; massacring some, converting others, he forced the celibate monks to marry. The lapse of the monks from celibacy, however, was not altogether due to the above source, but may be considered as due to the general decadence of Buddhism during this period. In addition to this,

Professor Levi puts forth a theory that to the marriage of the clergy is due the origin of the present complex social organization of the Newars. Living, as they did, in *Vihars* or monasteries, together with their families, they were forced to adopt secular professions, as the scant remuneration of their religious duties did not suffice to sustain both them and their families. In consequence, the Banras became a clearly defined social class, and the more material conditions of their new life, added to the fact that they were already influenced by the example of the Brahmans, quickly brought into being the question of caste. Forming, as it were, a religious aristocracy, they came to look upon ordinary laymen as inferior to themselves, and a not unnatural disinclination to share with them the privileges they enjoyed, as the result of their former condition, only served to tighten the bonds of caste. Other rigid supporters of all that pertained to caste were the royal families of Nepal, the Surajvansis and the Thakurs, whose tribes, having been grouped as inferior to the Kshetriyas or fighting men, were anxious to prove their qualification for admittance to that rank, to which they were finally admitted, but not without opposition. Their admission led to the formation of a Kshetriya caste in Nepal which professed a mixed faith of Buddhism and Hinduism, thus serving to unite the two religions. The regime of caste, though modified to suit the new conditions, had also been introduced by the Brahmans, who had brought the cult of Shiva from India, and this was further strengthened by the advent of the Hindu monarch, Harisinha Deva, who conquered Nepal in 1324, and is said to have brought with him seven castes. The work of this king was completed by the seventh king of the third Thakur dynasty, Jayasthiti Malla (1385–1429), who was the first to introduce systematic laws of caste for his subjects. Finally, the conquest of Nepal by the Gurkhas, Hindus of a stricter persuasion than the Newars, fostered the growth of Brahmanic ascendancy to an even greater degree, with the result that the Buddhist religion, customs and social rule became, to a certain extent, greatly minimized.

The original inhabitants of Nepal are said to have been wild and almost barbarian tribes, devoid of all knowledge of arts and crafts, while the immigrants from the plains of India are believed to have possessed a fairly advanced standard of culture. In consequence of this it follows that, after a time, the aborigines welcomed the introduction of agriculture and the various arts brought them by their more cultured intruders, and this probably accounts for the fact that they were peaceably received. The style of buildings and architectural ornament in Nepal is often attributed to Tibet or China, for the most characteristic types of Nepalese temples are in the so-called pagoda style; but Professor Levi thinks it not improbable that the pagoda style was in existence in Nepal long before it made its appearance farther east. He traces the origin of the form to the early wooden architecture of India, which preceded the ancient stone monuments of that country, and suggests that the pagodas of China and Japan are due to the influence of the Newars. He supports this hypothesis by the fact that Newar workmen have been, up to quite modern times, widely employed in Tibet, Tartary and many parts of China, and that it is admitted in the annals of the last-named country that art in China has been largely influenced by the Newars. Mr. E. B. Havell, in his *Ancient and Mediæval Architecture of India*, has arrived at the same conclusions, for he claims that the so-called pagoda style in Nepal can be found in the Asana type of temple architecture in India, which was subsequently modified to meet the conditions which prevailed in the Himalaya, where the rainfall is heavier

NEWARS PLOUGHING—SHOWING METHOD OF TERRACE CULTIVATION

than in the plains of India, and where flat-terr roofs are consequently unsuitable.

Other points which support the theory that t early culture of Nepal was not derived from Tibet o China are to be found in the fact that in such crafts as weaving, spinning and agriculture the appliances, implements and general methods of execution bea a much closer similarity to those in use in India. In the case of the first two, the loom and accessories for weaving differ but slightly from those still in use in India, while as regards spinning, an instrument closely resembling the spinning-wheel of India is still used in Nepal. These few instances will, it is hoped, show that there is a strong reason to believe that not only in matters of religion and social organization, but also in the arts and crafts of the Newars, the influence is more likely to have been from India than from anywhere else, but the various questions raised by this inference are, naturally, of too broad a nature to permit of detailed discussion in these pages.

The chief crop of the Nepal Valley is rice, and the method of agriculture is to level the land into terraces, each surrounded by a border of earth about a foot in height to aid in the retention of the water brought for irrigation purposes. This method of systematic irrigation is similar to that obtaining in the rice country of Bengal and Assam, and has always been considered as the chief characteristic of the cultivation introduced into Nepal by the earliest immigrants. The Newars have, since time immemorial, been skilful craftsmen in metal and stone, carpentry and related arts, and not only in their own country, but also in Tibet and Tartary, are many examples of their handiwork.

Before proceeding to describe some of the better known Newar festivals, and then their manners and customs, the following points should be noted with regard to the two immigrant cultures and the two

THE NEWARS

Buddhists and Hindus alike, and is looked upo
the guardian angel of the country. The Jatr
festival, takes place at Bhatgaon, being one o
three major festivals which take place annua
each of the three principal cities of the Vall
other two being the Machendrajatra and the
jatra, which are held at Patan and Kath
respectively. Commencing about the mic
April it lasts for two days, and possibly owir
fact that Bhatgaon is some eight miles dist
the capital, it does not, as a rule, attract
spectators as do the other festivals. It c
two parts, known respectively as the Rat
Lingajatra. In the former, two cars, in or
a figure of Bhairab, and in the other one o
is seated, are dragged in procession through the city. In the latter festival a large beam of timber, known as the *Linga* (phallic emblem), is erected in front of the temple of Bhairab, near the Darbar, and buffaloes are sacrificed and votive offerings made to the deity. The two cars subsequently take their stand beside the *Linga*, where they remain during the time that the religious ceremonies in their honour are being performed, on the completion of which the *Linga* is dismantled and the cars removed. Besides the Bhairabjatra there are two other festivals in honour of Bhairab, known as the Neta Devi Rajatra in Kathmandu, and the Devijatra at Nawakot. These do not call for any detailed description ; in the Devijatra the figure of Bhairavi Devi is brought from the temple of Nawakot to Devi Ghat, at the junction of the Trisulganga and Tadi rivers, and the festivities last for five days, during which time crowds of buffaloes are slaughtered. When the festival is over, the image of the goddess is escorted back with much ceremony to the temple at Nayakot, there to remain until it is required in the following year.

16
that, as a result, ens
rancy ever getting stronger has
d upon the people as the result of bitter struggle,
n the case of the Gurkha invasion, but appears to
ve been a gradual growth. Legends and tradition
elate that the conquest of what was, in those days,
a purely Buddhist country by Brahman kings was
not opposed with abnormal vigour, and the Banras
actually became the peers of the Brahmans in conse-
quence. Not only in the matter of food and drink,
but also in some of the ritual connected with marriage,
the social organization, both Buddhist and Hindu, of
the Newars often coincides, and in ordinary social
life the differences have never been sharply defined.

Besides the three purely Hindu festivals of the Holi, Dasehra and Diwali which are observed by all classes of Nepalese, in much the same way as they are in India, there are certain festivals in Nepal which are peculiar to the Newars, and which find no counterpart in the plains of India. The most important of these, which may be regarded as purely national festivals, are the Bhairabjatra, the Gaijatra, the Banrajatra, Indrajatra, Sheoratri, Great and Small Machendrajatra, and the festival of Narayan at Balaji and Bara Nil Kanta. As has already been stated, some of these festivals are so mixed in character that it is often difficult to say whether they belong more to the Buddhists or the Hindus. In consequence the only course open is to describe briefly those festivals as they at present exist, without any attempt being made to assign a purely Buddhist or purely Hindu character to any one of them.

One of the most important Newar festivals is that known as the Bhairabjatra, or, as its name suggests, a festival in honour of Bhairab. Bhairab being an incarnation of Shiva, a purely Hindu god, but having since time immemorial been adopted into the Buddhist mythology, is held in great veneration by

The Gaijatra, or Festival of the Cow, has been
named because the Hindu Newars, who have alw
been the most influential, if not the most numer
members of the population, have elected to cal
after their favourite animal. It takes place, dur
the month of July, at all the big cities in the Val
and is connected with the *Vihars*, or monaste
which exist in these places. On the first day an im
of a cow is carried in procession through the str
accompanied by a motley band of revellers, who w
horns and grotesque masks, a bevy of Brahr
virgins accompanying the procession. For the Hi
portion of the participants this day, devoted as i
to the worship of the cow, constitutes the wh
festival, but for the Buddhists who take part in
the festivities are carried on for some time, for du
the following fourteen days Newars of both se
come to visit the various *Viharas*, where they m
offerings of flowers, fruit, grain and rice, and
their devotion to the various deities to whom
Viharas are dedicated. On this occasion the w
of the *Viharas* are hung with pictures, painted
water-colours, usually of vivid hues, represent
Buddhist subjects. These remain upon the w
until the last day of the festival, when the ima
which have also been exposed during this per
are also removed to their storage places, there
remain until another year has passed.

The Banrajatra, or Festival of the Banras, ta
place every quarter, provided there happens to
some wealthy man who is willing to bear the he
expenses of it. The chief object of this celebrat
is to make a present of food and money to as m
Banras as the organizer of the entertainment
afford. On the day itself a platform roofed ab
and enclosed on three sides is erected in front of
house of the host, in the centre of which is an a
adorned with the copper-gilt coronet of Amitab

LOOKING TOWARDS GOSAINTHAN FROM KAKANI

DARBAR AND TEMPLE, TIRSULI, NAWAKOT

Buddha, and other sacred relics brought for the purpose from the temple at Swyambunath. On the platform, priests offer up prayers, and after consecrating offerings of rice, milk and flowers, they scatter them amongst the spectators who are collected in the street below. After paying their respects to the altar, the Banras who have been invited to the feast march in procession through some of the principal streets, and, as they pass along, receive alms from the numbers of women who line the route along which it is known the procession will pass. In front of each woman is a large basket filled with grain, fruit and flowers. As each Banra passes by he is presented with some of the contents of the baskets, which he puts in a special wallet brought for this purpose. For many Newars this day is made the occasion of performing an act of piety and generosity at a small cost and with a minimum of labour, for most of the women who distribute the alms have been sent at the express command of their husbands. After the women's contributions have all been disposed of, their baskets are replenished at the expense of the giver of the feast, and they remain at their post until every Banra, and there are usually many hundreds of them, has received a share of the offerings. On the following day the altar is dismantled and the sacred relics are returned to the temple of Swyambunath with much pomp and ceremony, escorted by a bevy of Newari maidens singing and accompanied by a band of musicians who perform on instruments of various shapes and sizes.

The Indrajatra, which takes place about the beginning of September, and lasts for eight days, is always held at Kathmandu. This festival, which is held in honour of Indra, the god of rain, is celebrated by all classes of Newars, Hindus and Buddhists alike, and is peculiar to Nepal, there being no festival of a similar kind held anywhere in India. During the eight days, the Newars observe a general holiday, spending the daytime either in prayer or in fasting. In the evening they sally forth to look on at the dancing and masquerading which take place in the streets of the city, which are illuminated for the occasion. In reality two festivals are celebrated at this time; one, the Indrajatra proper, in honour of Indra, and the other, the Rathjatra, in honour of Devi Kumari, but curiously enough, beyond the fact that they invariably occur at the same time, the two festivals have no connection with each other. During the period of the Indrajatra small images of Indra are erected all over the city, and much singing, dancing and masquerading take place in the streets. The Rathjatra, a comparatively modern festival, owes its origin to a legend concerning the monarch Jayaprakasa Malla, who reigned in the middle of the eighteenth century. It is said that this king banished a girl from the city who was possessed of an evil spirit and believed herself to be a *Kumari*, or deity. On the same night the King's *Rani* was seized with similar symptoms, and declared that the spirit of the deity has passed into her body. The King, now thoroughly alarmed, immediately took steps to make reparation for the wrong he had done to the girl, and amongst other tokens of atonement and respect, decreed that she should be drawn through the city in state in a *rath* or car. He further decreed that she should be attended by two Banra boys, one of whom was to personate Ganesh and the other Mahenkal, as her attendants and guardians. Three Banra children are nowadays selected to impersonate the rôles of Devi Kumari and her two custodians, being chosen from the Banra families whose hereditary privilege it is to furnish them. As this office, which is held for three or four years, carries with it considerable pecuniary advantages, there is usually no lack of candidates, although it is well known that the little girl of the party, usually chosen on account of her personal attractions, finds difficulty in securing a husband later on, as the public position she has thus occupied is considered to have unfitted her for the domestic duties and responsibilities which marriage entails. The Rathjatra, therefore, consists in dragging these three children, each situated in a triumphal car, through the main streets of Kathmandu. Three different routes are taken on three alternate days in three different parts of the city, after which the cars are stored away in a special building close to the Darbar.

The most important of all the Newar festivals is that known as the Machendrajatra. The origin of this festival is attributed to the following tradition. A disciple of Machendra, by name Gorakhnath, is said to have once visited Nepal, and considering that he had not received there the reverence to which he considered himself entitled, retired to a little hill near Deo Patan, where he remained immovable for twelve years. As a result Nepal was visited by a drought which, it was considered, would never disappear until Gorakhnath could be induced to leave his position. This was finally effected by the King of Bhatgaon, Narendra Deva, making a pilgrimage to the dwelling-place of Machendra and persuading the saint to visit Nepal. On the latter's arrival in the valley, Gorakhnath, abandoning his position on the hill, proceeded towards Patan in order to do homage to Machendra, and immediately after, rain fell copiously. The two saints thereupon proceeded towards a large tree to the south of Patan, where Narendra Deva had done homage to a vessel filled with sacred water before proceeding on his journey. The saints soon after returned to the plains of India, and the King instituted the festival of Machendrajatra, which has been held annually ever since. Although Machendra is particularly venerated by the Newars, all races hold him in great esteem, and rain, which is wanted at the time of the festival for the sowing of Indian corn, is always said to fall during the Machendrajatra, a further proof of the benevolence of the god; but the timely arrival of the south-west monsoon would seem to be a not unimportant factor of this last!

The Machendrajatra is divided into three portions. Firstly, the bathing of the image of the god near Narendra Deva's tree in Patan; secondly, the parading of the image in a car through the streets of Patan; and thirdly, the unrobing of the image and exhibition of his shirt to the people. The image is taken out of the temple of Machendra at Patan and, in the presence of a large crowd, is bathed and carefully washed on the stone platform beneath the sacred tree. After this he is carried back with much pomp to the temple, and there painted and got ready for his appearance at the principal ceremony. Seventeen days after the bathing ceremony, the image is dragged through the main streets, and on this occasion there are two cars, each consisting of a square chamber, covered with copper-gilt plates in the case of the larger and with thatch in that of the smaller. These are placed on rough waggons, some six to seven feet high, and in the larger one is placed the image of the god. The cars are dragged, by means of ropes, by about 150 men, and the whole circuit of about a mile and a quarter is performed in three stages, at the end of which a halt is made at some previously appointed spot, where sacrifices are performed and great feasting takes place. The third stage includes the circuit of Narendra Deva's tree, and at this place the cars stand for two whole nights. After this they proceed to an open space near the city called Puriya Tal, where they remain for another ten to twenty days, awaiting the auspicious day for them to be dragged to the parade ground for the disrobing

DARBAR SQUARE, PATAN

SUBMERGED STATUE OF VISHNU, AT BALAJI

of the image. On the day of the disróbing about six Banras, dressed in red and with shaven heads, bring the small car to the side of the larger one. The Banras then proceed to undress the image as he sits in his car, taking off his clothes piece by piece until they come to the shirt. This is then held aloft for all to see and worship, after which this also is packed away in a box. The Banras now take the unclothed image out of his shrine and place it in the smaller car which is now borne in triumph to Bhungmatti, a spot near Patan where Narendra Deva halted during his return from pilgrimage, where it remains for six months.

There are two shrines to Narayan, an incarnation of Vishnu, in Nepal; one at Balaji, at the foot of the mountain of Nagarjun, and another at Bara Nil Kantha, at the base of Sheopuri. At each place there is a figure of Narayan lying on a bed of serpents, sculptured in the middle of a small tank, but the image at Bara Nil Kantha is four times the size of that at Balaji. By a custom, dating from very long ago, the King of Nepal is never allowed to visit the Bara Nil Kantha—he himself being considered an incarnation of Vishnu—and so the smaller image at Balaji was built in imitation of the larger in order that the King and members of the royal family should be able to pay their devotions to the shrine. A yearly festival, known as the festival of Narayan—a deity popular in Nepal and worshipped both by Hindus and Buddhists, but especially by the former—takes place at both these shrines. On this occasion a canopy is erected over the god's head, which is decorated with marigold flowers, while his limbs are festooned with garlands. His forehead is marked with a caste mark and the sacred chest mark of Vishnu is painted on his chest. Flowers and rice are sprinkled over the figure, and the worshippers, muttering prayers the while, bow low to the ground, and with their foreheads touch the feet of the god. With the customary donation to the officiating priests the ceremony is terminated as far as the Hindus are concerned, but the Buddhists, in addition, make a pilgrimage to the top of the mountain of Nagarjun, where they worship at the small *chaitya*, or mound temple, on the summit. And now some Newar ceremonies.

On the birth of a child the infant is first washed with *Karuwa*, or Shishum, oil, after which it is wiped with a cotton towel. The towel and the clothes upon which the mother has been lying are next put into a basket which is placed in the corner of the room, where parched corn, salt, sugar-cane and ginger are offered to it. News of the birth is carried to the mother's parents by special emissaries, who take with them a salver containing ginger, salt, sugar-cane and a bottle of spirits. These gifts, however, are not kept, but are forthwith returned to the donor. Two days after the child's birth the umbilical cord is cut, after which the child is washed in sherbet. On the conclusion of this operation all the child's relations, other than parents and grandparents, are considered to have become impure for a period of four days, at the expiry of which a purification ceremony takes place in the room in which the child was born.

After six months in the case of a boy and five in that of a girl, the ceremony of feeding with rice takes place. On this occasion all friends and relations are summoned and a big feast takes place. The actual ceremony does not differ greatly from that performed by the other races of Nepal, where all the invited bring gifts for the child, either in money or in the form of clothing.

On attaining the age of seven or eight years a ceremony which involves the cutting of the children's hair is performed. On this occasion a barber is summoned to the house, but before he is allowed to carry out his part of the performance—which consists in completely shaving the child's head—the maternal uncle of the boy goes through a mock performance with a gold razor and scissors, but the significance of this appears to be unknown. When the barber has completed his work and has also pierced the child's ears, the shorn locks are collected in a brass or copper vessel by the maternal aunt, who subsequently presents the barber with a suit of clothes and a brass platter, while at the same time she gives the child two balls of sweetmeat with which he is supposed to pelt the barber. On the completion of the above the child is taken upstairs to a priest who is in waiting. Prayers are offered and the vessel containing the hair is taken and thrown into the nearest convenient stream. This being accomplished, the whole party, priest, family and child, go and worship at any convenient temple which is dedicated to Ganesh, after which the child is presented with a bow and arrow and is then supposed to make a pretence of running away from his parents. The ceremony concludes with the usual feast, and gifts (which should include ducks' eggs, a handkerchief, a sheet and a plate of curds) are presented to the child.

A Newar child is not considered to be fully admitted into the Newar caste until it has performed the ceremony of *Kaita Puja*. This consists in showing it, in the form of a ceremony, the correct method of girding on the *kaita* or loincloth, and on its conclusion the Newar boy is considered of age and must from that time onwards conform to all the rules dictated by caste.

At any time between the ages of five and twelve all Newar girls are married to a *Bel* fruit. In order to bring this about, the date of consecration of some such structure as a temple must first be ascertained by parents who have daughters of marriageable age.

On the day in question the virgins fast during the morning, and having bathed and arrayed themselves in clean clothes, repair to the spot where the particular edifice is situated. Arrived there, they go through a small ceremony, after which they return to their homes; but during this day they may eat nothing but fruit. On the following day they return to the appointed temple, and the *Kanyadan*, or giving in marriage of the virgin to the *Bel* fruit, is performed. Each girl is given a *Bel* fruit with four or five inches of stalk attached to it, and the officiating priest then performs the *Sankalpa* ceremony. The parents of the girls put the fruit into their daughters' hands, who in their turn deposit it in a brass plate provided for this purpose, and this concludes the ceremony.

On reaching the age of twelve, Newar girls are confined to their homes for twelve days, during which time they are not allowed to meet anybody, nor may they even see the light of the sun. After the period of confinement is over, an elderly female relative is summoned, who after making votive offerings to the child, puts a little betel nut and spice into her mouth and some vermilion paint on her head. Later on in the day a female barber is called and she pares the girl's nails and removes the blinds or cloths with which the windows have been covered during the whole of the preceding twelve days. The next part of this ceremony is performed by a priest, and consists in the girl offering a libation of water to the sun, the priest chanting the while. He gives her a mirror and a pot of red paint, and she thereupon sets off for any temple dedicated to Ganesh and offers prayers to that deity. At the close of this day a great feast is held, on the conclusion of which presents of parched corn, sugar-cane, ginger and salt are presented to all who have attended.

Amongst Newars marriages are usually arranged by the parents, and the following procedure is

IN THE FOOTHILLS

FOUNTAINS AT BALAJI

adopted. When a father wishes to arrange the marriage of his son he sends a friend to enter into negotiations with the parents of some girl he has previously selected. These last, if they agree to the match, send by the same messenger a plate of curds signifying their approval. On the following day the father of the boy, accompanied by a friend, proceeds to the girl's house, taking with him 2 lbs. of meat, 4 lbs. of toddy, 16 lbs. of sweetmeat, and 14 lbs. of betel nut, the last being given to the girl's mother for the purpose of propitiating the household gods. Some fifteen days later this proceeding is repeated, but on this occasion the bearers of the gifts are entertained to a feast in the girl's house. During the course of the feast the father of the prospective bridegroom inquires the amount of sweetmeat required for the guests at the wedding, and on returning to his house he sends the amount named, with a like proportion of fish, to the house of the girl's father. The despatch of these gifts is followed by a personal visit to the girl by her prospective father-in-law, who presents her with four duck's eggs and some gold bracelets. In the evening a feast is held, the guests on this occasion presenting the girl with rather more substantial gifts than usual, such as buffaloes, goats, sheep and household utensils. On the next day the father of the bridegroom prepares a load of two large copper dishes, in one of which he places flowers, betel nut and red lead, and in the other ten large pieces of betel nut, while at the same time he gives to a female attendant the articles necessary for worship. When all has been prepared the load is put on to the shoulders of an attendant, and taking in addition two loads of foodstuffs, an empty dandy, and accompanied by three dandy bearers and three torch holders, he sets off for the girl's house once again. On his arrival he deposits the dandy and gifts and returns to his own home, to return again on the following morning, when a big feast, in the presence of the bridegroom, is held. At the conclusion of this the girl's father, after exhorting the bridegroom's father to cherish her, gives his daughter his hand and raises her up. At this moment she is presented by her future father-in-law with four small packets, each containing betel nut. These she gives away to her parents and near relations as a token signifying that the hour of her departure from home is at hand. This is the signal for a general show of weeping and lamentation to take place, and while this is going on the bride takes her seat in the waiting dandy. The bride spends that night at the house of friends, and it is not until the following morning that her father-in-law, after taking her in procession through the main streets, escorts her to his house. On either side of the door stands a man with a vessel full of water; and as the party approaches, the mother-in-law rushes out and does obeisance to the girl and afterwards washes her feet. The bride is now given ten pieces of betel nut, which she offers up to the gods and afterwards distributes to the male members of the household. It is usual to hold a big feast during the evening, and when all have eaten and drunk their fill, the bridegroom's father addresses the guests, apologizing for the meagreness of the fare provided. Two days later the bride and her mother-in-law take their first meal together, and this, known as *Niksha Bha*, is carried out in the presence of friends and relations. On the fourth day the bride is visited by her father, who brings a small present. Before the bride, however, is allowed to visit her parents, she must perform a ceremony at a temple and offer a sacrifice to the god Ganesh. This ceremony is known as the *Pakna*, and consists in offering up goats and ducks. Four days after the conclusion of the Pakna ceremony the wedding may be said to have been concluded and the newly wedded pair are free to pursue their own ways.

Amongst Newars, widows are allowed to remarry, contrary to the custom, which does not permit the other races of Nepal to remarry, as a Newar girl is never really a widow, for the *Bel* fruit to which she was originally married is presumed to be always in existence.

On the death of a Newar, the family usually send for a *Guthi*, whose hereditary caste profession it is to ascertain the cause of death. Then, under the orders of an astrologer, the *Santi* ceremony is performed. In order to carry this out, four duck's eggs and four grass images of the deceased are procured, and one of each is placed at each corner of the corpse. The body is then washed and a clean loincloth put on it, and in cases where the deceased is an adult the father and brother must sit by the corpse and perform such daily religious ceremonies as would have been performed by the deceased had he still been living. Before the corpse is sewn up in the shroud, a duck's egg and a fried fish are placed in its mouth, over which are sprinkled a little curds and parched corn, the whole being covered with a cup. After this has been completed the body is shrouded and later buried.

If the deceased was married, his widow brings a little cowdung in a platter, with which she draws three lines on the ground. The corpse is then laid along these lines. Four lights are placed, one at each of the four corners of the corpse, and the wife and near male relations set up a wail of grief, at the same time removing the clothes from the body and throwing them aside. An earthen vessel is next filled with chaff and dry cowdung, and this is placed upon a little fireplace, composed of three bricks, near a wall of the dead man's house, and a fire lit beneath it. The funeral procession is now ready to move to the place of burning, and it accordingly sets out in this order : at the head of the procession a band ; then men carrying straw, wood and oil for the cremation ; next some women who scatter rice on the road ; then sprinklers of milk and water and a reciter of holy verses ; behind them the corpse, closely followed by the next of kin, their heads covered with sheets, making much noise and at least a pretence of weeping ; finally, the friends of the deceased, their heads covered, but not weeping. As the tail of the procession leaves the house, a woman issues forth and scatters cowdung round the door, while another comes out carrying the deceased's clothing, which she throws away. On arrival at the burning-place the corpse is placed on the pyre, and before the latter is kindled, the man appointed to apply the light circumambulates the corpse once, scattering rice as he goes. On completion of this he goes round the body three more times, on these occasions taking a lighted torch in his hand. After the pyre has been kindled the musicians and mourners remain hushed for a few moments, and leaving those responsible for the cremation, return to the home of the deceased. Before any one can enter, however, the ceremony known as *Bilampi* must first be performed. For this the widow brings out a chafing dish in which a little fire is burning, and on this she throws a little mustard seed, ginger, parched corn and water, which produces a thick smoke. The youngest mourner then steps forth, and holding a key in his hand fumigates himself by putting his face in the smoke. After doing this he places the key on the ground and enters the house. All follow his example, the man who lighted the pyre being invariably the last to enter. The women-folk never accompany a funeral party, but only proceed a short distance along the road and then return home. After entering the house the mourners rest for a short time, and then, taking with them a plate containing the various articles for worship, together with a cowrie or conch shell, return to the pyre. Arrived there, they make an effigy of the deceased out of his ashes, and to this they offer up prayers. This last completes the funeral ceremonies.

For the seven days following death no cooking may take place in the house of the deceased, and relations must subsist only on parched corn, curds, clarified butter, red pepper, salt and toddy. At dawn on the day following the funeral the family priest attends, and friends make a ceremonial call to inquire the cause of the death of the deceased and to offer their condolences. On the third day after death the priest draws three symbolical signs—*Dharma*, *Chakra* and *Mandal*—on the ground, and near them he places in a box the skull bones of the deceased. Above this a canopy is erected, around which a screen is built, and on the four sides of this four pictures, each representing some deity, are hung, while four candles, one in front of each, are lighted. The mourning lasts for about thirteen days, as in the case of the other races of Nepal, after which normal life is resumed.

CHAPTER XIII

MAGARS AND GURUNGS

CENTRAL NEPAL is, broadly speaking, that stretch of country to the west of Kathmandu which is bounded on the east by the Ankhu river and the ancient town of Gurkha, and on the west by the Birehi, and includes the districts of Piuthan and Sallyana. From here come the Magars and Gurungs, the two tribes who provide the greater part of the Gurkha battalions of the Indian Army.

Concerning the Magars and Gurungs, Brian Hodgson, in one of his miscellaneous papers, says :

" From lending themselves less early and heartily to Brahmanical influences than the Khas (Chetris) they have retained, in vivid freshness, their original languages, physiognomy and, in a less degree, habits. Their two languages differ materially, though both belong to the unpronominalized type of the Turanian tongues.

" The Gurungs are less generally and more recently redeemed from Lamaism and primitive impurity than the Magars.

" For though both the Gurungs and the Magars still retain their own vernacular tongues, Tartar faces and careless manners, yet what with military service for several generations under the predominant Khas (Chetris), and what with the commerce of Khas males with their females, they have acquired the Khas language (Nepali), though not to the oblivion of their

A TYPICAL THAKUR

A GURKHA MILITIAMAN

A MAGAR *HAVILDAR* (NON-COMMISSIONED OFFICER) NEPALESE ARMY

GURUNG BOYS FROM CENTRAL NEPAL

own, and the Khas habits and sentiments, but with sundry reservations in favour of pristine liberty.

"As, however, they have, with such grace as they could muster, submitted themselves to the ceremonial laws of purity, and to Brahman supremacy, they have been adopted as Hindus, but they have been denied the thread, and constitute a doubtful order below it."

It should be borne in mind that the above words were written some hundred years ago, and that this Hinduizing influence has been making itself felt all the time. With regard to the exact social status of the Magars and Gurungs, it has now been ruled that both they and, in fact, most of the military races of Nepal, excluding, of course, the dominant Chetris, shall be classed as *Sudras*, according to strict Hindu ideas a very inferior order.

Although Central Nepal is rightly regarded as the home of the Magars and Gurungs, they are, of course, to be found all over the country. Generally speaking, certain districts are usually regarded as the strongholds of certain tribes, where the finest specimens of that particular race are usually to be found. It should be pointed out, however, that the various races are not confined absolutely to certain districts, but are scattered about all over the country. Thus, in the Gurung country one finds an occasional Rai or Limbu, or *vice versâ*. It is interesting to note in this respect that the Magars and Gurungs who inhabit parts of Nepal away from their ancestral area are, as a general rule, greatly inferior to those of Central Nepal, though the same does not appear to be the case to anything like the same extent with the other castes.

The Magars, who are an agricultural race, inhabit the temperate regions which lie immediately to the north of the foothills, whilst the country to the north of this again may be said to be the home of the Gurungs, a purely pastoral people.

Owing to the geographical position of their

country, the Magars were amongst the first to receive immigrants from the plains of India. It follows, therefore, that a great number of their customs and ceremonies conform very closely to those of the Hindus of India. For the same reasons they do not exhibit quite such a decided Mongolian appearance as do, for instance, the Gurungs, or still more so, the Rais and Limbus of Eastern Nepal. Although now regarded as quite separate races there appears to be but little doubt that in former times a great deal of intermarriage had taken place between the Magars and the Gurungs, for they are much akin in their ways and character, and the Magars now have no affinity with the people of the plains of India.

Amongst themselves the Magars speak a language known as Magarkura. This language is, however, not spoken by the inhabitants of Gulmi and the large district of Piuthan. It is also curious to note that in other parts of the country, wherever colonies of Magars exist, this tribal language is invariably in use, even as far as the Darjeeling frontier of Nepal, in contradistinction to the Gurung who, when found away from those districts which one looks upon as peculiarly his own, such as Pokhra, Lamjung or Tanhu, never speaks, or even understands, the Gurung language.

It is difficult to account for this linguistic anomaly, but the following story, quoted by Sarat Chandra Dass in his book, *A Journey to Lhasa and Tibet* (Murray, 1904), may have some bearing on the subject :

"The legend which I heard of the Kangpachan people (a district to the west of Kinchinjunga) and of the Magars, the ruins of whose forts and towns we saw in the Kangpachan valley, is very interesting. People say the account is correct and true.

"The upper valley of the Kangpachan river,

through the grace and blessing of the royal Kinchinjunga, was peopled by men of Tibetan extraction, called the Sherpa, whose original home was in the mountains of Sher Khambu, or Eastern Kiranta. (The district referred to is probably that now known as Sola Khambu, situated in North-Eastern Nepal and the present stronghold of the Sherpas.)

" The lower valley, a few miles below the Kangpachan village, on account of the comparatively sluggish course of the river, contained many spacious banks fit to be the habitation of hillmen. The Magar tribe of Nepal occupied these tracts. Their chiefs, who had become very powerful, extended their sway over the people of Kangpachan, and exacted a heavy tax from them.

" Their deputies always oppressed the people to squeeze out money from them, so that at last they were driven through desperation to take revenge upon their enemies.

" The Magar chief, accordingly, was murdered with all his followers upon their visiting the Kangpachan village on a certain occasion.

" The wife of the Magar chief thereupon planned the best means of wreaking vengeance on the Kangpachan murderers.

" She therefore ordered grand funeral observances for the honour and benefit of the departed soul. The funeral was appointed to take place six miles up the river, midway between the two great villages of the Kangpachan valley, so that all the villagers might assemble there.

" After the Queen's followers had finished drinking, poisoned wine was given plentifully to the Kangpachan villagers, who, suspecting nothing, drank freely, and all died. In this way nearly one thousand men and women died, and the infants in arms were taken away by the Queen's followers.

" The place where this foul deed was committed

is now called Tong-songh-phug, or 'The place which witnessed a thousand murders.'

"In consequence of this a Tibetan army invaded the several jongs (forts) belonging to the Queen, when she shut herself up in one of her castles. She had made no preparations to fight the enemy, but her soldiers defended the place for three months.

"The Tibetans then tried to compel the Magars to surrender by depriving them of water. At last the Queen, aware of this intention, threw all the water she had in store towards the Tibetan camp. The Tibetans, thinking that she had abundance of water, raised the siege and went to a distance to watch the movements of the Magars. She immediately collected her men and pursued the enemy, when a skirmish took place, in which she fell, fighting nobly. The Tibetans expelled all the Magars from the country, viz. Kangpachan and Tamban valley, and left their property to the Kangpachan people."

Fantastic and improbable as the above story is, there must be elements of truth in it, for the few remaining Magar colonies in this far-eastern district of Nepal still adhere to their mother tongue. This fact leads one to reasonably suppose that, at one time, there must have been very large Magar colonies in this part of the world, or the Magar language would not have survived in this district, but would have disappeared in the same way as has that of the Gurungs and other tribes when they are found away from their own special districts.

Of the early history of the Magars nothing whatever is known. The first mention of them is the fact that in A.D. 1100, the Magar King of Palpa, one Makunda Sen, invaded and conquered the Nepal valley and committed fearful atrocities whilst there. It is always understood, however, that they have resided round about Palpa from time immemorial and that they were probably the earliest settlers of the Mongolian immigrants from the north. This part of the country was formerly divided into twelve districts, each under its own ruler, being known as the *Barah*, or twelve, Mangranth. This term has, however, entirely fallen into disuse, and to the modern Gurkha has no significance whatsoever.

The Magars are divided into six tribes as follows: Rana, Thapa, Ale, Pun, Burathoki and Gharti. Of these the first three are certainly superior to the remainder both in physique and breeding, and amongst Magars themselves the Rana class is undoubtedly given pride of place. It is generally understood that in former days any Thapa who had lost three generations of ancestors in battle became a Rana, so that it seems that the Ranas have always been considered the élite of the Magar race.

It is probably no exaggeration to state that only the first three-named castes are pure Magars, for the latter three do not speak the Magar language and are somewhat different in appearance. The Puns and Burathokis, who live in the high isolated parts of the Magar country, have languages of their own, which differ slightly from valley to valley. These languages have no affinity with Magarkura, and this fact alone is sufficient evidence to prove that they originally came of different stock. Of the Ghartis, little can be said. Their exact origin is obscure; they are chiefly shepherds and usually of very coarse appearance. There is no doubt, however, that every Gharti was originally a freed slave, for except in the case of the offspring of a slave-mother with a Thakur, which is called Khwas, up to recent time manumitted slaves were invariably called Ghartis, although it is not definitely known at the present time, however, if this will be applicable in the case of the 55,000 slaves recently freed by the decree of the Prime Minister. The Ghartis of to-day of Western Nepal would not themselves admit that any such stigma still attaches to their name, but amongst Nepalese of the extreme east of Nepal and of the Darjeeling district, the word "Gharti" implies a freed slave and nothing else. All the six Magar tribes may now intermarry one with the other, so that we may expect to find, eventually, a type of feature common to the whole race.

The Puns can usually be easily distinguished from other Magars by their somewhat wild, unkempt appearance, long hair and heavy limbs. In intelligence they are undoubtedly inferior to the other tribes, and are inclined to be somewhat quarrelsome. So obscure is the origin of the Puns that the Nepalese authorities do not acknowledge their existence as a separate race; but the fact remains they make excellent soldiers and are cheerful companions.

In general appearance the Magars differ but little from their neighbours the Gurungs, and in many cases can only be distinguished by their less nasal intonation when speaking Nepali, as opposed to their tribal language.

It has already been explained how the Magars were probably the first Nepalese to receive immigrants from the plains of India. Hence, it follows that the greater part of their customs and ceremonies differ but little from those of the Hindus of India and conform almost exactly to those of the Chetris.

An account of the customs and ceremonies of the Chetris will be found elsewhere in this volume, and it should be borne in mind that the ceremonies there described also apply equally to the Magars.

The home of the Gurungs is situated in a stretch of country immediately to the north of that occupied by the Magars, and extends right up to the snows. With regard to their early history it appears that a certain chief, who was Raja of the district of Kaski, settled in Ghandrung, a town due north of the modern

A HIGH CASTE NEPALESE LADY

GURUNG WOMAN (CENTRAL NEPAL)

MAGAR GIRL (CENTRAL NEPAL)

WOMEN OF CENTRAL NEPAL (MAGARS AND GURUNGS)

valley of Pokhra and distant some eight marches west of Kathmandu. At that time Ghandrung was the stronghold of the Gurungs, and the people of the place became much attached to the Kaski Raja and his descendants. They were undisturbed in their religious opinions and customs, and in their own homes they followed a form of Buddhism which was expounded to them by their *Lamas*, or priests. Situated as they are, in an inaccessible part of the country, their manners, customs and religion have not been subject to the same changes as have those of their neighbours to the south, and we find amongst the Gurungs many curious customs and institutions which are nowhere else to be found.

The Gurung race is of pure Mongolian origin, and no doubt its original religion when, in the dim past, it crossed the Himalaya and took up its abode on the southern slopes, was the same as that in vogue in Tibet at that time, and may or may not have been the Lamaïstic form of Buddhism existing in that country at the present day.

The actual date at which the Gurungs settled south of the range is not known, but even to this day they are, in their own homes, more Lamaistic than Hindu, although they have submitted themselves freely to the Hindu ceremonial law.

The Gurung race is divided into two great divisions, known respectively as the *char-* (or four) *jat*, and the *solah-* (or sixteen) *jat* Gurungs. The *char-jat* Gurungs are the undoubted aristocracy of the race and are much looked up to by the remainder. These two divisions are not supposed to intermarry, but with the gradual spread of progress and civilization the once rigid distinction between the two classes is beginning to break down. Of the *char-jat* Gurungs the Ghale is generally considered the leader, for he, in olden times, possessed a separate kingdom and ruled over the country now known as

Lamjung. The origin of the Gurung separation into two classes is said to be as follows :

A Thakur king asked the king of Lamjung for his daughter's hand in marriage. The Ghale king of this place accepted the proposal favourably, and sent a young and beautiful maiden as his daughter to the Thakur king, who duly married her, and by her begot several children. Some years afterwards it transpired that this young maiden was no king's daughter, but merely one of her slave attendants ; whereupon the Thakur king was very angry, and sent a message threatening war, unless the Ghale king sent him his real daughter. The king of Lamjung complied with this request, and this time sent his real daughter, whom the Thakur king duly married and by whom he begot three sons. From these three sons are descended the Ghotani, Lama and Lamchane clans.

It was now ruled that these three sons and their descendants should rank equal to the Ghale clan, and that they should be called the *char-* (or four) *jat* Gurungs, whilst the descendants of the former slave mother should be called *solah-jats*, and should for ever be servants to the *char-jats*.

In exactly the same way as the superior classes in Nepal all claim descent from the fashionable Brahmanical and Rajput ancestry, so also do the Gurungs try to show in their traditions that they too have Hindu forbears.

The Gurungs are loth to consider themselves as inferiors in the Hindu hierachy of Nepal, and in this respect they have an interesting legend.

Once upon a time the *char-jat* Gurung was entitled to wear the Hindu sacred thread, and the story continues that a Ghale was once travelling with his slave, who was a Gyabring. The Ghale is the priest of the *char-jat* Gurungs and the Gyabring that of the *solah*. The Ghale and his slave, feeling tired after a long journey, went to sleep. After a time the god Vishnu appeared in a vision to the slave of the Ghale, and ordered him to put spirits into his master's mouth and to steal the sacred thread from off his body. This the Gyabring did, and the Ghale, awakening, missed his sacred thread, and tasting the fumes of spirits on his lips he dolefully cried out, "My caste has been taken from me and I am ruined." He fled to the nearest Buddhist monastery and passed the next twelve years in prayer and contemplation.

The Gurungs divide time into circles of twelve years, known as *Barkhas*. Each of these circles is given a special name, which is in every case the name of an animal. Every Gurung child is carefully taught the *Barkha* in which his birth took place, and ages are calculated by this means. Thus a Gurung, on being asked his age, will reply that he was born in, say, the "snake" year. As the snake year occurs only once in every twelve it is fairly obvious from his appearance to which cycle he belongs, and a small calculation will thereupon determine the exact year of his birth.

On the birth of a child the Gurung mother is considered to be impure for a period of eleven days. During this time she must keep to her own apartment and is not allowed to come into contact with any one at all. On the eleventh day, known as the *Nuwaran*, a priest, who may be either Lama or Brahman, as fancy may dictate, is called in in order to perform the naming ceremony. The child is now washed, his *Barkha* is determined, and he is given two names, one of which is dedicated to the household god, and the other a family name by which he is called. On this occasion all the relations of the family are present and a big feast is prepared, the expenses of which are defrayed by the infant's parents. This ceremonial feast consists of cooked rice, meat, home-brewed beer, fowls and rum ; and on its completion the mother is considered to have become again pure, and is free once more to leave the house.

Six months after birth in the case of a boy, and five months in the case of a girl, the weaning ceremony takes place. The priest and relations are again invited to attend, and they are feasted once again. On this occasion all present place a caste mark on the forehead of the infant, put a little rice in its mouth, and deposit a coin in a large plate which has been put ready for this purpose.

Although infants are ceremonially weaned a few months after birth, it is a common practice throughout Nepal for mothers to suckle their children to a comparatively advanced age, it being not uncommon to see a child of ten years of age being so nourished.

The next important ceremony in the life of a Gurung is that of marriage, and this usually takes place at the age of fifteen. Gurungs are permitted to marry only within their own tribe, and, when living in Nepal, can never marry outside it. Should a Gurung, however, contrive to marry a Magar woman, for instance, and there is offspring, these cannot be admitted into the Gurung tribe until a certain sum of money has been paid to the headman of the village and the elders of the tribe. This entails a certain amount of ceremonial, which includes the usual feast, during the course of which the children's hands are placed upon a dish of cooked rice. After this all present partake of a portion of the rice so touched by the child, who is now considered to have been adopted into the Gurung clan.

In normal circumstances marriages are arranged by the parents of the contracting parties ; but before the actual marriage can take place there is an elaborate ritual, known as *Mangni*, or asking in marriage, which has first to be performed.

In the first place, the boy's father is required to present the mother of the girl with certain coins, and must also make a present of one rupee to the *Mukhya*, or headman, of the girl's village. As the question of marriage is considered too delicate a subject for personal discussion by those nearly related to the contracting parties, the services of two male representatives are enlisted, and these act as emissaries on the boy's behalf. Taking with them a wooden bowl, which must first be painted with green and red stripes, and which is filled with curds, and a long spear hung with strips of red cloth, the two emissaries proceed to the girl's home. On arrival they plant the spear in the ground just outside the door, and then enter the house, taking the bowl with them. They are now received by the girl's parents, who have, of course, been previously warned of this visit. They inform them of the object of the call and ask if the suggested marriage meets with approval. The next step is to summon all the available relatives of the girl's parents, and these are asked their views as to the suitability of the match proposed. When the marriage has been approved the red-and-green striped bowl is placed in front of the girl's parents, who deposit one rupee on the top of the curds. A brass dish is now brought, and in this are placed, in the form of a circle, the coins which were originally sent by the boy's father. It is usual, at this stage of the proceedings, for a feast to take place, on the conclusion of which the boy is summoned. On his arrival the girl's father, taking some of the curds from the wooden bowl, together with a little damp rice, places a small quantity first on the boy's forehead, and then on those of every one present. The betrothal is now complete and the actual marriage ceremony may take place in due course; but before the actual ceremony is solemnized it is necessary to commit the betrothal to paper. This is done in the presence of the assembled company and testified by the village headman.

An astrologer is now consulted in order to ascertain the most auspicious date on which the marriage ceremony may be performed. The day having been fixed, the boy's father sends two representatives to the girl's house in order that they may make the arrangements necessary for the marriage. Upon their arrival they inform the girl's parents of the day selected and ask permission to take her away on that date.

The day of the wedding has now arrived, and a procession consisting of the relatives and friends of the bridegroom, and accompanied by a band, proceeds to the house of the bride. Upon arrival they are, by way of welcome, besprinkled with curds and rice. The bride's father now walks in a circle once round the dooly in which the bridegroom is seated, making a trail of water as he goes, by pouring the liquid from a two-mouthed jug. He now takes in his hand a brass dish in which he places a little curds and rice, and, accompanied by his wife, walks three times round the bridegroom. During all the foregoing the bride remains concealed in the house. At this juncture the male guests join the women-folk inside the house, and the assembled company sit down to a feast, which is accompanied by singing and dancing; but it should be pointed out that no one may commence to eat until the bridegroom has tasted his food.

The remainder of the ceremony is performed under the direct orders of the officiating priest, and each stage must take place at a specified time, and in order to keep a check on the time the officiating Brahman, or Lama, as the case may be, orders a water-clock to be brought in and set.

It is now night and time for the ceremonial washing of the feet. The bride is now brought in and seated by the side of the bridegroom, each attended by their respective relations. The bride now crosses her feet, which are then lifted up by her sister and placed above a large vessel of water in which her feet are washed by her father. This procedure is now repeated in the case of the bridegroom, after which all the blood relations present wash the feet of the happy pair. Now comes the ceremony of *Dhok dinu*, which consists in making obeisance to the bride's relations.

The last-named ceremony is followed by the presentation of new clothes to the bride by her father-in-law. She is now arrayed in these by her friends, and is expected to make some pretence of weeping. On appearing in her new clothes she is ornamented with earrings, bracelets, nose-rings, anklets, and so on, also the gift of her father-in-law.

Now comes the ritual of the *Sindhur halnu*, or sprinkling of red-lead powder. The bridegroom produces a box of red *Sindhur* powder from his pocket, whereupon a white cloth is placed over the bride's forehead and held diagonally down in front of her. The bridegroom now lifts the end of the cloth, and pours the powder down it and on to her head. This is repeated three times, and the cloth, still covered in powder, folded up and presented to the bride, together with the box in which the powder was originally contained.

The bridegroom now lifts up his bride in his arms and sets her down close beside him.

The preceding ceremonies, interspersed with much feasting, singing and dancing, have been going on throughout the night, and it is now daybreak and time for the bridegroom to take away his bride. The bride is placed in the dooly, and, accompanied by her husband mounted on horseback, all the wedding guests, and the band at the head blaring defiance, proceeds to the home of her newly wedded husband.

Arrived in her new home the husband's sisters bolt the door, for which service they are presented each with a *mohur* (a coin).

One more small ritual needs to be chronicled before we can take leave of the newly wedded pair. The husband's mother hides in the loft and makes a pretence of refusing to come down. Perhaps she feels a little doubtful of being welcomed by the two young people so absorbed in their own happiness, and that she is somewhat in the way ; but on receiving a reassuring invitation from her son, she descends and once more joins the family circle.

Amongst Gurungs polygamy is permitted, but in actual practice the number of wives does not usually exceed two. Should the husband, for any reasons, leave home, the senior, or *jethi*, wife is, as a rule, left behind in order to look after the house and cattle. The younger, or *kanchi*, wife, often accompanies her master, and should he enlist in the army she it is who goes with him. Except in the case of the first wife no marriage ceremony is performed, and it follows therefore that the position of the second wife is somewhat insecure, as she may be cast off at the will of her husband. It is not unnatural that this practice often leads to amusing episodes, which do not as a rule take a very serious form. In this respect a story is related :

During the war a lad was at the front, but his wife, tired of waiting for him, went off with another man. On the husband's return from the front he invoked the full majesty of the law and took the case before his company commander.

The latter, when inquiring into the matter, seemed surprised at the soldier's lack of interest in the measures proposed for the return of his wife. He seemed still to have some matter on his mind, and upon being assured that the matter would be brought to a successful conclusion, replied, " I'm not worrying about my wife, but the other man has gone off with my umbrella."

Upon the death of a Gurung it is usual to bury the body in a place set apart for this purpose, which is generally situated just outside the village. This practice is in contradistinction to the funeral rites of most of the other tribes in Nepal who usually bury, or burn, their dead by the banks of rivers.

In the case of very near relations the period of mourning lasts for thirteen days. During this time only rice may be eaten, and that but once a day, and the *tupi* (top knot) is cut, and the rest of the head, eyebrows and moustache shaved. The period of mourning differs somewhat for more distant relations, but it is not thought necessary to enter into details here. During the period of mourning only white clothes may be worn, and these should be of one thickness only.

The principal ceremony in connection with death is that known as the *Aghun*, which is not dissimilar to an Irish wake. When money is available this ceremony usually takes place on the actual day of burial, and may last as long as three days. It is not attended by the chief mourners, and consists in the disposal of a gargantuan feast in which the consumption of large quantities of liquor is considered the most important feature.

The *Aghun* ceremony may take place at any time after death, and from motives of economy the ceremonies of several deceased people may be celebrated at the same time.

It is usually a very costly affair, and as it is considered to be the most important of all the Gurung ceremonies it does not take place until sufficient money has been saved with which to do full justice to the memory of the deceased. Cases have been known where this ceremony has been postponed for as long as twenty-five years after death, and in which the savings of a lifetime have been expended in these few days.

The Gurungs have a characteristic institution known as the *rodi ghar*. This is best described as a dancing-hall, and takes place, as a rule, in the house of the local headman of the village. It is held only during the harvest season, and is open only to the unmarried boys and girls of the village. This is made the occasion for a good deal of licence, and here are sung and composed songs of a somewhat doubtful nature. It is interesting to note that this institution is held nowhere else in Nepal. It exists, however, under the name of *Rang Bang* in the upper parts of Garhwal, which border on Tibet, and this fact leads one to believe that the custom must be of Tibetan origin.

In a country where distractions are few and far between, village life is naturally of the simplest description. Singing and dancing are the favourite forms of amusement, and through the songs of the country we get an excellent insight into the character and outlook of the people.

Of the songs common to Central Nepal, the majority are sung in the Nepali language, a fact which accounts for there being practically no difference between those of the Magars and Gurungs. There are various kinds of songs which are sung at special times and considered appropriate for certain ceremonies. Amongst these are the *Ramayan*, *Chalitra*, and *Mahabharat*, which are in reality Hindu classics, and mythological songs. Another popular form of song is the *Sorati*, which may, perhaps, be best described as a kind of Hans Andersen fairy-tale put to music. Amongst the songs which are unconnected with any questions of ceremonial and are sung on all occasions, the best known are the *Juwāri Kheliako* —a popular type of song in which a boy and a girl take part in question and answer form—and the *Saleju* and *Jhàmre*.

In connection with Gurkha songs it is worth while mentioning that the ceremonial songs, such as the before-mentioned *Ramayan*, *Chalitra* and *Sorati*, are only sung by Magars, Gurungs and Chetris, and never by the races of Eastern Nepal, such as the Limbus, Rais and Sunwars. The tunes or *ràg* of the old-established and ancient songs do not change, but the composition of new songs and tunes is in the hands of the *Gainis*, professional female singers, who wander from village to village exhibiting their talent. The music to which the songs of Central Nepal are set is invariably written in the Pentatonic, or black-note scale ; but this is not the case in Eastern Nepal, where the songs approximate more nearly to the music of Europe.

The words of many of the songs are founded upon local traditions, and in many cases contain descriptions of local scenery. These latter are of particular interest, for they form practically the only account we have of the scenery of Central Nepal.

A few small tribes that are to be found chiefly in Central Nepal, although their homes cannot be said to exist in any particular part of the country, merit mention before proceeding further. These are the Kusundas, Chepangs, Thakales, and the two salt-carrying classes known as Binge and Kolme. The first-named, the Kusundas and Chepangs, are nomadic tribes, of which the former are to be found chiefly in Central Nepal, and the latter a little farther towards the east. They are obviously of Dravidian or Turanian extraction, resembling the Kols and Uraons of the plains, and speak their own languages, but no account or history of them has ever been known to exist. Few in number, they are very shy, and live in caves and under trees. Although both tribes are as near a state of nature as it is possible to be, the

Chepangs have, of recent years, made a slight advance in their civilization, and have, it is said, learnt to build houses. In physique they are small, puny and ill-formed, and in appearance dark, with features that betray their Dravidian origin.

The Thakales are a race of undoubtedly Mongolian extraction who inhabit the region of Muktinath and the hills surrounding it. Prosperous, and great traders, especially in sheep, the Thakales are of mixed religion and are closely allied to Tibetans; they also speak a language akin to that of Tibet. In appearance they greatly resemble Magars and Gurungs, from whom they can sometimes hardly be distinguished.

The Rohanis, who inhabit the head of the Tarkhola, not far from the same region as the Thakales, are a small tribe somewhat similar to the above, their name affording a good description of them, as it implies "mountain man."

The Binges and Kolmes are the salt-carrying classes who trade in salt, which they bring from Muktinath and Montichettra, above the gorge of the river Kali, and barter in the bazaars.

CHAPTER XIV

A JOURNEY TOWARDS PALPA

By W. B. N.

IN December of 1922, His Highness the Maharaja kindly gave me permission to visit the Massiang ridge, in the Palpa hills, ten miles north-west of Batoli. This last is an important Nepalese town some twenty miles to the north of Nautanwa, a large village on the frontier, between the United Provinces of India and Nepalese territory. As no European had ever set foot in the Palpa country, save perhaps an occasional Jesuit missionary in the dim past, it was with the greatest interest and pleasure that I started off from Gorakhpur.

I was accompanied by Lieutenant Ganesh Bahadur Regmi, a Nepalese officer detailed for special duty at the Gurkha Recruiting Depôt at Gorakhpur, and my guide, philosopher and friend in more than one adventure in Nepalese territory.

Although a railway now runs to Nautanwa, and a road, though unmetalled, has, I believe, been made between that place and Batoli, until quite recently both journeys had to be performed on foot, but once past Nautanwa the disadvantage of finding no road was amply compensated for by the joy felt in traversing new ground. The actual frontier is about a mile distant from the village, marked by stone cairns placed at intervals. The first place of any importance after entering Nepalese territory is

Baitheri, the headquarters of a Nepalese official, whose house, built in the orthodox style, high and imposing, with white-painted projecting eaves, formed a landmark which could be seen for many miles round. For the greater part of the journey the track led through open cultivation and past occasional clumps of trees, a characteristic of the scenery of Northern Behar. For the last five miles, however, the fields of corn and sugar-cane gave place to the ordinary scrub jungle and high grass of the Terai, and after crossing the Tindho Khola, on the right bank of which Batoli stands, our journey was at an end, for waiting to receive me were a Nepalese officer and a party of men, sent by His Highness to look after my comfort during the trip.

The praises of Batoli have been sung in countless Gurkha songs, and in far-off Nepalese villages the name is uttered with bated breath ; for it conjures up in the mind of the simple villagers visions of the bustling, cosmopolitan life of a frontier town. To the European traveller, however, who approaches it from the plains of India the place does not present a picture of any particular charm, and only the romance attached to the unknown—for the village is at least well away from the beaten track—prevents it appearing to the eye as a somewhat drab and very ordinary Indian village. A stroll in the one long and straggling street—almost the whole place—does not remove this impression, for there are but few buildings which can be said to be typically Nepalese. On the far side of the Tindho river, however, the atmosphere is different, for here, below the barracks which form the winter quarters of the Palpa regiments, numbers of lusty hillmen, many of them with bales of simple merchandise for the marts of India, make their camp. The smoke of their fires can be seen in every direction, and the hardships of the long and toilsome journey—for among them are many women and children—

ON THE WAY TO BATOLI—FOOTHILLS IN DISTANCE

BRIDGE OVER THE DOBHAN KHOLA

seem quickly forgotten. It was on this side of the river that my camp had been laid out, a veritable work of art in green brushwood, with trim-cut paths and garden seats, the whole surrounded by a high fence to shield the stranger from the gaze of the curious.

Above the town, and standing in its own grounds, is the palace of the local Governor, and this worthy, a kinsman of the Maharaja, bade me enter and sit for a few minutes before starting on the ten-mile march ahead.

Although the bazaar of Batoli is, in some ways, strikingly unNepalese, yet no sooner does one ascend the steep path that leads past the palace to the hamlet of Nawakot than an entire change of everything—scenery, people and surroundings—takes place. The sudden transition from the plains, with their Aryan inhabitants, to the rough mountain by-paths, peopled with sturdy Mongols, is very striking, for on crossing the spur of the hill on which Nawakot stands one bids farewell to India, and from thence no trace of it is discernible.

Nawakot consists of a few small huts and a guardhouse, before which a sentry, wearing the picturesque headdress with its silver badge, stands on guard. A few yards away, at a place overlooking the whole of the plain below, stood a small stone cairn. This was, I learned, in memory of a Gurkha bugler, who performed some act of great gallantry in the campaign against the British in 1815—a simple, yet lasting, reminder of a humble hero.

Leaving Nawakot the path descends through pretty wooded scenery, until, passing the village of Jhirdi, it comes out at the unexpectedly fine suspension bridge over the Dobhan river. In the few shops skirting the road by the bridge-head a few Newars plied a brisk trade; and it was interesting to notice the hill-folk as they passed through, heavily laden, on their way to Batoli, or fingered the bright bead necklaces and other wares displayed to their admiring gaze.

As this district, Palpa, is essentially the home of the Magars, it follows that the greater part of the people we saw on the road or in the villages belonged to that race. On the other hand, as the road along which we travelled was, in spite of the fact that it was little more than a rough track, one of the main routes from Central Nepal to the plains of India, men of many other races were also to be seen. Though outwardly the various tribes of Central Nepal appear to the uninitiated to differ but little, yet to one who has had experience of them it is not a matter of great difficulty, after a time, to distinguish between them, for each has certain small but definite facial characteristics. For the benefit of those who do not know the people, therefore, I will endeavour to describe the few points by which typical specimens of the two main races of Central Nepal, the Magars and Gurungs, may generally be distinguished. Gurungs from what may be described as the true Gurung country—places such as Gurkha, Lamjung, Kaski Pokhra, Tanhu, Bhirkot, Andhi Khola * and the Ghandrung district of Parbat—are more agile and spare and less thick-set than the Magars, while their features, though distinctly Mongolian, are narrower and finer, their noses particularly being longer and less flat. I think that Gurungs are inclined to be more intelligent and quicker to learn than the more stolid and simple-minded Magars, while those who hail from the Pokhra district are usually particularly sharp and alert. This last may possibly be accounted for by the fact that, next to that of Nepal, Pokhra is the largest valley in the country, and its large bazaars and many villages thus offer opportunities for intercourse with outside

* Khola is the Nepali word for river.

people which do not come in the way of those living in more isolated districts. Lamjung Gurungs, and, indeed, all those coming from the higher valleys, invariably wear a blanket made in the form of a hood. This is woven by their women-folk from sheep's wool, and is known as a *Rari Kashto*. Another characteristic garment is the coarse sheet, known as *Aingti Bhangro*, which is worn knotted in such a way as to leave the arms bare and to form a kind of loose bag on the back. The Magars from the real Magar country—Palpa, Gulmi, Bhirkot and Piuthana—do not wear this last, although it is not infrequently worn by some Magars, such as the Puns, for instance, who live in the higher parts of the country.

The dress of the women does not differ greatly, although the true Gurung woman may usually be distinguished by the fact that the *Majetro*, or shawl which she wears over the head, is invariably of the same colour and pattern—a dark background with a pattern of red roses, as opposed to those of white or other colours often affected by women of the Magar and other tribes. Other small features of the Gurung woman's dress, which differs from that of the other tribes, are the *Kramo*, a cloth band worn bound round the forehead, and the *Tikia*, a cloth worn wrapped round the waist; and it may be noted that a Gurung woman never wears the *Bulaki*, or nose-ring. But I must continue my journey.

After crossing the suspension bridge we followed the road, which now ran beside a beautiful stream of clear water, until we reached the customs house of Morek. My imposing retinue, and the rank of the two officers accompanying me, produced a friendly welcome from the Brahman official in charge, but it was interesting to watch his subsequent interview with a group of long-haired Puns, real wild men of the woods, on their way to the plains for the first time.

Passing Morek the path drops gently down to the Siswa Khola, a small stream celebrated amongst the local inhabitants for the coldness of its water, and follows its left bank for several miles, until a steep ascent brings one to the Massiang ridge. From here a beautiful panorama unfolded itself before my eyes, a picture rendered all the more alluring by the wealth of historic episodes and legends which have the surrounding country for their setting. Before us lay the ridge on which Palpa stands, to the west of which the white roofs of a temple stood out hard and clear, although the main portion of the town is invisible from here. A small track which ran under the western flank of the ridge and disappeared on the other side arrested my attention, for this was the road to Riri, a well known market-place on the banks of the Kali, and a place said to have been visited during the fifteenth century by one of the Rajput kings who laid the foundations of the family of Gurkha. Farther still to the west, a prominent spur, thickly wooded, was pointed out to me as the hill on which Gulmi was situated, but the town was only visible to the eye of faith. To the east, distant some four miles, I could clearly see the town of Tansen with its parade ground, palace and temple. The houses, chiefly red in hue owing to the clay with which their walls were coloured, surrounded by a patch of cultivation, looked comfortable and cheerful. Towards the north, from west to east, rose tier upon tier of lofty mountains crested with groves of dark-coloured firs, the highest of all snowcapped and standing out clearly against the vivid blue of the sky.

It was difficult to tear one's self away from a scene so beautiful and so rich with memories of the past, and it was not until the shadows were lengthening that we started on our return journey; for although the longing to go to the next ridge had been almost unbearable, I had reached the limit imposed by

MAGAR GIRLS MAKING MUSTARD OIL

TYPICAL PALPA COUNTRY

His Highness, and after all I had been fortunate to see as much as I had. As we started down we met a party of Gurungs on their way to Tansen, where they were to spend the night. On the morrow they would again set off on their long journey to far-away Lamjung, over a week's travel from here. Though heavily laden they were stepping out manfully, and as I listened to their cheerful laughter I could not help feeling that perhaps after all the greatest charm of this little kingdom lay in the uncomplaining spirits of its simple inhabitants.

PART V

EASTERN NEPAL

CHAPTER XV

LIMBUS

ACCORDING to tradition, the country to the east of the valley of Nepal was, prior to the Hindu dynasties of historical times, peopled by a race of shepherds. These shepherds were subsequently subdued by a race known as the Kirantis, a people who, at the time of the Gurkha conquest in 1768, were still an independent nation, and whose domain was situated to the east of the kingdom of Bhatgaon and distant some five or six days from that place.

At the present day Nepalese custom still designates under the name of Kiranti all the country lying between the Dudh Kosi and Arun rivers; but in reality the tribes grouped under this name occupy territory still more extended, and are in possession of the country right up to the eastern boundary of Nepal. Although the eastern frontier of Nepal is formed by the Singalela ridge, the country east of this, comprising the British district of Darjeeling, is peopled almost entirely by members of the Kiranti race, and large numbers of them are to be found still farther east in the little hill state of Sikkim.

It appears, from the bulk of the evidence available, that in ancient times the Hindus designated under the name of Kirantis all the people of the Tibeto-Burman family who spread themselves over the high plateaus of the Himalaya and the country round about the mouths of the Ganges. Pushed back and absorbed by the Hindu influx from the plains, the Kirantis became confined to the mountains to the east of the Nepal valley.

The name Kiranti has from time immemorial been familiar to India, and occurs in many of the early Hindu sacred writings. With regard to this aspect, Sylvain Levi says : " A Vedic poem, associated with the distant reminders of human sacrifice, ' drives back the Kiranti to his caverns.' The mountain is, in fact, his domain. It is there that he continues to live and to dominate during the epic period : Bhima meets the Kirantis on leaving Videha during his victorious march towards the eastern regions ; Nakula meets them also on his journey when he conquers the west ; Arjuna, whilst penetrating the Himalaya towards the north, is arrested and defied by a Kirant, or rather by Shiva in the guise of one. The word Kiranti occurs times out of number in the Mahabharat in company with the names of strange people whose territories border upon the frontiers of India—the Yavanas, Shakas, Pahlavas—but it is, above all, with Chinese that they are associated. Kirantis and Chinese fraternize under the banners of the glorious Bhagadatta, Emperor of Pragjyotisa (Kamarupa). They form a contingent of ' the yellow men.' ' The Chinese and Kiranti soldiers seem to be made of gold. Their troops gave the impression of a forest of yellow flowers.' The Ramayana also makes note of the golden colour of the Kirantis."

The following story, collected by Sarat Chandra Dass, gives a somewhat more picturesque account of the origin of the Kiranti race :

" The village of Yangma, from whence spread the Kiranti race, in ancient times was not inhabited. Once upon a time a cowherd from Tashi-rabka (in Tibet) lost one of his yaks which, grazing in towards the Kangala Chen pass, entered the Yangma valley. Here the cowherd, having followed the tracks, found his hairy property lying on a rock with a full stomach. In the morning he again missed his yak and, proceeding farther down into the interior, met it at a place called Shophug, grazing in a rich pasture land. Here, being charmed with the luxuriance of the pasture as compared with his own bleak and barren country, he sowed a few grains of barley which he had obtained from a certain priest as a blessing.

" On his return to his village in Tibet he gave a good account of this place to his fellow-countrymen, but nobody would believe him, nor would any one undertake to visit the place of his discovery on account of its position beyond the snows.

" The cowherd, however, with his wife went to the Yangma valley to tend his flock, and to their surprise they found the barley well grown. On his return he showed the barley ears to his friends, who were now induced to emigrate to the new land to grow corn.

" Thus was the village of Yangma first inhabited. It is indeed a purely Tibetan settlement as the houses testify."

The Kiranti race comprises the clans of the Khambus, Yakhas and Limbus. There are a few other tribes, such as the Danuars and Thamis, who claim, more or less legitimately, to belong to the Kiranti family, but these are of somewhat mixed origin, and being of comparatively little importance will not be treated as separate races.

The term " Kiranti " should by rights be applied only to the Khambus, but as the three before-mentioned races have for many generations freely intermarried, it is applied indiscriminately to all three, although they were formerly quite separate races.

It is interesting to note that although the manners and customs of the three main tribes do not greatly differ, yet each has retained its own language.

When the Khambus first, and the Limbus later,

were conquered by the Gurkhas, the Gurkha king, anxious to conciliate his recently vanquished enemies, conferred upon their leading men commissions, sealed with the royal signet, in which they were given powers to rule over certain districts. With these commissions were given to the Khambus the title of Rai, and to the Limbus the title of Subha, each title having practically the same significance and meaning " chief." These titles were originally given only to the most influential men of the races concerned, and the title remained hereditary. In these days, however, the use of these titles has been somewhat abused, and they are often employed by many who have no legitimate right to them.

Khambus and Yakhas, having become very much mixed, are now both regarded as Rais. They both speak the Rai language, and there is practically no difference between them.

The Kirantis have, of course, been subject to Indian influence in the same way as have the races of Central and Western Nepal, but living as they do in close touch with Tibet and the Buddhist religion this influence has been considerably less marked. Sylvain Levi says :

" The religious indifference which Father Giuseppe noticed amongst the Kirantis has hardly altered at all. In a Buddhist country they mumble the ' Om mane padme hum ' and make presents to Lamas ; in a Hindu country they give themselves out to be followers of Shiva and worship Mahadevi and Gauri. Like all the peoples of the Tibetan race the Kirantis are extremely partial to beef, and it is only by force of arms that the Gurkhas have introduced amongst them obligatory respect for the cow."

The stretch of country known as Kirant, the limits of which have already been defined, may be divided roughly into two parts. Of these, that known as Limbuana, or the country of the Limbus, lies between the river Arun on the west, and the Singalela ridge on the east. The country which is inhabited chiefly by the Rais lies to the west of this again, and extends nearly as far as the Nepal Valley on the west.

The Limbus race is now divided into a large number of tribes. These tribes were formerly centred, in groups, in ten different districts of the Limbu country, and from the names of these ten districts come the names of the ten tribes from which the Limbus themselves say they were descended.

Owing to the lack of historical evidence it is practically impossible to gauge with accuracy the origin of most of the tribes now inhabiting Nepal. What little we do know is based almost entirely on mythology and legend, handed down by word of mouth from one generation to the next. Many of the tales are very conflicting, and it is only by viewing them as a whole and selecting those which are most in accordance with facts already proved that we can, with any certainty, trace the origin of these various races.

The remarks at the beginning of this chapter on the origin of the Limbus are based on the most generally accepted facts. It is interesting, however, to see what the Limbus themselves say of their early history, and the following account is translated from a *Vanshavali* which was examined by Colonel Vansittart :

" God is called Mojingna Khiwagna. He made the world and all the creatures in it.

" Limbus were first known by the name of Yakthumba, and they are descended from ten brothers. With these ten brothers came three spiritual advisers.

" The above-mentioned brothers and priests did not know how to read or to write, but they knew some prayers and traditions.

"These prayers and traditions were handed down by word of mouth, and according to them were the people ruled.

"These thirteen men were all residents of Benares, and they agreed to make themselves homes in the mountains of Nepal.

"Five of the brothers marched straight from Benares to Nepal, but the other five went to Tibet, and from Tibet through Lhasadinga, until they met their five brothers in the mountains of Nepal.

"The first five brothers and their descendants are called Kashigotra, and the second five brothers and their descendants are called Lhasagotra, because they respectively journeyed from Benares to Tibet, and from Lhasadinga to Nepal. [*Note.*—In the Hindi language Benares is known as Kashi.]

"All ten brothers should rightly be called Kashigotra, for they all came from Benares.

"Now, these ten brothers settled in a placc called Ambepojoma Kamketlangma Sumhalangma. The ten brothers had many children, and their descendants multiplied very quickly, till they became a nation and were called Limbus.

"The Limbus were, however, subject to the kings of the country, and they were very much oppressed. The kings ruled them with such a hard rule, and oppressed them so greatly, that eventually the Limbus, having joined together, decided to fight the kings of the country and drive them out.

"Every Limbu swore upon the holy place that he would conquer in the fight or die, and every man swore that he would not return from the war until the kings had been driven from the country, and that he would sooner die than run away in battle.

"There was a great war between the Limbus and the kings, and the former won many victories and drove out the kings from the land, and the Limbus seized the country as their own and fixed its boundaries: on the north Tibet; on the south the plains of India; on the west the Arun river; and on the east the Mechi.

"The Limbus now assembled together again and consulted, and they determined to elect unto themselves ten chiefs, one from each tribe. In this way ten chiefs were elected, and each chief built himself a fort and called it by his name, and each chief marked the boundaries of his country and called it by some name.

"After this division of the country the Limbus remained rulers of their country until the Gurkhas waged war against them.

"For twelve years did the Limbus fight with the Gurkhas, after which they were defeated. The Gurkhas then killed all the Limbus whom they could catch, whether men, women, or children, and the Limbus had to hide in the mountains because of the cruelty and oppression of the Gurkhas.

"After some time the Gurkha king, thinking of all the heavy troubles that were upon the Limbus, called them together, and on their promising to look upon him as their king, he granted unto the chief men amongst the Limbus commissions with certain ruling powers for the chief of each district.

"Each holder of the commission was granted full power, according to his warrant, to try all cases in his district, and to rule in every way as he deemed fit, with the exception only of cases of murder, cow killing, and with regard to taxes or money matters, which had to be referred to and settled by the King of the Gurkhas.

"The Limbus after this ceased making war with the Gurkhas, and became their friends, and acknowledged the King of the Gurkhas as their king."

So much for the origin of the Limbus. Let us now examine some of their customs.

When it is known that a child is about to be born,

a Brahman, or, failing him, a *Phedangma* or Limbu priest, is summoned. He notes the exact time of the child's birth, and in return for his services receives five *paisa* in money and a small amount of rice. It is customary amongst Limbus who can afford the expense to have the child's date of birth committed to writing. This paper is known as the *China Kagaz*, and is retained by the parents, who consult it on all important occasions—such as marriage—throughout the child's life. The cost of a *China Kagaz* amounts to some five or six rupees.

On the fourth day after birth (on the third in the case of a girl) a big feast is held at which, in addition to the immediate relations of the child, a priest is present. The actual ceremony is as follows: A cup is taken and filled with water, and into it is placed any gold object, such as a ring or ornament. To this are added a small quantity of sugar, cow's urine and milk. Into this mixture a small branch is dipped and the assembled company besprinkled. The house, and particularly the actual spot where the child was born, is similarly treated.

At the conclusion of the ceremony every one present is feasted and given a portion of the remains to take home. On this occasion there is neither singing nor dancing.

The next ceremony to be performed is that of weaning. The details of this are practically the same as already described for other tribes, but the date at which it is to take place is determined by a *Phedangma*. There is, again, no singing or dancing, and the child is presented with small gifts of money, according to the means of the guests.

A Limbu may marry any girl he likes, provided she does not actually belong to his tribe. In common with other parts of Nepal, the date of marriage is usually determined by means of astrology.

A common way of selecting a bride is by open

singing competitions held for this specific purpose. Thus, either the boy or girl will commence by singing a couplet to which the other must reply. The couplets are composed on the spur of the moment, and each succeeding one should improve on the one before it in wit and humour. The contest goes on until neither party is able, for lack of further ideas, to continue, and in order to win a bride the man must produce such a couplet that the girl is unable to reply.

If the man is defeated in the contest he at once runs away, leaving some other competitor to win his fair victor's hand.

A successful suitor, before proceeding further, now presents his future father-in-law with the carcase of a pig, which is divided up and laid out in pieces according to custom.

Unlike the races inhabiting Western and Central Nepal, marriages are usually contracted without the parent's consent, and take place, as a rule, at a somewhat later age. It is not uncommon amongst the poorer people for the parents of the bride to know nothing at all about the marriage of their daughter until she returns from the wedding ceremony a married woman.

To take first the case when the parents have not been informed of their children's intentions. On the day fixed for the ceremony the parties meet in some convenient place attended by a few of their intimate friends. These latter, be it noted, bring their own victuals for the feast which precedes the ceremony. A little singing and dancing takes place, in the course of which the bridegroom beats a drum, to the accompaniment of which his bride dances.

The officiating *Phedangma* now commences his incantations and murmurs a few words over the bridal pair, who are now sitting cross-legged on the floor holding each other's hands. The *Phedangma* now takes a cock and a hen, cuts off their heads and allows the blood to run into a plantain leaf which is held below. From the blood thus collected he seeks for omens and explains their portent to the assembled company.

The *Phedangma* now places a little *Sindhur*, or red powder, on another leaf, and the bridegroom applies it to his bride's face from the nose up to the crown of the head.

The ceremony is now complete and the officiating *Phedangma* is presented with a new white *pagri* and a few rupees.

On the following morning he visits the newly married pair and enjoins them to live happily, to which they reply, " We will do as you command."

The bride now returns to her parents, who are made aware, for the first time, of what has happened. A few days later an intermediary calls and intercedes on behalf of the newly married pair. He brings with him the carcase of a pig, a bottle of rum, and one rupee with which to pacify the anger which the girl's parents are supposed to exhibit. They make a show of refusing to acknowledge the union, but eventually give their consent. Whereupon the intermediary pays the price of the bride, which varies according to the means of the bridegroom, but is usually about eighty rupees in cash.

In cases where the consent of the parents has been obtained previous to marriage the preliminaries of the ceremony are somewhat different.

When about to set out from his parent's home the boy, who is dressed completely in white, first makes obeisance to his parents, who put a caste mark on his forehead. This is composed of curds and rice.

Before he is allowed to take his seat in the waiting dooly, the unmarried girl friends of the party, each bearing a brass plate in which there is some rice and curds, and a bowl filled with water, circumambulate the dooly six times, sprinkling it with the water from their bowls as they go.

The bridegroom now makes obeisance to the dooly four times and takes his seat. He must be careful not to assume a recumbent position, but is expected to sit cross-legged and with his hands holding on to a handkerchief, which is suspended from the roof.

The bridegroom is now carried to some prearranged place where the bride has been hidden, and which is not necessarily her home.

The bride comes out of her hiding-place and the bridegroom gets out of the dooly. The girl makes obeisance to her future husband three times and puts a caste mark on his forehead. The bride's unmarried attendants now walk three times round the dooly, after which she herself takes her seat in it, and accompanied by the bridegroom, mounted on a horse, proceeds to her father-in-law's house.

On arrival at the house the bride enters it, passing on her way two large earthen vessels of water which have been placed one on either side of the door. Her future parents-in-law then welcome her by placing a caste mark on her forehead and claim her as their future daughter-in-law, and the ceremony proceeds as previously explained.

When a Limbu dies the fact is first reported to a priest who is called to the house for this purpose. The priest examines the corpse to see that death has really taken place; he then inquires how long the deceased had been ill and also the cause of death. Having satisfied himself that death has taken place, he orders the *China Kagaz* of the deceased to be thrown away.

If death occurs on a Tuesday, Thursday, or Saturday, the corpse is left in the house for one whole night, and is buried on the following day.

Should death occur on any of the remaining days of the week, it is buried immediately after death.

On the day of burial the corpse is taken by the priest into the woods. He takes with him a coin which has been given him by the parents of the deceased with which to propitiate the gods and goddesses of the ground in which it is proposed to dig the grave. Having selected a suitable spot, the priest takes a little sacred grass (*Dubo* grass) and places it on top of the coin, together with a little rice. Holding these offerings in his hand, and uttering prayers the while, he places them in the centre of the plot of ground which he has selected as the grave. He cries out, "Here is the money with which we purchase this land"; the ground is dug and the offertory coin thrown into it.

The corpse is placed in the grave with its face towards the setting sun and the hands at the side. A large flat rock is placed over the grave, and on this a small quantity of earth is thrown by each person present. After this earth has been smoothed over the grave a small rough flag is placed in the centre in order to mark the spot.

After the burial ceremony there is no big feast, but every one repairs to the house of the deceased, where a light repast is provided.

In the case of rich men the corpse is enclosed in a coffin in which is placed grain of every kind. Earth is piled over the coffin and on top of the earth a monument of stones is erected. Should the body have been buried near a road the top of the grave is finished off in such a manner as to provide a resting-place for passing travellers, and a tree is planted to give them shade.

The period of mourning lasts, in the case of grown-up people, for seven days, and in the case of boys for four days, and of girls for three days. During this period no meat, *dal* (split pulse), salt, oil, or chillies may be eaten, and the hair, moustache and eyebrows are shaved in varying degrees according to the relation of the deceased to the mourner.

After the above period of mourning has elapsed comes a further period known as *Barkhi*, or half-mourning. This may last for as long as six months, and during this time mourners may wear only one thickness of clothing, and only the lining of their caps. During the *Barkhi* it is obligatory for all mourners to wear their caste marks.

The date for the conclusion of the *Barkhi* is determined by the *Phedangma*, who gives permission for normal life to be resumed. The people are now free to eat what they please, and also to sing and dance, and the occasion is marked by a big feast in the deceased's house.

A few miscellaneous customs remain to be noted.

Three months before a child is born it is customary to give a feast. This usually takes place in the woods, and never inside a house. The feast is attended by the friends and relations of the expectant mother, and the indispensable *Phedangma* offers prayers to the gods for the successful delivery of the child.

In cases where the delivery of the child is attended by complications a most curious custom prevails. The *Phedangma* takes a few chicken's eggs, feathers, rice, oil and spices and places them in a wicker receptacle. This is then pierced with a stick, and the *Phedangma* raises it aloft and gently waves it to and fro, muttering exhortations the while.

If a Limbu marries a woman of a tribe foreign to his own—such as a Magar, Gurung, or Rai—and there is an offspring, the child can be accepted into the Limbu caste. In order to effect this a special ceremony is held which is attended by ten Limbus selected by the *Phedangma*. At this ceremony black pulse is ground up and applied to the mouths of the children, who are thereupon considered as Limbus.

When the mother dies she may be buried according to Limbu custom, provided the above ceremony on behalf of the children has been carried out ; she cannot, however, be admitted into the Limbu tribe during her lifetime.

Limbu songs and dances differ somewhat from those performed in other parts of Nepal. Songs fall into two chief divisions known as the *Laivari* and *Hakpara* respectively, the former being sung only by children and the latter only by their elders. Dances, again, are divided into two main categories known as the *Langma* and *Ke Langma*. Dancing is carried on more or less generally throughout the year, but is especially indulged in during the season of harvest.

Generally speaking, the dances of Eastern Nepal are much more graceful to watch than those of the West, and the songs, being based on the same scale as our own music, are therefore much more melodious to Western ears.

As will be observed from the accounts of the foregoing ceremonies it is the *Phedangma* who may be described as the tribal priest of the Limbus, for it is he who generally officiates at their sacrifices, weddings and funerals. His duties are not, however, confined merely to attendance at these ceremonies, for his advice is also generally sought, not only in cases of sickness and distress, but also in the warding off and propitiation of the higher of the many evil spirits with which the Limbu imagines himself to be surrounded. He is occasionally assisted by a lower class of the priesthood, known as *Bijuwas*. These latter are, in reality, a class of wandering mendicants, common to Sikkim and the eastern parts of Nepal, who spend their lives travelling about the country singing and dancing, prescribing for the sick and muttering prayers and incantations. They are, generally speaking, wholly illiterate men who may be regarded as mere exorcists and charlatans. They have no qualifications and their ranks are open to all and sundry, and they earn their living by preying on the credulous peoples—both Rais and Limbus—of Eastern Nepal.

The *Bijuwas* are considered by the Limbus as being somewhat inferior to the *Phedangmas*. They have become, however, the accepted priesthood of the Rais; and the *Homes*, or *Gurus*, of the *Bijuwas* now occupy the same place amongst Rais as do the *Phedangmas* amongst the Limbus.

Both of the above-mentioned classes of the priesthood work according to custom, which has been passed on from one generation to another. Neither are subject to any supreme head, nor are their teachings dictated by any set doctrine. It follows, therefore, that slight differences are observable in the ceremonies as performed in different parts of the country. In the course of our interrogations we have often obtained conflicting accounts of the various ceremonies. It is obvious that space will not permit of every variation being noted, and the ceremonies described above are those most generally in use.

Practically nothing is known of the country of Eastern Nepal. In the year 1850 Sir Joseph Hooker was granted permission to visit certain parts of the country, but charming as his narrative is it is written primarily from a botanical point of view.

In 1926 His Highness the Maharaja granted us the great privilege of making a small tour into Eastern Nepal. As the country we visited has only been seen by one other European—Sir Joseph Hooker—it may not be out of place to describe it in some detail.

We left Darjeeling on November 25, and leaving our car at the Nepalese frontier climbed on to the Singalela ridge to Tonglu, which is situated just inside British territory.

Arriving at the bungalow, we found an escort awaiting us. This was kindly provided by His

Highness, and consisted of Subedar Dhanbahadur, of the Naya Sirinath Regiment, a Jemadar, Havildar and three soldiers. All were dressed in the semi-military costume favoured by the soldiery of Nepal when not actually on parade. This consists of a dark-coloured, double-breasted shirt, fitting tightly over the breast and arms, and fastened at the shoulders and waist with tapes. With this are worn a pair of trousers of the same material, which are made so as to fit closely below the knee and very loosely above; round the waist is worn a white or coloured cloth, usually several yards in length. Into this is tucked a *khukri*, a weapon the Gurkha is seldom without. A tweed or serge coat of European pattern is worn over the above, and the usual headdress is either a white cotton cap or the regimental head-dress. Many of the people go barefoot, but when shoes are worn they are of local manufacture.

For transport we had engaged the services of ten sturdy Sherpas, men from North-Eastern Nepal who usually contrive to spend a part of their lives in Darjeeling. Being extremely strong and impervious to hardship they make ideal carriers in this sort of country.

Early on the following morning we set off and were soon in Nepalese territory.

The road was rocky and uneven, but bad though it was, from what we had been led to expect we considered ourselves lucky to find a path at all. After a mile or so of steady descent we came to a Bhotiya village, but beyond a smiling welcome from its hordes of dirty children there was little or nothing of interest. At the bend of the road, where it descends abruptly and is lost to view, there stands a white-washed *Chorten;* clearly visible from the Tonglu spur above, it stands alone, a sentinel guarding the approach to the forbidden land.

The road so far had been none too good, but

INGLA VILLAGE, EASTERN NEPAL

compared with that which now confronted us it was a veritable high-road: it ran between rocks and trunks of trees, and was hardly distinguishable from the moss-grown forest on either side. It was, in fact, little more than a channel cut in the side of the hill by the periodical streams which gush down its side; down it we stumbled and crawled until we reached the village of Ingla, perched on a tiny plateau.

Ingla—a curiously unNepalese name, by the way—is a collection of small houses strung out loosely over the hillside. Each is surrounded by a patch of cultivation, and here and there can be seen a small and smooth mud platform, the threshing-floor of the homestead. We noticed a number of long white strips flapping in the breeze. These were Buddhist prayer flags and were covered with emblems of the Buddhist faith; the people of Ingla, though, are not all Buddhists, for here the Brahman's fields adjoin those of the Bhotiya, and the Rai and Limbu rub shoulders in the diminutive bazaar and live peaceably side by side.

Here, as in most valleys similarly situated, rice forms the staple crop. Of this there is as a rule only one sowing a year, and after the harvest in October barley takes its place. Besides rice, Indian corn, or maize, buckwheat, millet and potatoes are also grown. Of these, Indian corn—the most common cereal grown in the higher altitudes—has also only one crop, and after being cut it is usually replaced by potatoes, or some such vegetable. It is interesting to note that in Nepal fields are never allowed to lie fallow as we are accustomed to see them in Europe: as soon as one crop is gathered another is quickly sown and the fields are given no chance to recover.

Beyond Ingla the path meandered through the cultivation and was finally lost to view behind a distant spur, beneath which, so our escort told us, lay Jamuna, our halting-place for the night. Now and again we descended through hedges of sunflowers, then in full bloom, and were a source of amazement to the inhabitants of the numerous dwellings we passed on the way.

The path now dropped steeply down to the Ingla river. As we came to the ford a party of Limbu boys were just returning from a fishing expedition. Their method of fishing was somewhat unusual and as effective as it was unorthodox.

A number of large stones are collected and a dam is made across the stream. Here are stationed a few of the party whose duty it is to see that no fish pass the obstruction. The remainder of the party proceed a hundred yards or so upstream, and arrived at the starting-place, walk slowly through the water, driving the fish in front of them as they go. As they near the dam they close in and scoop the fish out of the water with their hands. A great number of fish escape, of course, but on occasion quite considerable catches are landed in this fashion.

After a welcome drink in the stream we continued on our way and soon came in sight of the village of Jamuna. News of our impending arrival had evidently preceded us, for the headman of the village, as indeed most of the population, came out a short distance to welcome us.

The *Mukhiya* of Jamuna was a Brahman and displayed in his conversation and bearing the intelligence and breeding of his caste. He spared no pains to make us comfortable, giving us quarters in an empty house.

We stayed in Jamuna one night, and during this time were the objects of the greatest curiosity. So long as we stayed behind doors all was well, but we had only to set foot outside to send the villagers—and in particular the belles of the village—scuttling into their homes. This did not last, however, and

THE MUKHIYA OF JAMUNA—A TYPICAL BRAHMAN

curiosity gained the day. Doors were gradually opened and we were soon surrounded by a crowd of gaping rustics.

The few small shops which line the one small street of Jamuna are for the most part owned by Newars; side by side with rows of umbrellas and the inevitable hurricane lantern, that indispensable adjunct of Eastern life, we noticed necklaces of bright blue beads, red cords or tassels for the hair, and glass bangles of size and colour to suit the fancy of the most fastidious village maiden. In other houses are to be found tailors, carpenters and goldsmiths, men of low caste and easily distinguishable by their darker complexion and features of coarser stamp.

At the entrance to the village, and nearly opposite our resting-place, stands the *Adda*. This is best described as the local court house, and one of these buildings is a prominent feature of most of the larger Nepalese villages. Here the *Mukhiya* holds his court; here taxes are paid, passes issued and customs dues levied; and when sufficient letters have been collected it is from here that the local postman—known as *Hulaki*—starts on his rounds.

Jamuna lies on the left bank of the Mai Khola, and from the wooden bench outside the Adda where we sat the river could be clearly seen winding away along the bottom of the valley, its banks dotted here and there with dark-coloured trees. It was up this river that our path of the morrow lay.

We were early away from the village, and escorted by the *Mukhiya* and his myrmidons, started to ascend at once. After the first steep climb the path descends gradually for several miles through beautiful rock-strewn woods, and bending away from the river, crosses a small side valley. This is spanned by a small wooden bridge over the stream which pursues its turbulent course into the Mai Khola below.

Here we halted a minute while our escort murmured a prayer and threw flowers into the stream—an offering to the goddess of the river.

From here the path ascends steeply through patches of cultivation, and as we climbed we halted every now and then in order to admire the wonderful panorama gradually unfolding itself before our eyes. To the south we could see the suspension bridge a little below Jamuna, beneath which the Mai Khola roars and foams its way between steep and wooded banks, while on the far distant hills the houses of Ilam could be clearly seen. To the north our eyes rested on the village of Mahbu nestling amidst yellow fields. Above it, on either side, the hills rise steeply, sometimes dotted with pine forest, sometimes conical and bare; below, terraced fields fall in gentle contours to the valley, through which the blue Mai river can still be seen as it flows in varying mood.

Mahbu presented a delightful picture with its bright red houses and still brighter mustard fields, then in full bloom. The houses of Mahbu are clean and tidy—a contrast to those we find in the higher elevations, where conditions are harder and life is less easy.

In the veranda of one of the houses a man was lying fast asleep. He was not of the village, and his travel-stained clothes and sack of worldly belongings by his side proclaimed him a traveller like ourselves.

Nepalese villages do not as a rule possess any hostel for passing wayfarers, though in the larger towns and on the highroads are to be found occasional *powas*, or rest-houses—usually erected to the memory of a departed relative.

Distractions for those who dwell in these Himalayan villages are few and far between. The large fairs, however, that are held from time to time in various places are the means of attracting large numbers of people from far and wide, and contribute

THE VALLEY OF THE MAI KHOLA

VILLAGE OF MAHBU, EASTERN NEPAL

not a little towards bringing a touch of colour into their somewhat drab but happy lives. At these, as can be readily imagined—especially by those who know the Gurkha well—every means is employed to combine business with a proportionate amount of pleasure. Besides the brisk and lively trade at the booths, presided over by every conceivable type of hillman, from the business-like Newar from the bazaars of Ilam to the wild-looking Bhotiya from the Tibetan border, the usual simple amusements which accompany fairs in all parts of the world are to be found. The gaudy wooden horses and noisy steam organs of Europe are missing, but the primitive structure which does duty as a swing in this part of the world is there, and the screams of delight of those who sample it are no less loud.

One of the most celebrated of the fairs held in this district is that which takes place at Maibeni, a place on the river below Ilam. This is held at certain seasons of the year and is attended by large numbers of people from the surrounding country. These fairs are held all over Nepal and usually take place at the junction of rivers. The junctions of rivers have no special significance in themselves, but in a country badly provided with roads they are the places most easy of access.

From Mahbu we followed the path through fields of mustard and wheat and occasional clumps of bamboo, until, skirting the Mai Khola, we saw on a cultivated plateau before us, lying at the foot of a thick forest, the white houses of Maimajua, our halting-place for the night.

The inhabitants of Maimajua are Gurungs : they do not speak the Gurung language, nor do they wear the dress common to Central Nepal, but they resemble the Gurungs of that part in that they follow the same occupation, that of shepherds, rather than cultivators of the soil.

Here it might not be out of place to remark on the one great divergency of dress between Eastern and Western Nepal, which, though small in itself, is easily noted by the observant eye. In Eastern Nepal, the *suruwal*, or loosely fitting trouser already described, is almost universally worn; in the West this is usually replaced by a long strip of white cloth—known as a *patuka*—wound round the waist so as to give rather the appearance of a kilt.

The headman of the village, himself a Gurung, received us kindly, and quarters were quickly found for us. This time no house was available, but the evacuation of a cowshed by its four-footed tenant was the means of providing us with a shelter, which, with the assistance of our escort and willing helpers from the village, quickly became not only habitable, but even comfortable.

From the village we looked down, in the fading light, on the valley up which we had come, and in the distance the high spurs which overlook the Ingla valley from the south stood out dimly against the sky; to the west of us we saw, spread out over a spur, a large straggling village inhabited, so we were told, entirely by Rais.

The *Mukhiya* showed us with pride his gun, a single-barrelled, muzzle-loading weapon of somewhat antique pattern. No one, he told us, is permitted to keep a gun without a licence, which in every case, however distant the village, must be procured from the central Government in Kathmandu. Similarly, the sale of intoxicating liquors, and even of cigarettes, without a licence is prohibited; but the brewing of the rice beer, known as *Janr*, is permitted throughout the country.

Game appeared from all accounts to be plentiful in the district. It comprised all the animals usually met with at similar altitudes all over the Himalaya—*ghural*, or Himalayan wild goat, bears, and barking deer, and most kinds of Himalayan pheasant and partridge.

After a peaceful night we started early the following morning on our journey to Banduki. For a mile or so our path led over bare and uncultivated country, and save for occasional small groups of houses, inhabited chiefly by people of the Limbu tribe, there was nothing much to interest us. After this, however, we struck a patch of pretty, undulating country dotted here and there with prosperous-looking houses. The houses bore a striking resemblance to Swiss chalets, and what with the blue of the sky and green of the grass and trees, the whole scene was strangely reminiscent of that little mountain country.

As we rested a moment, the owner of the largest house, a Rai of distinguished appearance, caught sight of us and bade us a friendly welcome to his home. We sat on wicker seats on the pleasant turf outside his door, and partook of eggs, milk and sweetened tea, provided by our kind friend. Objects of great interest to his family and retainers, we were fortunate to find amongst them some fine specimens of the Rai tribe, of whom we were able to secure some good photographs. Refreshed and ready for the stiff climb that, as we could see from afar, lay in front of us, we bade farewell to our courteous host, and began to climb the wooded slope that rose steep, and in places almost sheer, straight behind the house.

The track, for path it could not be called, ascended through dense, dark green forest, up the southern slope of the spur that comes down from Sandakphu, on the Nepal frontier road. As we climbed higher we became enveloped in a thick mist—such a common phenomenon in this part of the world—and it was not until we had arrived, as it were, right on the top of it, that we saw Banduki, our camping-place for the night.

Banduki appeared to consist of a single, small and humble-looking Nepalese house and a few low sheds roughly constructed of wicker hurdles. The occupant of the house proved to be a *Nausinda*, or Customs House official, whose duty it is to inspect the loads and baggage of wayfarers who pass through along this path, one of the main tracks leading into the Panch Thar country.

Situated in a clearing of the forest, Banduki afforded us no view whatsoever, though the ever-thickening mist would have prevented us seeing far even had there been one. Situated as it is, miles from anywhere, life in Banduki must be simple in the extreme; but the Customs official appeared cheerful enough and was no less willing than the previous officials we had met to afford us every possible assistance.

Although apparently unimportant, many travellers pass the little Customs House at Banduki. Toll is levied on many things, such as animals, cloth and salt, which are brought in from across the border, while the import of other articles, such as cigarettes, not to mention the domestic cow, is prohibited without special permission.

From Banduki we had been able to see but little of what lay before us, but some few miles after leaving it we were more than rewarded by the beauty of the scene unfolded before our eyes. From where we sat we saw, rising in fold upon fold, a mass of beautiful wooded hills, while to the north the mountain of Kinchinjunga raised aloft its mighty head. Seen thus, from a point of view denied to the many, it appeared " a dazzling mass of snowy peaks intersected by blue glaciers which gleamed in the slanting rays of the rising sun like aquamarines set in frosted silver " (Hooker).

The country into which we had now passed is known as the Panch Thar, or land of the Five Tribes.

TYPICAL PANCH-THAR COUNTRY

A LIMBU HOUSE, EASTERN NEPAL

It is mentioned in the Limbu history as being one of the ten original homes of their race, and the villages in this district are almost entirely inhabited by Limbus. Here, in the occasional patches of cultivation through which we passed, rice had given place to Indian corn, while in the forests the bamboos, plantains and tree-ferns of the lower valleys were replaced by the oaks, chestnuts, maples and mangolias of these higher elevations.

Our path lay sometimes through thick verdant forest, sometimes over ridges crowned with stunted pines. As we climbed higher, rhododendrons became plentiful, some grown into great trees, others clothing the hillside with a thick mass of shrub, whilst the pines and firs were often blasted by lightning. We stopped short of the village of Myeimeng, as we considered this beyond the limits imposed by His Highness, but from the crest of the hill where we sat we took a last view of the beautiful country before us, the home of so hardy and valiant a race.

We climbed slowly up to the bungalow of Sandakphu high above us on the Singalela ridge, whence we were to return to Darjeeling by the frontier road; but, so far as Nepal was concerned, our journey was now at an end.

CHAPTER XVI

RAIS

As in the case of the Limbus, the Rais have a tradition that they, too, came originally from Benares. In the history of Nepal it is related that the Rais conquered the Nepal valley, and after ruling over it for a very long time were supplanted by the gods. All this, of course, is mere conjecture, and in actual fact the origin of the Rais is more or less of a mystery.

Traces of the tradition of the emigration from Benares survive up to the present day to the extent that the many sub-divisions into which the Rai race is divided are grouped into ten main *thars*, or tribes, known as the *Das Kirant*.* Of these, three claim to have come originally from Lhasa, known as *Lhasagotra*, and seven, known as *Kashigotra*, from Benares. At the present day Rais are divided into no less than seventy-two tribes, but the above-mentioned ten original sub-divisions may be regarded as the most important of them.

In appearance the Rai is, perhaps, more Mongolian than any of the other races inhabiting Nepal. His complexion is fairer and has a decided yellow tinge, while his eyes are set rather far apart. Nice mannered and cheerful, they are much more amenable

* 1, Atpahare; 2, Bantawa; 3, Chamling; 4, Kulung; 5, Lohorong; 6, Nawahang; 7, Nechali; 8, Sangpang; 9, Tulung; 10, Chaurasia.

and far less quarrelsome than their neighbours, the Limbus.*

In contrast to the Limbus the Rais have no common tribal language, but each sub-tribe—and there are nearly seventy—has its own. Naturally, many of these languages are very similar, and several could almost be grouped as one. In all probability there are no more than ten actual languages, the remainder being classed more correctly as dialects. Of these languages nothing is known.

The Rais, in common with most of the Nepalese, are Hindus, or at any rate, nominal followers of that religion. They worship Shiva and Parbati, known also as Mahadeo and Devi, and occasionally the former, in the guise of a mythical ancestor known as Parubhang, is still looked up to by some as a household deity.

The customs and manners of the Limbus and Rais are gradually becoming more and more assimilated, but exhaustive inquiry has elicited the fact that great differences still exist. There follows a description of Rai customs which it is as well to place on record before they become finally merged into those of the Limbus, as it appears to be merely a matter of time before the two races become one in all essentials.

On the birth of a Rai there is no ceremony involving the presence of a Bijuwa, or tribal priest, but the following ritual is carried out in the house by friends and relations. A fowl—cock in the case of a boy, hen for a girl—and some rice beer are first procured, after which an old woman proceeds to tie the umbilical cord with a piece of thread, and the knot thus made is laid over a rupee and severed. The child is then washed with hot water, while the

* Though the characters of Rais do not differ much where their *thars* are concerned ; the Yakkas and men of the Lohoron thar are generally considered less tractable than the rest.

mother's clothes are changed and others put on her. The gullet of the fowl is now put on one side, while the rest of the bird is placed in a utensil containing oil, spices and rancid butter. The gullet is next placed on top of the mixture and the whole cooked together. In the meantime rice has been simmering in another pot, and two plates are brought—one for the mother and one for the child—in which the rice is heaped, while into two other vessels is put the flesh of the fowl. The gullet is now placed on the top of the plate of rice which has been set aside for the child. After this, three leaves are placed on the ground, and on to each leaf is placed a little rice and meat over which rice beer is poured. Of these three portions, one is offered to the family gods—known as *Pitri*—another to the gods in general, and the third as a propitiatory offering to the evil spirits. The mother now partakes of a little food.

During the period of the mother's ceremonial uncleanliness she lives quite apart from the rest of the family and is not allowed to associate with any one. This period lasts, in the case of a son, for six days, and in the case of a daughter for five, and until it is ended only rice may be eaten, and that but once a day.

On the sixth day all the relations are called to the house, when the father of the child provides a feast at which all freely partake of meat, cooked rice and rice beer. On the conclusion of this, all present, and the house itself, are besprinkled with a mixture of water and cow's urine, and the period of the mother's uncleanliness is considered to have been terminated.

The ceremony of weaning takes place six months after birth in the case of a boy, and five in the case of a girl. On the day preceding the actual ceremony a pig is killed, preparations for a feast are made, and the child's clothes are got ready. On the day itself all relations are invited to be present. A plate

RAIS AND LIMBUS—EASTERN NEPAL

A RAI BOY MAKING HURDLES

containing curds, rice and a lighted wick, together with a vessel filled with water, in which the heads of some flowers have been placed, are put on the ground. The child, dressed in its new clothes, is then put on a blanket, and the plate and the vessel containing the water are placed by its side. The child's father and mother now put a coin into the plate and apply a caste mark to the child's forehead. After this they feed it with a little rice and meat, using a rupee or similar coin as a spoon. The guests now act in a similar fashion, and all present partake of the feast, on the conclusion of which all make obeisance to the child, and the ceremony concludes.

Amongst Rais, as a rule, the men marry between the ages of fifteen and twenty, and girls between twelve and fifteen, but in many cases marriage is deferred, by both sexes, for a further period of some five years or so. In order to effect a betrothal preliminary negotiations are entered into by the bridegroom's family, and usually take the following form.

An emissary of the boy, taking with him jars of spirits corresponding in number to the senior relations of the girl—such as her father, mother, uncles and aunts, but not her brothers and sisters—a small wicker basket containing pig's flesh, together with two rupees in cash, proceeds to the girl's house. On arrival there he places the jars of spirits and the basket containing the pig's flesh on the ground, and presents one of the rupees to the girl's representative. All the girl's relations are now summoned, and in their presence she is asked if she is willing to marry the man in question. If she consents, the boy's emissary is told to return after a certain period. On the conclusion of this period he proceeds once more to the girl's house, taking another gift of pig's flesh and jars of spirits; but on this occasion he does not make any monetary present. On arrival, he places his offerings on the ground, and is thereupon told to come back on some definite date, when the actual marriage will be solemnized. In former days it was customary to pay a standard price of eighty rupees for a bride, but this practice has now fallen into disuse, and a bride is never now purchased.

On the day of the marriage, the boy, dressed entirely in white, proceeds to his bride's house. If he can afford it he is carried in a dooly; otherwise he rides on horseback, or may even go on foot. He is accompanied by one whose duties correspond, more or less, to those of a "best man" in Europe. This should be, if possible, a younger brother, otherwise a very near friend.

The emissary who carried out the preliminary negotiations on behalf of the boy also accompanies the party, but he goes on a little in advance in order to arrive at the bride's house before the others.

On his arrival he informs the girl's representatives —not necessarily her parents—of the approach of the party, and they in turn inform the bride and her parents.

The ceremony opens by the girl giving a large feast, which takes place at some convenient place outside the house, and never in it. For this all the provisions have been provided by the girl's relations, by whom, on their arrival, the boy and his retinue are plentifully besprinkled with a mixture of rice and curds. The bride herself does not attend this function, which is known as the *Lamtumpa*, but remains hidden in the house.

After the conclusion of the feast, the girl's mother and younger (maternal) uncle are presented with gifts, the former receiving the leg of a pig, a jar of spirits, and about nine rupees in cash, the latter fifteen rupees in cash, some meat and a little spirits.

In addition to the gifts just mentioned the head-man of the village and the girl's paternal uncle each receive five rupees in cash, a jar of spirits and a basket of pig's flesh.

The bride is now summoned and is arrayed in her nuptial finery by her two attendants, who also adorn her with the usual gold ornaments—gifts of the bridegroom. When ready she is brought out of the house and made to sit near what is known as the *Jage*, or sacred fire, where the bridegroom is already seated and awaiting her.

The girl's attendants now give the " best man " a little food, after which they wash his hands and give him some tobacco.

Now is the moment for the appearance of the family priest, who demands a cock and a hen, a jar of rice beer, and another of spirits, to be brought from the bride's house. The priest places two plantain leaves on the ground and puts into each a little rice and vegetable. He now takes each bird in turn, puts some rice and vegetable on its head, invoking the name of the deity as he does so, and, calling out the names of the bride and bridegroom, pours a little spirit on the bird's head and slits its throat, taking care to see that the blood flows on to the plantain leaves below.

The blood is carefully examined, and if it has not flowed as satisfactorily as it should, the above ceremony is repeated with another fowl.

When the ceremony of the blood has been successfully performed, the bride and bridegroom put a little curds and rice into one another's mouths, and place their heads close together. This last takes place to the accompaniment of the singing and dancing of the assembled guests.

After the completion of the above, the boy's original emissary informs the bride that her groom wishes to make obeisance to her parents, and on her approval being obtained, he makes a monetary present, not only to them, but to all the assembled relations of the bride, both male and female, the value of which depends upon the closeness of their relationship. As each relation receives the present, he or she, as the case may be, applies the caste mark to the foreheads of both the bride and bridegroom.

All the relations having performed the above act of obeisance, it is now the turn of the attendants of both contracting parties. These receive one rupee each, and in turn apply a caste mark. It is the duty of the bridegroom's attendant to ascertain that no one has been overlooked in the performance of the preceding ceremony, and having satisfied himself on this point, he sits down to a feast provided for him and the other attendants who have been helping in the preparation and distribution of food up to date.

Singing and dancing goes on throughout the night, until, at break of day, the attendants ask the bride's parents for some reward for their services, and are thereupon given five rupees each, together with some spirits, rice beer and a leg of pork.

The feasting, however, is by no means yet over, for there still remains another banquet that takes place near the high-road. This, like an earlier ceremony mentioned above, is also known as the *Lamtumpa*, and is provided, this time, at the expense of the bridegroom. The ceremony being concluded, the boy's parents are informed of the fact and order the happy pair to be brought to their house.

The mother now procures a brass plate and bowl. In the former she puts a little curds and rice, setting a lighted wick in the centre of it, and in the latter pours a little water in which are placed the heads of a few flowers. As the bride approaches the door of the house, the mother takes up the two vessels and sprinkles her with water, and throws a little rice towards her at the same time. Then, holding the plate in her left hand, she seizes the girl with her right and drags her into the house, the bridegroom following behind. Both are now made to sit on a blanket, which is spread on the floor for this purpose.

Some rice is now put into a vessel, and into this a few coins are dropped. The rice is then tipped out on to the plaited strap, known as *Namlo*, with which loads are carried. Into this the bride and her mother-in-law put their hands and are allowed to keep as many coins as they are able to grab.

The marriage ceremony is finally concluded by the interchange of gifts between the parents of the newly wedded pair. These consist of the inevitable leg of pork and jar of spirits.

In the case of a runaway marriage, the boy, as a rule, keeps the girl for a period of some fifteen days, after which he appeases the wrath of the supposedly injured parents by a monetary present amounting to some twenty rupees.

When a Rai dies, all his relations are summoned to the house and a priest is called. The father sends for some white cloth, in which the body is presently enshrouded, and also for some bamboos or other suitable lengths of wood. Out of these a kind of rough stretcher is made, which can be carried either on the shoulders or by hand. On to this the white cloth is now laid, with the ends projecting over the sides, and on the top of this is laid the corpse. The cloth is now folded over and sewn along three sides.

A fowl and some rice beer are now procured, while into a cooking-pot are placed some rice, Indian corn, buckwheat and plantains which are mixed up and set to cook. The resultant dish is thereupon put into a cloth and secured by knotting one corner.

A rough flag is now made by inserting a piece of white cloth into a cleft stick. It is now time for the priest to take an active part in the ensuing ceremonies.

Holding a vessel of water in his left hand and a flower or a piece of some special kind of grass in his right, he sprinkles the corpse with the water, murmuring incantations the while. After this he addresses the corpse, exhorting it to go peacefully to its last resting-place. The funeral procession now starts off. This is preceded by a man carrying a bag of grain, who scatters some on the ground as he walks, while behind him follows another man bearing a lighted torch. On arrival at the burial place a grave is dug, and the priest, taking a jar of rice and a coin, addresses the grave, which he sprinkles with water and into which he throws the coin. He now places a large stone at the head of the grave, and taking the fowl dashes it against the stone and casts away its dead body. The corpse is now placed in the grave, and all present throw, with the left hand, three handfuls of earth over it. The grave is now filled in, especial care being taken to ensure that no traces of the gravedigger's footprints remain visible. On the top of the grave the priest empties the contents of the bag containing the rice and coins and places the flag in position.

On completion of the above the whole party proceeds to the nearest convenient spring or river, where they all wash themselves thoroughly. While this is going on the head of the deceased's brother is shaved and covered in a white cloth. All now adjourn to the house of the deceased and the burial ceremony is held to be completed.

The period of mourning in the case of a Rai is much the same as for that of the other races—six days in the case of a man, and five in the case of a woman. On the morning previous to the expiration of this period all the relations of the deceased are summoned, and a pig and some rice beer procured. On the last day the pig is roasted, and to each person present is given a small cup, known as a *dona*, made of leaves sewn together. After this all the people stand in a line while the priest mutters exhortations. The chief mourner now brings a cup of water and passes it to each person in turn in order that he may wash his hands. Into one of the *donas* is now put a mixture of oil and salt ; into this the chief mourner dips his little finger, and with a snapping motion of the finger and thumb, he flicks a little of the mixture from him. The remaining relations now follow suit, and on the conclusion of this all again wash their hands.

The chief mourner now removes his white head-covering and places it over some rice which has been put there for the purpose. He next dresses himself from head to foot in white clothing, takes some curds and rice, and anoints all present with a caste mark, giving at the same time a money present to each of the unmarried females present at the ceremony. The presentation of coins is concluded by the customary feast, after which all present disperse to their homes and the period of mourning is at an end.

CHAPTER XVII

A JOURNEY ON THE NORTH-EASTERN FRONTIER OF NEPAL

By C. J. M.

TOWARDS the end of June 1922 I was fortunate enough to find myself in that part of Tibet which adjoins the north-eastern corner of Nepal. My companion and I had been sent from the Mount Everest Expedition to explore the gorge of the Arun, and to find out in what manner the river drops 4,000 feet in the short distance of twenty miles.

The Arun, one of the principal tributaries of the Kosi, rises behind the main chain. It drains the plains of Tingri and Khamba in Tibet, and then, with the force of its accumulated waters, carves its way through the main chain of the Himalaya directly between the gigantic mountain massifs of Everest on the one side and Kinchinjunga on the other.

The prospect of carrying out this journey was sufficiently attractive in itself, but for me there was the added attraction of possible glimpses into Nepal, as, in order to get up the gorge, we had first to go down to the Tibeto-Nepalese frontier at Kyimateng.

The weather at this time was just about as bad as it could possibly be, and no one would normally choose to explore a thickly wooded Himalayan valley at such a season of the year. We had, however, no other alternative, as we should be out of Tibet before

ARUN VALLEY SCENERY

THE ARUN VALLEY LOOKING SOUTH

the end of the monsoon, and the opportunity to visit this part of the country might possibly never recur.

We had been in camp at Sakyateng, in the Kama valley, for some days, and had been enveloped in cloud during most of this time. The rain hardly ever ceased, and photography—the principal object of our visit—was well-nigh impossible. From Sakyateng there is, I believe, a magnificent view of Makalu, but, personally, I never saw it. Occasionally an ice cliff or part of a hanging glacier would be visible for a few moments, and one would hasten towards the cameras—permanently set up in readiness—in the hope that the pall of cloud was about to be lifted. We spent hours in this way, looking towards the spot where the mountain ought to have been visible; sometimes the base would be visible, sometimes a spur, looking in the evening glow as though carved in coral. We saw many parts of the mountain, but she was always too shy to vouchsafe us even a fleeting glance of her stately summit.

Sakyateng itself is merely a small collection of grazing huts. These are used by Tibetan shepherds who bring their flocks to graze on the rich pastures all around. I imagine that the huts are unoccupied during the greater part of the year, and the position of the camp probably changes from year to year according to the quality of the grazing.

Hearing that a party of Tibetans had come up the Kama valley with supplies of salt, I went over to interview them in the hope that they might be persuaded to carry our kit for us. They agreed to come as far as Kyimateng, and with the help of our own Sherpa porters we were able to make a start.

We set off from Sakyateng on June 27, in heavy rain. The steep hillsides were clothed with dense green forest, and a steady downpour soaked the undergrowth and dripped from every leaf. We had hoped to reach Kyimateng on this day, but after marching for some three and a half hours we met one of our men, who had been sent forward to try and buy supplies, and was now on his way back to meet us. He gave us the cheering information that we were not even halfway to our goal, so we thereupon decided to camp for the night at the first suitable spot.

A short distance on we came to the bridge leading across to the Popti La, at one time a much-frequented pass between Nepal and Tibet, but now discarded in favour of the more direct route straight up the Arun valley. I had hoped to ascend to the top of the Popti, for from here there must be a magnificent view right into Eastern Nepal with, possibly, a sight of Dhankuta. The weather, however, made this out of the question. We were already wet through, and the rain showed no signs of abating. The whole valley was now filled with dense white clouds, and the chances of seeing anything from the summit of the Popti were practically nil.

Near the Popti bridge is a small clearing, known as Chotromo. There were a few stone huts dotted about, but they appeared not to have been occupied for some considerable time, and provided a welcome shelter for our staff.

There was no rain when we started the following morning, but thick clouds were drifting slowly up the valley. We were soon level with the path leading off to the Popti. In spite of the humid atmosphere of the valley there was still a little snow lying in the shadows on the pass.

The forest now became still more wonderful, and the trees were very much larger as we got lower down the valley. Here and there by the bed of the river we came across delightful little glades, carpeted with moss and thick with purple iris. The path became almost invisible at times owing to the thickness of the undergrowth, and for about two miles was some four inches under water; but here the Tibetans had cut down large trees and laid them end to end along the path, which enabled one to keep fairly dry as long as one did not fall off—a not infrequent occurrence.

At last the forest ended abruptly and we were walking across grassy slopes, high above the river. Just before the end of our march we came across a party of Gurkhas, the first real Nepalese we had yet met. They had come up from Dhankuta, one of the largest towns in Eastern Nepal and a few days' march down the Arun, to graze their flocks, and were halting here a few days before going on to the rich grass-lands above the gorge. After a steep descent we crossed the river by a quaint little bridge, almost hidden by the overhanging trees, and commenced the short, but very steep, climb up to the village of Kyimateng. We camped a little outside the village, which is perched on the high cliffs overlooking the junction of the Kama and Arun rivers. Looking up the Arun from our camp we could just see the tiny village of Tsanga, but the river here bends sharply to the left and is lost to view; while looking down the river we get a glimpse into the forbidden land of Nepal.

Kyimateng, though strictly speaking in Tibet, is a typical Nepalese village. The neat little houses are each surrounded by well-kept fields of Indian corn, wheat and barley. The fields are bounded by substantial stone walls, and each contains a light bamboo structure from which a look-out is kept for bears at night.

Kyimateng and the surrounding villages are so inaccessible that the people do not appear to come under the influence of either Tibet or Nepal, leading a more or less independent life.

On the following morning I went to call on the headman of the village, who was, indeed, expecting me. To my consternation I found that practically the whole village was in attendance, anxious to see what was going on. Bamboo matting had been laid on the ground, and on this we took our seats. We conversed on general topics for a time, and then I thought it best to find out what hope we had of proceeding up the Arun valley. The headman at first said that there was no road through the gorge, and in any case no one was willing to go with us, as all the men in the village were occupied in the fields at this time of the year. I knew the information about there being no road to be incorrect, as the Gurkhas we met on the road the day before had told us they were on their way there. However, after a promise of double pay he guaranteed to find us coolies for the following morning.

It was necessary to pay the porters in advance, and in so doing I had an insight into the method of bookkeeping in this part of the world. A large board and a bag of beans were produced. The beans were laid out in rows, a row for each man, and a bean for each anna of the amount we agreed to pay per head. After counting the total several times the amount due from us was arrived at, and the board with the "account" on it was carefully removed inside the house.

There are a number of Nepalese living in the village, and in consequence most of the inhabitants are bi-lingual, speaking both Nepali and Tibetan indiscriminately and with equal fluency.

In addition to Nepalese and Tibetans we also find, in this part of the world, a race known as Sherpas. Their particular stronghold is a place called Sola khambu ; situated in North-Eastern Nepal it is quite near the Tibetan frontier.

The Sherpas speak as their mother tongue a dialect of Tibetan, but they all know Nepali equally well. Originally of pure Tibetan stock they have

RAI FAMILY FROM DHANKUTA—A TYPICAL *GOTH* OR GRAZING CAMP

KYIMATENG—ON THE NORTH EASTERN TIBETO-FRONTIER

mixed with the local inhabitants and are now extremely proud of being considered as Nepalese subjects.

The word " Sherpa " is Tibetan, and means simply " an easterner."

As far as I can remember I believe Sola khambu is situated at a height of about 14,000 feet above the sea, and the Sherpas are probably the highest livers in the whole Himalayan range. They are usually men of tremendous physique and can carry heavy loads at very high altitudes. It was from this race that the Mount Everest porter corps was recruited who performed such prodigious feats of endurance. Their normal occupation consists in carrying work and pushing *rickshas* in the hill station of Darjeeling, where large numbers of them are always to be found.

Although they have a certain amount of Nepalese blood running in their veins the Sherpas exhibit many of the bad characteristics of the Tibetans. Left to themselves they are extremely lazy, and will spend the whole day in gambling for drink, of which they are inordinately fond. With a firm hand over them they will, and do, work extremely hard, but they lack that standby in times of distress—an innate sense of discipline—which makes the Gurkha the wonderful fighter he is.

In their own homes the Sherpas are almost wholly Tibetan in their manners and customs. Extremely superstitious, their religion appears to be almost the same as the somewhat corrupt form of Buddhism followed in adjacent Tibet ; but surrounded as they are by followers of the Hindu religion it is not unnatural that they should have adopted certain Hindu practices. They have, however, no system of caste, but it is not improbable that this may follow as the Sherpas come more and more, as they are almost bound to do, under Hindu influence.

On leaving Kyimateng we turned away from Nepal in order to explore that part of the Arun which lies in Tibet. It would be out of place—since this is a book on Nepal—to describe the remainder of our journey here, but one incident I must describe, as it gives an account of a Gurkha summer grazing camp—a *Goth* as they are called—the normal hot weather life of the pastoral part of the population of Nepal.

We had been walking for hours, up and down over spurs and through dense forests, and were hoping to find some spot where we could camp for the night. Presently we came upon a small matting hut, unoccupied but guarded by two savage dogs which were chained up inside. We decided to halt here for the night. Strangely enough, there was no sign of water near, and we had to wait until the return of the occupants of the hut before we found out where they obtained it. Fortunately they soon returned, warned of the strangers' arrival by the savage barking of the two canine guardians. They turned out to be Gurkhas—of the Rai tribe—and, like those we had previously met, also from Dhankuta. The old man, who must have been nearly eighty, had been, many years ago, in one of our Gurkha regiments, and was soon talking of weapons and systems long since obsolete. He was able to tell us a certain amount about our route ahead, and also said that this tract of country was yearly visited by large numbers of people from Dhankuta. Dhankuta—I would give almost anything to see it—has, I believe, been seen by only one European, and he, the late Dr. Hooker, saw it only from the south. His charming book has long been out of print, so perhaps it may not be out of place to quote his description.

" . . . the Ghorkas led me aside to the top of a knoll, 9,300 feet high, covered with stunted bushes, and commanding a splendid view to the west, of the broad, low, well-cultivated valley of the Tambur, and the extensive town of Dunkotah on its banks, about twenty-five miles off; the capital of this part of Nepal, and famous for its manufactory of paper from the bark of the Daphne. Hence, too, I gained a fine view of the plains of India, including the course of the Cosi river, which, receiving the Arun and Tambhur, debouches into the Ganges. . . .

" . . . . It was a goodly sight to one who had for his only standard of comparison the view from Sinchul, of the gloomy forest-clad ranges of 6,000 to 10,000 feet, that intervene between that mountain and the snowy gurdle of Sikkim; though I question whether a traveller from more favoured climes would see more in this than a thinly inhabited country, with irregular patches of poor cultivation, a vast amount of rugged forest on low hills of rather uniform height and contour, relieved by a dismal background of frowning black mountains, sprinkled with snow."

Some ten days later we rejoined the expedition at Kharta, and after a brief halt, during which we developed photographs and wrote up our journals, the whole party set off once more on the long homeward journey across the plains of Tibet.

CHAPTER XVIII

MISCELLANEOUS TRIBES OF EASTERN NEPAL

THOUGH the Limbus and Rais are perhaps the best known of the tribes who inhabit the country to the east of the Nepal Valley, there are two others which cannot be overlooked and which merit a short description. These are, firstly, the Sunwars, and secondly the Murmis, known also as Lamas or Thamangs.

The Sunwars live in the country which lies to the west of the Sunkosi river, and their territory extends as far as Tibet on the east, and to the valley of Nepal on the west. There are numerous traditions as to their origin; one states that they originally hailed from Tibet, whence they migrated to the Ganges, thence working their way, via Simraghur, up to the country they now inhabit. Others seem to imply that they found their way through such widely separated routes as Kashmir and Assam.

Whatever credence may be placed in the foregoing theories as to the routes of their original migration, it appears fairly evident that at the time of their being at Simraghur, they consisted of three distinct tribes, the Jetha, Maila and Kancha, signifying the elder, second and youngest brother respectively, which divisions have been, in a modified form, retained up to the present day.

Of these three original tribes the former has been now divided into ten subdivisions, known as the *Das thar*, or ten tribes, and these retain, to a much greater degree than do the two remaining tribes, their Buddhist religion and ideas ; but in the case of all the Sunwars, as indeed all over Nepal, it would appear to be merely a matter of time before Buddhism is completely effaced as the people pass to complete Hinduism.

The other two tribes, the second of which is known as the *Bara thar*, or twelve tribes, have become almost entirely of the Hindu faith, and the priests who officiate at their religious ceremonies are said to be, nowadays, exclusively composed of Brahmans, of the Upaddhe class, although some of their tribes are said to employ a form of ceremonial akin to that of the Magars and Gurungs, and are considered to resemble those tribes in many respects. The resemblance to the Magars and Gurungs is not strong, however, and the Sunwars retain, to a large extent, the characteristics and manners of the other main races of Eastern Nepal, the Limbus and Rais, into the latter of which many of their subdivisions are, it is said, rapidly being absorbed.

To those who know them intimately, the Sunwars may be described as being the best mannered, and perhaps the most attractive, of all the races inhabiting Eastern Nepal. Somewhat reserved, and inclined at first to be dirty, they quickly adapt themselves to new conditions, and are much liked by those who have any dealings with them, whether in a civil or a military capacity.

One point deserves special mention, as it applies to no other race in Nepal. The Sunwars are almost entirely confined to the country already described as their dwelling-place, unlike people of other tribes, who are to be found living in localities far away from what one may describe as their " ancestral " part of the country. Generally speaking, Sunwars are never found outside their tribal territory, a fact which may perhaps account for their marked shyness when meeting strangers for the first time.

The Sunwars are few in number, and are, as a rule, easily recognizable by certain marked characteristics in their features. They have, as a rule, very prominent cheek-bones and a reddish complexion, while in stature they are very small and distinctly below the average in Nepal. In the oval shape of their faces they rather resemble Lepchas, though in all other respects they bear little or no resemblance to that race.

With regard to the second race, the Murmis, Lamas, or Thamangs. The origin of this race is veiled in the same mystery which surrounds those of the others. It would seem, however, most probable that they were originally a Tibetan tribe that somehow or other had managed to find its way into Nepal thence to settle and never to return. They possess a tradition of their own relating to their origin which is sufficiently interesting to merit its inclusion in these pages.

It is said that there were once three brothers, Brahma, Vishnu and Mahasur, by name. These went out shooting one day, and after wandering about for some hours without seeing any game, eventually came upon a *gauri gai*, or bison. This was killed by Vishnu, and thereupon all set to work to prepare it for eating. Mahasur, being the youngest, was given the entrails to wash in a stream nearby.

During his absence the other two, after cooking the meat, divided it into three equal portions, but being about to partake of it themselves, they suddenly realized that they could not eat it, as it was cow's meat, and so they concealed their share. On Mahasur's return, however, they pretended that they had eaten the meat, thereby inducing him to eat his portion in front of them. On their showing him their uneaten portions and abusing him for his action in eating his share, Mahasur became very angry and struck his brothers with the intestines, some of which hung about their shoulders, and which now accounts for the wearing of the sacred thread.

Mahasur was, however, degraded for having eaten the flesh of the cow, and hence the cow-eating Murmis are followers of his, and Murmis themselves relate that from Mahasur are descended the present race called Murmis, Lamas, or Thamangs.

To-day Murmis are divided into two main divisions, the *Bara*, or twelve Thamangs, and the *Athara*, or eighteen Thamangs, and although differing but slightly where questions of ritual or ceremonial are concerned, the former are supposed to be socially the superior, intermarriage between the two divisions being usually not practised.

The Thamangs, no less than the other races, lay claim to be adherents of the fashionable Hindu religion, but their priests are Lamas and they have obviously become Hindus more from compulsion than from choice. They make, as a rule, no pretence of disguising the fact that they are eaters of cow's flesh, although they draw the line at killing the animal themselves, preferring to send Lepchas, or men of low caste, to perform this duty for them. Their cow-eating propensities are further manifested by the fact that a Murmi, or Thamang, will always use a cowhide head strap, or *namlo*, for carrying loads.

While the exact social status of the Murmi is not very easy to define, it is certainly below that of the Magar, Gurung, Limbu, Rai and Sunwar, and the men of these tribes would always consider themselves superior to them.

Their obvious Tibetan origin, which shows itself very markedly, lays them open to the name of *Bhotiya* (Tibetan), and although the laws of caste are perhaps less rigid in the east than in the west, even their subsequent adoption of the Hindu faith and many of its customs cannot entirely save them from the thinly veiled contempt and opprobrium attaching to this name.

In physique and stature they are, perhaps, unsurpassed amongst all the races of Nepal, and they are generally industrious, hard working, and amenable. In the Nepalese Army they are never recruited in the combatant ranks, but are employed exclusively for such work as the pitching of tents, carrying of loads, and general work connected with transport, being known there as *Pipas*, or *Khalassies*.

In appearance they differ but little, if at all, from the other races, and many of them pass easily for Magars and Gurungs of good class. Their language, which is very akin to that of the Gurungs, also renders them still more difficult to distinguish.

The Murmis are to be found practically all over Eastern Nepal, and are very numerous in the hills round, and especially to the north of, the Nepal Valley. Both sexes are fond of necklaces of bright-coloured beads, and as a general rule can be fairly easily recognized by this fashion, which is certainly more indulged in by them than by the other races.

One more caste inhabiting Eastern Nepal remains to be mentioned. This is the Thami. Only about three to four thousand in number, they live chiefly on the banks of the Sunkosi and Tamburkosi rivers. Coarse in appearance, and the inferior of the other races in social and religious matters, they do not merit further description.

PART VI

NEPAL AND THE GREAT WAR

CHAPTER XIX

NEPAL'S WAR EFFORT

BEYOND a few casual words in the Press, practically no mention has anywhere been made of the part played by Nepal in the Great War. Out of all proportion to her size and means—far exceeding that of any Indian Native State—the help given by Nepal to the British Government is of such interest as to merit detailed description.

As early as August 3, 1914, His Highness the Maharaja called on the British Envoy and informed him of his readiness to place the whole military resources of Nepal at the disposal of the British Government, should they be needed. The Government of India gratefully accepted the offer, which subsequently took the following form. Firstly, the loan of a contingent of Nepalese troops. Secondly, assistance rendered in connection with the special recruiting measures necessary for the maintenance of the existing Gurkha regiments, and the provision of additional battalions. Lastly, gifts of war material which were provided from Nepal's natural resources.

Not long after the outbreak of war, the Maharaja, considering that such a force might prove of considerable assistance to the British, offered to provide a Nepalese contingent for use on the North-West Frontier of India, to be ready in the early spring of

1915. This suggestion was received with favour, and accordingly 10,000 troops, fully equipped, left Kathmandu on the 3rd and 4th of March, 1915, under the command of General Sir Baber Sham Sher, the second son of the Maharaja. Commanding-General Sir Padma Sham Sher, a nephew of His Highness, was sent in command of four regiments, which proceeded straight to the North-West Frontier, and General Tej Sham Sher, another nephew, with two others which were posted to the United Provinces. The 1st Rifles and the Kalibahadur Regiment, the crack corps forming the bodyguard of the Maharaja, also formed part of this contingent.

In February 1916 a second contingent, fully officered and equipped as the previous one, was despatched to India. Both these contingents were kept at full strength by drafts from time to time.

Primarily intended for general service in India, and stationed for the most part on the North-West Frontier, the Nepalese contingents proved of incalculable assistance during their stay in India, where their general bearing and discipline elicited universal praise.

Several of the regiments took part in the Waziristan Campaign of 1917, and distinguished themselves by their bravery and steadiness under fire, the Mahindradal Regiment being especially mentioned for their gallantry in assaulting a strongly-held position.

The Gurkhas form no inconsiderable part of the British Indian Army—to be exact, there are ten regiments of two battalions each. The gallantry of these hill people so favourably impressed the British at the time of the Nepal war that soon after friendly relations were restored they took into their service such of the Gurkhas as were willing to enlist, thereby creating a nucleus for the Gurkha battalions which exist to-day.

Up to the year 1914 the number of recruits

required annually to maintain the twenty Gurkha battalions at full strength was about fifteen hundred, and these were, with the sanction of the Nepal Government, recruited by Gurkhas specially deputed from the various regiments. Almost immediately after the outbreak of the war the Government of India intimated that the demand for recruits was expected to be high, and the Maharaja took immediate steps to evolve an organization which would prove capable of being able to cope with the situation at once, abnormal and unprecedented as it was.

Officers were specially appointed to various places in the country, and local officials in the hills, both in the eastern and western districts, were ordered to put forward their best efforts. Available recruits were collected at different centres, which were increased from seven in the first to ten in subsequent years, with a view to facilitating the collection of men at points nearer their homes.

As the men were passed fit they were sent to the newly opened depôts and outposts, which were situated at convenient places on the Nepal frontier. To avoid the chance of any likely locality being left untapped, special officers were instructed to move from place to place, while the valley of Nepal and the adjoining districts, where recruiting was normally prohibited, were also thrown open for what supply they could yield. While the people were encouraged in every way to seek enlistment in the British Army they were at the same time repeatedly given to understand that in serving the British Government they would be considered to have rendered equal service to their own, and that every available means would be employed to provide employment and the means of livelihood for them on their return from service.

In spite of the fact that a certain amount of time was taken in perfecting the arrangements made to obtain the extra recruits, the results obtained in the first season were eminently satisfactory, many thousands of recruits having been obtained. That of the second year was a record one, during which the country was thoroughly exploited from end to end. It was inevitable that after such brisk and active recruiting in a restricted field and amongst a limited class of the population, a dearth of suitable men began, in course of time, to make itself felt. The task became more and more difficult, and though it could not expect to equal those of the preceding years owing to the constant drain on the manhood of the country, the result was still as satisfactory as could be expected. In the fourth year the work had to be carried on in a still more depleted field, but even so, considerable numbers of recruits were obtained. Recruiting from amongst the non-fighting classes was even attempted, though the result obtained did not quite come up to expectations. The returns of the local officers showed that the number of men taken out of the country since the outbreak of the war had exceeded 200,000. When it is recollected that the bulk of these men came from the martial classes, of which the total male population, according to the census of 1911, amounted to 907,000—from which total those who were too young, too old, or physically unfit must be excluded—it can be seen to what extent the country had been denuded of its manhood.

In consequence of the strenuous efforts made by the Maharaja of Nepal the British Government were not only able to make good the heavy losses in the regular Gurkha regiments, but were also able to raise many new battalions and such non-combatant units as the Army Bearer Corps and many Labour Battalions.

While no trouble and expense had been spared by the Nepal Government in sending the flower of her manhood to fight in the Allies' cause, help in money, materials, and in other ways was also forthcoming.

The first monetary contribution, made in September 1914, was a grant of 500,000 rupees, of which 250,000 were contributed from the Maharaja's private purse. On the New Year days of 1916 and 1917, a further sum of 300,000 rupees was presented on both occasions, and in 1918, on the occasion of the silver wedding of Their Majesties the King Emperor and Queen Empress of India, yet another 200,000 were given. There were, besides the above, many minor donations to the various hospitals and funds.

Of the produce of the country, 5,000 maunds of cardamons, 85,000 lbs. of tea, and numerous parcels of hill clothing were from time to time offered and accepted, while from the Nepal forests in the Sarda valley 200,000 broad-gauge *sal* sleepers were also presented free of cost.

Thirty-one machine guns from Vickers Maxims were presented on the occasion of His Majesty The King Emperor's birthday in 1915, and in the same year some 400 mechanics of the Nepal Government workshops were offered for work in India, and the services of a number of these were utilized.

One further item deserves special mention in this brief record. In 1917 and 1918 the financial position in India threatened to be critical for want of rupees and the necessary silver with which to mint them. The urgent appeal for help in this direction was met by a remittance of 10,100,000 British-Indian silver rupees, and 2,500,000 rupees in Nepalese coin, specially withdrawn for this purpose from the currency of the country.

During the war no less than 200,000 Gurkhas joined our service, and 55,000 of these were enlisted in the regular Gurkha battalions of the Indian Army. Nepal suffered some 20,000 casualties on our behalf, and its men fought in almost every theatre of war, cheerfully enduring tropic heat and the cold of northern winters. We feel that the British public at large have no clear realization of what Nepal did for the Empire's cause during the eventful years of 1914–18; and if, in these few pages, we have succeeded in bringing to notice, even though somewhat late in the day, the magnificent efforts of this little Himalayan kingdom, we shall feel more than rewarded.

APPENDICES

APPENDIX I

A Table of the Festivals observed by the Gurkhas

Basant Panchmi ; in honour of Spring.
Shibratri.
Holi.
Sawan Sakrati.
Rikhi Tarpan.
Janam Astami.
Dasehra.
Diwali.
Maghia Sakrat ; the Hindu New Year.

Except where stated in the text the above festivals do not differ from those celebrated all over India by Hindus.

APPENDIX II

A List of the Gurkhali Kings and Prime Ministers of Nepal

Gurkhali Kings of Nepal

Prithwi Narayan Sahi.
Pratapa Sinha Sahi.
Rana Bahadur Sahi.
Girbhan Juddha Vikram Sahi.
Rajendra Vikram Sahi.
Surendra Vikram Sahi.
Prithwi Vira Vikram Sahi.
Tribhubana Bir Bikram Jang Bahadur Shah Bahadur Shamsher Jang.

Prime Ministers of Nepal

Bhimsen Thapa, 1811–1837.
Matharsing Thapa, 1843–1845.
Sir Jang Bahadur Rana, G.C.B., G.C.S.I., 1847–1877.
Ranodhipsing Rana, 1877–1885.
Sir Bir Shumsher Rana Bahadur, 1886–1901.
Dip Shamsher Jung Bahadur Rana, 1901.
General Sir Chandra Shumsher Jang Bahadur Rana, G.C.B., etc., 1901–

BIBLIOGRAPHY

BELL, SIR C. Tibet: Past and Present. London, 1924.

BENDALL, C. A Journey of Literary and Archæological Research in Nepal and North India. Cambridge, 1886.

BROWN, P. Picturesque Nepal. London, 1912.

BRUCE, MAJOR HON. C. G. Twenty Years in the Himalaya. London, 1910.

BRUCE, BRIG.-GENERAL HON. C. G., and NORTHEY, MAJOR W. BROOK. Nepal. *Geographical Journal*, vol. lxv, No. 4. London, 1925.

CHATTERTON, E. Mission Work in Chota Nagpore. London, 1901.

CHATTOPADHAY, K. P. An Essay on the History of Newar Culture. *Asiatic Society Bengal*, vol. xix, 1923, No. 10.

CROOKE, W. Tribes and Castes of N.W.P. and Oudh. 1896.

DAS, SARAT CHANDRA. Journey to Lhasa and Central Tibet. London, 1904.

ELWES, H. Nepal. *Supplement of the Scientific American*, vol. lxxix. New York, 1915.

ENCYCLOPÆDIA BRITANNICA. All editions. Nepal.

GIUSEPPE, FATHER. The Kingdom of Nepal. *Asiatic Researches* vol. xi, 1799.

GRIERSON, SIR GEORGE A. Linguistic Survey of India, vol. iii, Part I.

HAMILTON (BUCHANAN). An Account of the Kingdom of Nepal. Edinburgh, 1819.

HODGSON, BRIAN H.

On the Languages, Literature and Religion of Nepal and Tibet.

On the Chepang and Kusunda Tribes of Nepal.

Sketch of Buddhism.

On the Geography of the Himalaya.

The Origin and Classification of the Military Tribes of Nepal.

On the Kiranti Tribe of the Central Himalaya.

On the Kochh, Bodo and Dhimal Tribes.

On the Law and Legal Practice of Nepal.

The first five of the above-mentioned are found collected under the title of "Essays on the Languages, etc., of Nepal and Tibet," London, 1874; the remaining papers are in his "Miscellaneous Essays," London, 1880.

HOERNLE, R. Inscribed Seal of Gupta. 1889.
HOOKER, J. D.
  Himalayan Journals. London, 1854.
HUC, E. R. Travels in Tartary. London, 1927 (reprint).
HUNTER, SIR W. W. Life of Brian H. Hodgson. London, 1896.
KILGOUR and DUNCAN. English-Nepali Dictionary. Darjeeling, 1923.
KIRKPATRICK, W. An Account of the Kingdom of Nepal. London, 1811.
LEVI, SYLVAIN.
  Note sur la chronologie du Nepal. *Journal Asiatique*, 1894.
  Le Népal. *Annales du Musée Guimet*, 1905.
MASSIEU, I. Nepal et pays Himalayens. Paris, 1914.
MONEY, MAJOR G. W. P. Gurkhali Manual. Bombay, 1918.
MORRIS, CAPTAIN C. J. The Gorge of the Arun. *Geographical Journal*, vol. lxii, No. 3. London, 1923.
O'CAVANAGH, CAPTAIN. Rough Notes on the State of Nepal. Calcutta, 1851.
OLDFIELD, H. A. Sketches from Nepal. London, 1880.
RISLEY, H. H. Tribes and Castes of Bengal. 1891.
SMITH, CAPTAIN T. Five Years' Residence in Nepal, 1841–1845. Unknown.
TEMPLE, R. Journals kept in Hyderabad, etc., and Nepal. London, 1887.
TURNBULL, —. Nepali Grammar and Vocabulary. Calcutta, 1920.
TURNER, R. L.
  The Infinitive in Nepali. *Philologica*, London, vol. i, 1921.
  Specimens of Nepali. *Indian Antiquary*, vol. l. Bombay, 1921.
  Further Specimens of Nepali. *Indian Antiquary*, vol. li. Bombay, 1922.
  A Dictionary of the Nepali Language with Etymological Notes. London (in the Press).
VANSITTART, LIEUT.-COL. E. Handbooks for the Indian Army, Gurkhas. Calcutta, 1915.
WRIGHT, D. History of Nepal. Cambridge, 1877.

MANUSCRIPTS

A large collection of manuscripts on various subjects connected with Nepal, but mostly concerning the Newars. All are in the writing of Brian Hodgson and may be examined at the India Office Library.

INDEX OF NEPALI WORDS

INDEX

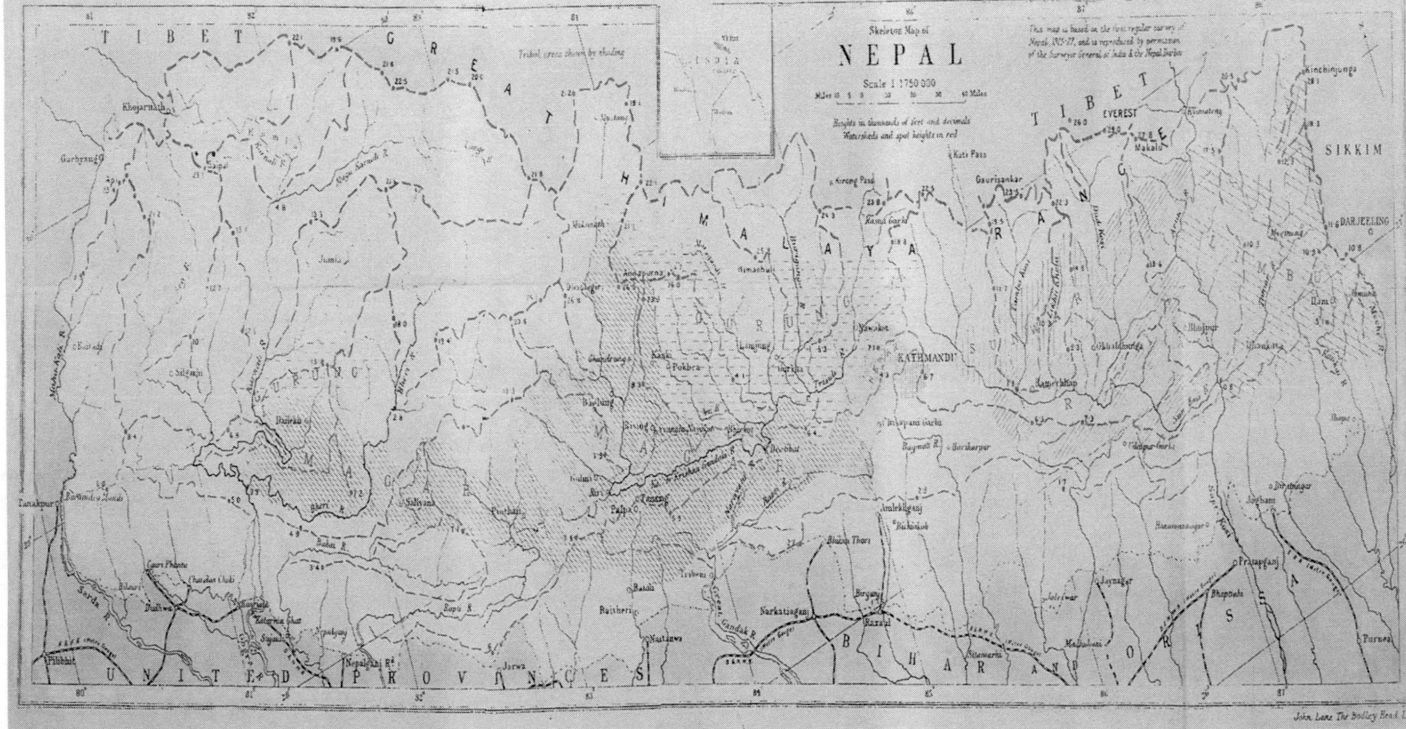

Skeleton Map of
NEPAL
Scale 1:1750 000
Heights in thousands of feet and decimals
Watersheds and spot heights in red
This map is based on the first regular survey of Nepal, 1925-27, and is reproduced by permission of the Surveyor General of India & the Nepal Durbar
Tribal areas shown by shading
TIBET
GREAT HIMALAYA RANGE
SIKKIM
EVEREST
Makalu
Kinchinjunga
DARJEELING
Gaurisankar
Kuti Pass
Kirong Pass
KATHMANDU
Annapurna
Pokhra
Kanki
Palpa
Tansing
Baglung
Jumla
Khojarnath
Garbyang
Taklakot
Kasna Garhi
Nawakot
Himachuli
Chisapani Garhi
Hariharpur
Udaipur Garhi
Dhankuta
Ilam
Bhojpur
Okhaldhunga
Amlekhganj
Bhichhakhori
Birganj
Raxaul
Narkatiaganj
Sitamarhi
Madhubani
Jaynagar
Jogbani
Biratnagar
Purnea
Pratapganj
Bhaptiahi
Nepalganj Rd.
Sujauli
Katarnia Ghat
Tanakpur
Pilibhit
Dailekh
Silgarhi
Salliyana
Pyuthan
Butwal
Bhairawa
Nautanwa
Tribeni
Trisuli
Dud Kosi
Sun Kosi
Tamur
Arun
Mechi R.
Sarda R.
Bheri R.
Rapti R.
Kali Gandak R.
Great Gandak R.
Bagmati R.
Babai R.
Mahakali R.
Nepalganj
Lamjung
Jajarkot
Mustang
Khatmandu
Bhotiya
GURUNG
MAGAR
LIMBU
SUNWAR
NEWAR
RAI
KIRANTI
UNITED PROVINCES
BIHAR AND ORISSA
John Lane The Bodley Head Ltd.